Z 50

THE UNCONQUERED

Ayn Rand

THE UNCONQUERED

With Another, Earlier Adaptation of *We the Living*

Edited by

Robert Mayhew

palgrave
macmillan

THE UNCONQUERED
Copyright © Robert Mayhew, 2014.

All rights reserved.

First published in 2014 by
PALGRAVE MACMILLAN®
in the United States—a division of St. Martin's Press LLC,
175 Fifth Avenue, New York, NY 10010.

Where this book is distributed in the UK, Europe and the rest of the world,
this is by Palgrave Macmillan, a division of Macmillan Publishers Limited,
registered in England, company number 785998, of Houndmills,
Basingstoke, Hampshire RG21 6XS.

Palgrave Macmillan is the global academic imprint of the above companies
and has companies and representatives throughout the world.

Palgrave® and Macmillan® are registered trademarks in the United States,
the United Kingdom, Europe and other countries.

ISBN: 978–1–137–42873–8

Library of Congress Cataloging-in-Publication Data

Rand, Ayn.
[Plays. Selections]
    The unconquered : with another, earlier adaptation of We the living /
by Ayn Rand ; edited by Robert Mayhew.
        pages cm
    ISBN 978–1–137–42873–8 (hardback :alk. paper)
    1. Soviet Union—History—Revolution, 1917–1921—Drama. 2. Rand,
Ayn. We the living—Adaptations. I. Mayhew, Robert. II. Title.

PS3535.A547U53 2014
812'.52—dc23   2014005572

A catalogue record of the book is available from the British Library.

Design by Newgen Knowledge Works (P) Ltd., Chennai, India.

First edition: September 2014

10 9 8 7 6 5 4 3 2 1

Contents

PREFACE

Ayn Rand's first novel, *We the Living*, was published in April 1936. That summer, the producer Jerome Mayer approached her with the idea of adapting it for the stage, and she agreed to undertake the adaptation. The play was ultimately produced and directed by George Abbott, however, and appeared on Broadway—with the title *The Unconquered*—in February 1940, closing after just six performances.[1]

In the 1960s, Rand twice discussed her misgivings with the adaptation. In an interview she said,

> I didn't really want to adapt it, but my main purpose [in doing so] was [that] since the book had done so *little* in this country, I thought that a play might help the sale of the book. And it was for that motive only that I took the time to dramatize it. And that first version [for Mayer] was better than what was finally produced [by Abbott]. But I would say I was satisfied with it as an adaptation.[2]

And in a course on nonfiction writing a few years later, she said of it,

> I had a terrible time writing the play, and I disliked every version of it, from the original to the many rewrites...The play never was—and I came to realize, never could be—good. It grew out of somebody else's suggestion plus my own irrelevant motive. So, no matter how conscientiously I tried, I could not make it good. The final version was more or less competent, but no better.[3]

These two (extemporaneous) comments might seem to offer different evaluations of the relative merits of the first and final versions. But I expect that what she meant to convey was that the first version is better as an adaptation of the novel, which leaves open whether she thought the final version (especially as realized by George Abbott) was better or worse as a play considered apart from the novel. In any case, she held the final version to be merely competent.

Of the several attempts, "from the original to the many rewrites," at least five versions survive (depending on what one considers a version; see Appendix 1,

---

[1] For a fuller description of the history of this adaptation, see Jeff Britting, "Adapting *We the Living* for the Stage" (an essay included in this volume).

[2] Biographical interviews, 1960–61 (transcripts in the Ayn Rand Archives).

[3] Ayn Rand, *The Art of Nonfiction: A Guide for Writers and Readers*, ed. Robert Mayhew (New York: Plume, 2001), 80–81.

"Sources," p. 349). Included in this volume are the two referred to above: the original and the final versions (or at least the earliest and the latest of those that have survived). In addition, I have provided a number of excerpts from the other versions, including two alternative endings. By considering the earliest and latest versions, and these other materials, the reader can see the extent to which Ayn Rand, over the years in which she worked on the adaptation, changed the events, dialogue, and even the cast of characters.

It is useful (at the very least, as a justification for including two versions of the play) to indicate briefly some of the key differences between the original novel and the two theatrical adaptations included herein (for the purposes of this comparison, Play 1 and Play 2). The novel opens with Kira and her family arriving in the St. Petersburg train station, having returned from the Crimea. Play 1 begins in a street outside the Technological Institute in Petrograd, where students (including Kira) are attempting to leave a compulsory Marxist meeting early. (These are the circumstances under which Kira meets Andrei.) Play 2 is quite different, opening in Leo's apartment, with Leo and Kira already living together. In the novel, Kira's family is quite prominent; in Play 1 Kira's mother has a small role, and in Play 2 none of her family members appear. In the novel, Kira and Leo meet when she is wandering the streets of St. Petersburg, and at first he believes she is a prostitute. There is a similar scene in Play 1; but as indicated, they are already together at the beginning of Play 2. In the novel and in Play 2, Kira meets Andrei only after meeting Leo; in Play 1 she meets Andrei first. In the novel Leo attempts to escape to Germany with Kira via ship over the Baltic Sea, but they are stopped by the Red Baltfleet. Leo makes no attempt to escape in either play. In the novel and in Play 1, Kira works at the House of the Peasant; in Play 2, she works at the Railroad Office. A scene involving the Soviet purging of noncommunist students (from the university in Leo's case, from the Technological Institute in Kira's) appears in the novel and in both plays. The basic plot-situation (what Ayn Rand calls the plot-theme) is established fairly similarly in the novel and in the two plays: Leo contracts tuberculosis and is told he must go to a sanatorium in the south or die; he is unable to secure a place at a state sanatorium (because of his aristocratic status) or at a private sanatorium (for lack of money); Kira becomes Andrei's lover in order to acquire the money necessary to send Leo south and save his life. (Part 1 of the novel ends here, as does act 1 in each version of the play.)[4] In the novel, and in both plays, the events that follow—whatever their differences—are *essentially* the same:[5] Leo returns from the Crimea cured of tuberculosis, and immediately becomes involved in an illegal moneymaking scheme with Morozov and Syerov. This culminates in the

---

[4] Rand says she began with a "trite plot-theme: the woman who sells herself to a man she does not love for the sake of the man whom she does love," but transformed it into "a much more dramatic conflict": "Suppose the woman sells herself, not to a villain who forces her into it, but to a man who really loves her, whom she respects and whose love she takes seriously. He does not want to buy her, and she must hide from him that it is a sale—but she has to sell herself to save the man she really loves, a man who happens to be the particular person the buyer hates most." Ayn Rand, *The Art of Fiction: A Guide for Readers and Writers*, ed. Tore Boeckmann (New York: Plume, 2000), 38.

[5] An important subplot emerges in Part 2 of the novel, but does not appear in any version of the play, involving Irina (Kira's cousin), her boyfriend Sasha, and her brother Victor.

climax of the story: Leo's arrest by Andrei, who thereby discovers Leo's relationship with Kira. Kira confronts Andrei and explains her actions, and consequently Andrei works to have Leo released. The events following the climax—especially the final scenes—differ quite a lot: the novel and Play 1 end with Kira on the Soviet border (though they have little in common besides the setting), the final scene of Play 2 is set in Leo's apartment.[6]

Now some of these (and other) variations do not essentially affect the basic story or its theme. For example, changing Kira's work place from the House of the Peasant to the Railroad Office (where Syerov works) was no doubt done so that the action of the play could be integrated more economically, and it does not alter the theme of the play or the nature of any of its characters. Nor does the addition to Play 1 of the character Olga Ivanovna (who does not appear in the novel or in Play 2): she serves the same function as Kira's sister Lydia in the novel, who in response to Soviet oppression seeks (unsuccessfully) consolation in traditional Russian mysticism; but as Kira's family is not featured in the play, changing Lydia into Kira's neighbor makes sense.

Some variations, however, arguably do alter key characterizations, and perhaps even the theme as well. For example, without Leo's attempt to escape the country with Kira, he comes across as less of a man of action than the corresponding character in the novel, and so even more defeated earlier on, and consequently it is not as clear why Kira loves him. Or, in the novel, when Kira is desperately trying to get Leo into a sanatorium, a commissar tells her: "One hundred thousand workers died in the civil war. Why—in the face of the Union of Socialist Soviet Republics—can't one aristocrat die?" In Play 1, the identical words are given to Kira's boss (Voronov) and so make the same point. But in Play 2, they are delivered by *Andrei*, which makes him worse—much less sympathetic—than he is in the novel. Rand once said that the theme of *We the Living* is "the individual against the state, and, more specifically, the evil of statism. I present the theme by showing that the totalitarian state destroys the best people: in this case, a girl and the two men who love her."[7] This is certainly part of what is projected in the plays (especially the earlier version); but by the time we get to the final version, there is arguably a subtle shift in thematic focus, less on the evil of the state and the masses, and relatively more on the intransigence of a heroic human being (Kira) in the face of totalitarianism. This must be part of the reason why Ayn Rand changed the title to *The Unconquered*.[8]

Although the two versions included in full are presented in chronological order in this volume, I feature *The Unconquered* in the title. Doing so should prevent prospective readers from confusing this material with the novel—which should certainly be read before either theatrical adaptation. Further, *The Unconquered* is Rand's final attempt at this material—and as indicated is further

---

[6] See the chapter "Excerpts from Other Versions: Two Alternative Endings" (p. 322) in this volume, where I briefly explain the difficulties Ayn Rand had adapting the ending of the novel.

[7] Ayn Rand, *The Art of Fiction: A Guide for Readers and Writers*, ed. Tore Boeckmann (New York: Plume, 2000), 17.

[8] In Rand's novella *Anthem* (written in 1937), the hero—whose state-given name is Equality 7-2521—is at first called "the Unconquered" by the woman who loves him.

from the novel than the earliest version—and so *The Unconquered* can more accurately be described as new material from Ayn Rand.

One may ask, why publish material with which Rand was herself not entirely satisfied? First, as works of fiction—the first "new" fiction of Rand to appear in nearly 20 years[9]—these plays will be of interest to the legions of fans of her fiction, and I expect *they* will be satisfied.

Further, this material is of value to historians and others interested in the life of Rand and the development of her thought and fiction. For example, scenes presenting the student purges (see act 2, sc. 3, in both *We the Living* and *The Unconquered*), which were based on Rand's own experiences at the University of Leningrad, provide details not included in the corresponding scenes in the novel. For scholars and fans of Rand's fiction, this material offers insights into the original novel—especially into the characterization of Leo Kovalensky (who states more explicitly the motives behind his self-destructive behavior). For instance, he explains to Antonina why he has been spending so much time going out with her:

> Throwing money away, night after night, in contemptible dives, among people I loathed, on drinks that tasted rotten, with a companion like you. Knowing all the while that I was paying with my life for every ruble and every minute of it...Well, that was my only answer to them. You don't fight with beautiful gestures today. Let the gestures fit the adversary...What do you think is easier? To go before the firing squad, quivering with love for that life you're leaving behind? Or to be so sick of it, so sick that even the squad comes to you as the sublime relief? (*The Unconquered*, act 2, sc. 5)

We are even given specific information about where Kira likely attempted to cross the border out of the U.S.S.R.: "Down on the Latvian frontier. North of Ostrov" (*The Unconquered*, act 2, sc. 3). Further, some of the scenes that take place in the Railroad Office foreshadow the portrayal of government control over Taggart Transcontinental and other industries in *Atlas Shrugged*.

Those interested in the development of Rand's philosophical thought should find fascinating an exchange between Andrei and Syerov about which of them is in fact an egoist (see "Excerpts from Other Versions," pp. 304–305). Moreover, in this scene Rand explicitly connects egoism and capitalism, arguably for the first time in print.[10] Syerov says to Andrei, "Self-respect, self-pride, self-admiration. Do you realize how much you think of your own precious self? You're worse than a capitalist. You're a capitalist of the spirit. A hoarder of your own soul." In her Foreword to the 1959 edition of the novel, Rand insisted, "*We the Living* is not a story about Soviet Russia in 1925. It is a story about Dictatorship, any dictatorship, anywhere, at any time, whether it be Soviet Russia, Nazi Germany, or...a

---

[9] Leonard Peikoff, ed., *The Early Ayn Rand: A Selection from Her Unpublished Fiction* (New York: New American Library, 1984). There is one exception: the short story "The Night King" was published in 2005 in the expanded edition of *The Early Ayn Rand*. (Note that *The Early Ayn Rand* contains the story "Red Pawn" [1931], Rand's only other work set in the Soviet Union. It has many interesting parallels with *We the Living* and its theatrical adaptations.)

[10] I owe this point to Darryl Wright.

socialist America." In one version of the play only (and not in the novel), she makes explicit the connection between the political philosophies of Communism and Nazism, and even claims that the former is responsible for the latter (see "Excerpts from Other Versions," p. 319.) This is just a sample of the never-before-published material this volume contains.

Note: Original material in this volume is presented as it is found in the extant typescripts, with little editorial intrusion. *We the Living* is a transcription of Version I (ARP 075–01x/076–04x); *The Unconquered* is a transcription of Version V B (ARP 077–11x). (See Appendix 1, "Sources" for more details.) Aside from the correction of obvious typographical errors, the few revisions I have made are indicated in footnotes.

ACKNOWLEDGMENTS

I wish to thank Leonard Peikoff for granting me permission to use this previously unpublished material of Ayn Rand, and for leaving it to me to determine just what to include and how to present it. Special thanks to Jeff Britting (curator of the Ayn Rand Archives) for his assistance in accessing this material and for contributing an essay on the history of the production of *The Unconquered*. I am extremely grateful to Seton Hall University for granting me a sabbatical (2013–14), and to the Ayn Rand Institute for a research grant that made a full-year-long sabbatical possible, during which I was able to complete my work on this volume. Many thanks to Brigitte Shull and the staff at Palgrave Macmillan for all their help in seeing this project through, from original submission to published book, and to Samita Narain for her superb copyediting of my typescript. One of the highlights of my scholarly life (both professionally and personally) has been the opportunity to participate in many of the BB&T workshops organized by Tara Smith. At one such workshop in October 2011, in the early stages of this project, I discussed *The Unconquered* with Onkar Ghate, Ann Ciccolella, and Tara. My thanks to them, as the feedback I received was very useful in first drafting the preface and selecting the excerpted material, and in general planning the entire volume. Finally, I wish to thank Shoshana Milgram, David Hayes, and Tore Boeckmann, for pointing out numerous typographical and factual errors in various drafts of this volume, and Greg Salmieri, for suggestions that improved my preface, notes, and other editorial additions.

Chronology

Feb. 1905	Born Alisa Rosenbaum in St. Petersburg, Russia, on February 2
Feb. 1917	Witnesses the first shots of the February Revolution
Oct. 1924	Graduates from the University of Leningrad
Jan.–Feb. 1926	Leaves Russia on January 26; arrives in New York on February 19
Oct. 1934	*Woman on Trial*, her first play, opens in Hollywood
Sept. 1935	*Night of January 16th* (formerly *Woman on Trial*) opens on Broadway[1]
Apr. 1936	*We the Living*, her first novel, published by Macmillan
Jul. 1936	Jerome Mayer purchases rights to the theatrical adaptation of *We the Living*
Jan. 1937	Completes adaptation. "I have just completed it, but it is too late for a production this winter and we plan to open it in early fall. The play is being cast now." (Letter to John Temple Graves, Jan. 30)
Sept. 1937	First printing of the novel (3,000 copies) sells out, and Macmillan destroys the plates, thereby letting the novel go out of print
Oct. 1937	Mayer "dropped his option on it recently, and for a very sad reason: he is afraid of producing an anti-Soviet play…Right now, I have a very big producer interested in the play and expect to hear from him definitely within this week." (Letter to Marcella Bannett Rabwin, Oct. 14)
Jul. 1938	"Ayn Rand…is having difficulty casting her new play. Its theme is anti-communist." (*Chicago Times*, Jul. 13)
Aug. 1939	Signed contract with George Abbott (Aug. 31)
Dec. 1939	*The Unconquered* plays at Maryland Theatre (Baltimore), week of December 25
Feb. 1940	*The Unconquered* plays at Biltmore Theatre (Broadway); opened February 13, closed February 17 after six performances[2]

---

[1] It is not clear whether the title was at the time *Night of January 16th* or *The Night of January 16*. See David P. Hayes, "Is *Night of January 16th* the right title of Rand's first play?" (http://actorsinaynrandroles.dhwritings.com/Appendices.html), last accessed April 26, 2014.

[2] At both venues, Ayn Rand's husband Frank O'Connor played the assistant G.P.U. chief.

PART I

Two Theatrical Adaptations by Ayn Rand of Her Novel *We the Living*

We the Living

A play by

Ayn Rand

(Adapted from her novel
of the same name)[1]

(1936/37)

---

[1] "*We the Living* A play by Ayn Rand (Adapted from her novel of the same name)" is found on the title page of every version, with the exception of the last two (which bear the title *The Unconquered*).

SYNOPSIS OF SCENES

ACT 1

Scene 1:   November 1923. Street in Petrograd.

Scene 2:   Spring of 1924. Technological Institute in Petrograd.

Scene 3:   Same evening. Leo's home in Petrograd.

Scene 4:   Fall of 1924. The House of the Peasant.

Scene 5:   Same evening. Andrei's home.

ACT 2

Scene 1:   Summer of 1925. Leo's home.

Scene 2:   Three weeks later. Andrei's home.

Scene 3:   Winter of 1925. Syerov's home.

Scene 4:   Same evening. Restaurant.

ACT 3

Scene 1:   A few days later. Office of the G.P.U.

Scene 2:   Same evening. Leo's home.

Scene 3:   Same night. Andrei's home.

Scene 4:   Two days later. Leo's Home.

Scene 5:   A week later. Frontier post on the Russian-Latvian border.

CHARACTERS

PAVEL SYEROV
COMRADE SONIA
KIRA ARGOUNOVA
ANDREI TAGANOV
LEO KOVALENSKY
GALINA PETROVNA ARGOUNOVA
CITIZEN LAVROVA
OLGA IVANOVNA
COMRADE BITIUK
COMRADE VORONOV
ANTONINA PAVLOVNA
KARP MOROZOV
G.P.U. OFFICIAL
G.P.U. CHIEF

STUDENTS, CLERKS, GUESTS, SPECULATORS, SOLDIERS

ACT 1

SCENE 1

November, 1923. A side street in Petrograd. Late evening. Dark houses, bluish in the glow of the snow-laden pavement. Heavy snowflakes flutter down lazily, sparkling in the single ray of one lamp post on a corner. Upstage Center, the back wall and side door of the Technological Institute; a red flag flutters in the wind over the door; a few windows in the building hang as yellow squares in the blue dusk. The street curves Right, disappearing upstage in the darkness. Downstage Left an old bench stands under a bare, snow-covered tree.

(All directions from audience)

As the curtain rises, the sound of the Internationale[2] comes from the Institute, played by a military band. A few ragged soldiers and sailors drift aimlessly past the building. Two or three street-walkers pass hopelessly back and forth, fat, unattractive women in red kerchiefs, short skirts, tight-laced high shoes; they blow on their frozen fingers, one chews sunflower seeds, another smokes a cigarette.

(During the following action, streetwalkers accost passersby, some unsuccessfully, some going off with men; the street is obviously not a respectable one.)

The door of the Institute opens soundlessly and two ragged YOUNG STUDENTS slip out, with a cautious glance up and down the street.

First Student

We can go now. They won't notice.

Second Student

Look! Snow! The first snow of the year!

First Student

Isn't it wonderful! Such a night to be locked up for hours in a stuffy hall listening to speeches about young Red engineers and the future of proletarian construction!

Second Student

Sh-sh! They'll hear you.

---

[2] For more information on this and the other music that appears in these plays (as they do in the novel), see Michael S. Berliner, "The music of *We the Living*," in Robert Mayhew, ed., *Essays on Ayn Rand's* We the Living, 2nd ed. (Lanham, MD: Lexington Books, 2012).

First Student

Whoever said "Proletarians of the world, unite!" never had to sit in a room full of proletarians for three hours with all the windows locked!

Second Student

For God's sake, have you lost your mind? Someone will hear you!

First Student

(Breathing deeply)

I don't care. Not tonight. God, isn't it beautiful to be alive on a night like this? I feel like working for hours, doing things, great things. If only they'd let one study more and sit at meetings less!

Second Student

(Hearing steps beyond the door)

Oh, shut up! Let's go or they'll notice that we slipped out before the meeting ended.

(They hurry away, up street Right.)

(THIRD STUDENT and YOUNG GIRL slip out of the door.)

Third Student

Come on, the coast's clear.

First Girl

Are you sure it's all right? Someone may report us.

Third Student

Oh, don't be afraid. Look, it's snowing. You promised me you'd go for a walk tonight.

First Girl

Yes, but...

Third Student

What would you rather do? Walk with me now or listen to speeches about your duties as a Soviet engineer in the future?

First Girl

Let's go!

(Exit, Right)

(FOURTH STUDENT, a puny little scholarly type with glasses and an armful of books, opens the door cautiously and peers, frightened, up and down the street. Just as he is about to slip out, a strong hand clasps his shoulder; the FIFTH STUDENT, a tall, husky lad, stands glowering at him ferociously.)

FIFTH STUDENT

What's this, Comrade? Sneaking away before the meeting is closed?

FOURTH STUDENT

(Trembling)

Comrade...I...I...I didn't mean any sabotage...I...it's just that my mother is waiting for me, and it's so late, and...

FIFTH STUDENT

(Laughing)

I feel just as you do, pal. Come on!

(Throws his arms around the other's shoulders and the two exit together.)

(A GIRL slips furtively out of the door; a SAILOR approaches her tentatively, but she jerks away from him terrified and hurries off. A BOY comes out of the Institute.)

STREET WALKER

(Approaching him)

Good evening, Comrade. Lonely?

SIXTH STUDENT

A pound of bread, Citizen—and I'm yours.

(Exits, while the STREET WALKER spits angrily)

(COMRADE SONIA and PAVEL SYEROV come out of the Institute. COMRADE SONIA is young, husky, broad-shouldered and short-legged; she wears a masculine leather jacket; flat masculine Oxfords and a red kerchief tied carelessly over short, stubby, uncombed hair; her whole demeanor is full of a brisk, imperious, over-cheerful activity. SYEROV is a youth in his middle twenties, but looks older, pale with an unhealthy, washed-out blond grayness, immaculately dressed, his manner alternating between obsequious servility and arrogance.)

SYEROV

This is where they slip out, the counterrevolutionary rats. Let's just hang around here and see who leaves before the meeting is closed.

(The Internationale ends offstage.)

COMRADE SONIA[3]

Really, the Communist Cell isn't strict enough. If I had my way I'd lock this side door during meetings and I'd simply expel anyone who took no interest in collective activity and tried to leave.

SYEROV

It's amazing, the number of bourgeois studying here, in our Red Technological Institute. Future engineers of the Soviet Republic! If I had my way, I'd kick them all out and make room for the children of workers and peasants who've never had a chance.

COMRADE SONIA

And who know how to subordinate themselves to the collective.

> (A YOUNG BOY comes out, sees Syerov and Sonia and quickly ducks back into the building. SYEROV chuckles.)

SYEROV

We'll just count those who sneak out tonight and make a note of it for the Communist Cell. It will come in handy some day, and the Cell won't forget this kind of service.

> (A YOUNG GIRL hurries out and stops short seeing Syerov and Sonia.)

SECOND GIRL

Oh!

COMRADE SONIA

> (With a charming, friendly smile)

Good evening, Comrade. Leaving?

SECOND GIRL

> (Terrified)

No! Oh, no! I wouldn't think of it! I...I was just running after someone I saw leaving, to call them back, but since it's you, Comrade Sonia, and Comrade Syerov, I know it's perfectly all right and...and...I'm going right back!

> (Turns quickly and collides with someone in the darkness of the hall. In a warning, terrified voice.)

Comrade, you...you're not leaving now?

KIRA'S VOICE

> (In the hall)

---

[3] The typescript is inconsistent, sometimes reading "Sonia," other times "Comrade Sonia." I always print the latter.

Of course, I'm leaving!

> (She pushes aside the terrified girl who rushes back into the building, and comes out. KIRA ARGOUNOVA is slender, eighteen, with wild, disheveled hair, a proud, arrogant, face dressed in an old faded black coat and tam. She stops short seeing Syerov and Sonia.)

KIRA

Oh, good evening. Doing a little spy work?

SYEROV

Really, Comrade Argounova, I don't know what you're talking about.

COMRADE SONIA

Comrade Syerov and I just came out for a breath of air. How about you? What are you doing here?

KIRA

I'm going home.

COMRADE SONIA

Before the meeting is dismissed?

KIRA

You know, I've heard the Internationale about four times a week in the last five years. It's a beautiful song, only don't you think it can be overdone?

COMRADE SONIA

Comrade Argounova, I would be careful, if I were you. With your social past, daughter of a former factory owner and this kind of talk...

KIRA

Daughter of a former factory owner, hell! Who cares whose daughter? A future engineer, that's all *I'm* thinking about, and I have a lot of studying to do tonight.

SYEROV

Oh, your own personal career—that's what you're most interested in?

KIRA

No, not *most* interested in—that's *all* I'm interested in!

COMRADE SONIA

You won't get far with that kind of attitude.

> (Applause in the building as a speech is finished)

KIRA

That depends on what direction I want to go.

(The Internationale starts again.)

You know, I love the Internationale. When all this is over, when the traces of your Soviets are disinfected from history—what a glorious funeral march it will make!

ANDREI

(Coming out, has heard her words. Seizes her wrist and wheels her about sharply.)

You little fool! What are you talking about?

(ANDREI TAGANOV is tall, slender, in his middle twenties, with a hard, uncompromising face, a scar on his temple, a Communist black leather jacket and a harsh, military bearing.)

KIRA

(Trying to disengage her wrist, he holds it.)

How much are you paid for snooping around?

ANDREI

Are you exceedingly brave? Or just stupid?

KIRA

I'll let you find that out.
(He drops her hand.)

COMRADE SONIA

Comrade Taganov, Comrade Argounova has been talking like that openly, everywhere. As head of the G.P.U. at the Institute, you must put a stop to it and...

ANDREI

What are you two doing here?

SYEROV

Oh, we...we just came out to...to...

ANDREI

I know. Who asked you to spy?

COMRADE SONIA

But, Comrade Taganov, we only...

ANDREI

If I need any information I'll ask you for it. Now go back.

SYEROV

But surely, Andrei, you're not implying that our motives...

ANDREI

(Without raising his voice)

Go back.

COMRADE SONIA

(Shrugging)

It's amazing how some Communists act as if they were better than anyone else and...

SYEROV

Come on, Sonia.

(SYEROV and SONIA exit into building.)

ANDREI

(To Kira)

You must be new here. I'd advise you to be careful.

KIRA

I am new here. It's my first year. I came here to study. I'm sick of having to waste my time at fool meetings, listening to your Red drivel. You may as well know it. If you want to arrest me—go ahead.

ANDREI

I haven't said anything about arresting you, have I?

KIRA

I am *not* studying here to serve you and your Red state, as those speakers of yours are yelling over there. I've always wanted to be an engineer—ever since I can remember. I want to build—just because I want to build. I've never had another thought, another wish in my life. I want to create, and say: This is mine. *Mine.* Do you hear? Not ours!

ANDREI

(Calmly)

You've heard Comrade Sonia say that I'm a secret police agent, haven't you?

KIRA

Yes!

ANDREI

And you still talk like that?

KIRA

Yes!

ANDREI

(Calmly)

I admire you. Even if you are a damn egotist.

KIRA

Thank you. It's nice to hear from one of those new masters of ours, who hold a safe job and enjoy nothing in life but the sheer delight of seeing men crawl!

ANDREI

(Calmly, with the faintest shadow of a smile)

That's not quite correct. I've always belonged to the Party, since before the revolution—ever since I can remember. My father died in Siberia for it. I want to serve the people—just because I want to serve them. I've never had another thought, another wish in my life. I want to create a state where all men will be men—and say: This is ours. *Ours*—you see?—not mine. A state where everyone will be—what you are.

KIRA

What . . . *I* am?

ANDREI

Yes. Brave and free and not afraid to live. I haven't seen enough people like that around me. The old world didn't encourage them. I'm fighting to make it possible.

KIRA

(Smiling suddenly)

I admire you. Even if you are a damn fool.

ANDREI

Thank you. Will you do me a favor?

KIRA

Yes?

ANDREI

Don't make it necessary for me to arrest you. Don't talk too much around the others. With me—it's all right. I understand. And I trust you—though I don't know why I should.

KIRA

All right. I'll try to keep my mouth shut. Because I trust you—though I know I shouldn't.

ANDREI

You can go home now if you wish. Only get off this street. It's no place for you to be late at night. Good night, Comrade Argounova.

KIRA

(Smiling)

Hasn't your G.P.U. a secret bureau of information about all the students?

ANDREI

(Puzzled)

Why?

KIRA

You could find out from them that my name is Kira.

ANDREI

(Smiling)

But that won't give you a way of finding out that my name is Andrei

KIRA

I'm afraid I'm going to like you, Andrei.

ANDREI

I'm afraid I'll be glad, Kira. Good night.

KIRA

Good night.

(He exits into the building. She stands looking thoughtfully after him. The sound of applause is heard in the building as a speech is finished. The Internationale starts again. A SOLDIER approaches Kira.)

SOLDIER

(With obvious intentions)

Good evening, Comrade.

(One look from her is enough. He hurries away, muttering.)

Oh, I beg your pardon!

(Hurries off)

(KIRA is about to go when she stops suddenly, stunned, looking at LEO KOVALENSKY who enters Left. LEO is tall, slender, young, unusually attractive, with a defiant, irrepressible arrogance in his face, his body, his every movement; he is wearing an old coat that had obviously been expensive long ago. He stops, looking at Kira, smiles a haughty, contemptuous smile, and approaches her.)

Leo

Lonely?

Kira

(Her voice breathless, incredulous)
Terribly—and for such a long time!

Leo

Want to come with me?

Kira

Yes.

Leo

I want you not to ask any questions.

Kira

(Staring at him incredulously)
I have no questions to ask.

Leo

Why do you stare at me like that?
(She does not answer. He takes her arm, starts to lead her away.)
I'm afraid I'm not a very cheerful companion tonight.

Kira

Can I help you?

Leo

Well, that's what you're here for.
(Stops suddenly)
What's the price? I haven't very much.

Kira

(Jerks away from him, startled, realizing suddenly for whom he had taken her. Looks at him. Then says resolutely, her voice calm and firm.)
It won't be much.

LEO

Where do we go?

KIRA

(Pointing at bench)
Let's...let's sit here first—for a while.

LEO

Any militia-men around?

KIRA

No.
(They sit down.)
Take your hat off.

LEO

What for?

KIRA

I want to look at you.

LEO

Sent to search for someone?

KIRA

No. Sent by whom?
(He doesn't answer and takes his hat off.)

LEO

Well? You've never seen me before anyway, have you?

KIRA

No. But I think I've always wanted to see you.

LEO

Forget the compliments? Have you anything to drink at your place?

KIRA

Oh...yes.

LEO

I warn you I'm going to drink like a sponge tonight.

KIRA

Why tonight?

LEO

I thought I told you not to ask any questions.
   (Silence)
You know, I envy you.

KIRA

Why?

LEO

You have the ideal profession of today. Everything for everyone—and everything for sale. Will you teach me how one can stand it? I want to go down, as far down as a woman like you can drag me.

KIRA

Why?

LEO

If I don't—how will I go on? What can one do today? Crawl. Compromise. Lick boots. Not one pair, mind you, but two hundred million pairs of boots. *Collective* boots. That's the lowest kind there is.

KIRA

One can always fight.

LEO

Fight what? Sure, you can muster the most heroic in you to fight lions. But to fight lice! No, that's not good construction, Comrade. The equilibrium's all wrong.[4]

KIRA

You're saying that only because you know you want to fight, you want it too much.
   (The Internationale ends.)

LEO

   (Looks at her closely, surprised)
How long have you been in this business?

---

[4] This is an inconsistency in the adaptation. In the novel, Leo speaks virtually this same line, but *after* learning that Kira is an engineering student. But here, as he still believes her to be a prostitute, it makes no sense.

KIRA

Oh...not very long.

LEO

I thought so.

KIRA

I'm sorry. I've tried my best.

LEO

Tried what?

KIRA

Tried to act experienced.

LEO

You little fool! Why should you? Tell me something! How can you lead your kind of existence and still want to remain alive?

KIRA

But it's beautiful to be alive. Haven't you ever felt it? It's like a strange treasure, waiting for you somewhere, something promised to you and you can't even name or explain it, you don't even know that it's a promise, it's like a hymn and you don't know the music, but you feel it, beating, like steps, your steps into your own future, yours to do with as you please, and so much can be done, so much is possible!

LEO

(Amazed, watching her closely)

Yes?

KIRA

Some day, I'm going to be an engineer. I'm going to build a skyscraper, some day, the tallest one on earth. And a bridge, a white aluminum bridge sparkling in the sun across a blue river. And just to see it, my work, mine alone...isn't that worth living for?

LEO

Are you a...street woman?

KIRA

No.

LEO

(Jumping up)

Who are you, then?

KIRA

Sit down.

LEO

Answer.

KIRA

I'm a respectable little girl who studies here at the Technological Institute, whose parents would throw her out of the house if they knew she had talked to a strange man on the street.

LEO

(Stares at her, amazed)
Why did you do it?

KIRA

I wanted to know you.

LEO

Why?

KIRA

I liked your face.

LEO

Why?

KIRA

Because you look like the kind of man that shouldn't have been born in Soviet Russia.

LEO

You little fool! Don't you know such things are not being done?

KIRA

I don't care. I wanted to know you.

LEO

Weren't you afraid that...

KIRA

I'm never afraid of what I want. Who are you?

LEO

A respectable young man who studies at the Red University of Petrograd. And...who has no parents to throw him out for talking to strange women on the street.

(Brusquely)

Want a confession from me?

KIRA

Yes.

LEO

This is the first time I've ever tried to...to buy a woman. Only...I couldn't make myself approach one of...of them. But you...I liked your funny smile.

KIRA

Why did you try it tonight?

LEO

I've walked for hours. There isn't a house in this city that I can enter tonight.

KIRA

Why?

LEO

I told you not to ask any questions? Oh, I'll tell you. They executed my father this morning.

(She stares at him.)

For counterrevolutionary conspiracy. He was an admiral. A Czarist admiral. Wounded in the war.

(Applause in the building as the meeting is closed)

KIRA

And...you...?

LEO

They're after me. I have to hide. I can't go home. If I can escape them for a few days, it will be all right. They have nothing on me. They'll cool off. They usually do. But if they catch me now...well, it's the firing squad.

KIRA

How can you hide?

LEO

Get a woman and go to her place. Or to some hotel—the kind where they won't suspect you if you're with a woman.

KIRA

And in a few days you would be safe?

LEO

I think so.

(SYEROV and SONIA come out of Institute door. KIRA sees them and draws Leo to her suddenly, her body shielding him from the street behind them.)

KIRA

(In a whisper)

Don't move!

(SYEROV and SONIA disappear up the street Right. KIRA releases Leo, tries to draw aside, but he holds her.)

I didn't want them to see you . . . Communist spies from the Institute.

LEO

Oh.

(Still holds her, draws her closer)

Will you go with me to that hotel?

KIRA

(Calmly)

Yes.

LEO

(He didn't expect it. Releases her, rises. Looks at her silently. Then)

Do you know what you're saying?

KIRA

Yes.

LEO

You don't know anything about me.

KIRA

I don't have to know.

LEO

And your parents?

KIRA

They'll throw me out when they hear of it. I don't care.

LEO

And if the G.P.U. gets me?

KIRA

They'll get us together.

LEO

Do you know what they'll do to you?

KIRA

You want me to go with you, don't you?

LEO

Yes.

KIRA

That's all I have to know.

LEO

I want you to go. I want you so much that I don't care what happens after-wards...even if they do get us...And if they don't...if they don't, perhaps you'll save me from more than the G.P.U. Perhaps you have already...It's funny. I found you because I thought you'd finish me. Now I'm afraid you'll be the one who'll save me. But I don't know whether I'll thank you for it.

(Draws her into his arms and kisses her. She does not resist.)

(Lights go out in the Institute windows.)

KIRA

Let's go. Before they see you.

LEO

(As they start walking away)
What's your name?

KIRA

Kira Argounova. And yours?

LEO

Leo Kovalensky.

CURTAIN

SCENE 2

About six months later. Spring of 1924. Hall in the Technological Institute. Late afternoon. A bare, dim, vaulted room. Door in back wall Left. An arch opening upon a corridor in Right wall upstage. A few uncomfortable wooden benches. A great profusion of gaudy posters, with red predominating: smokestacks, tractors, large workers in red blouses, appeals for donations to the Red Air Fleet, pictures of Lenin and Karl Marx with red bunting, a huge cotton streamer dominating it all, upstage Center, red with a white sickle and hammer and white letters proclaiming: "Proletarians of the World, Unite!"

Eight or ten STUDENTS, boys and girls, are loafing aimlessly in the hall; pale, tense, obviously undernourished faces, ragged clothes; some are smoking, some passing up and down restlessly, chewing sunflower seeds; all glance too often at an old clock on the wall and at the door leading into the Institute office. There is an atmosphere of tense, anxious waiting, of fear and hopelessly resigned despair.

The FIRST STUDENT of the previous scene is sitting on a high stone ledge in a niche, his green student's cap pushed recklessly to the back of his head, chewing sunflower seeds, spitting shells out noisily and singing softly, monotonously, as a flat, bitter wail.

FIRST STUDENT

(Singing, in Russian)

Hey, little apple,
Where are you rolling?

SECOND STUDENT

(Stopping abruptly in his nervous pacing)

Oh, shut up!

FIRST STUDENT

(With a weary, indifferent arrogance)

'Smatter, Comrade? Not getting nervous, are you? Because if you are, it won't help, you know. You'll still be expelled. All of us will. Why worry?

(Spits a shell out loudly and continues with his singing, louder and more defiantly)

FIRST GIRL

(Crushing a cigarette out viciously)

God damn it, I wish *they'd* hurry!

FIRST STUDENT

(Speaking lazily between snatches of song)

Patience, Comrade, patience...the purging committee will take its sweet time...They don't give a damn about you and your feelings.

COMMUNIST STUDENT

(Wearing a leather jacket and a red badge)

(Menacingly)

Look out, you! Found a good time to shoot your mouth off!

FIRST STUDENT

Oh, me—I've nothing to be afraid of—I know I'll be the first one kicked out. I've nothing to lose but my chains.

COMMUNIST STUDENT

(Making a step toward him)

What's that?!

FIRST STUDENT

(Pleasantly)

Marx. Karl Marx. Surely, there's nothing wrong in quoting Marx, now is there, Comrade?

SECOND GIRL

(Nervously)

They say there will be hundreds, *hundreds* expelled!

SECOND STUDENT

God, I wish they'd hurry and get it over with!

(Silence. The FIRST STUDENT sings through his teeth. The FIRST GIRL breaks down suddenly with a shrieking, hysterical sob.)

FIRST GIRL

(Screaming)

Oh, I can't! I can't! I can't lose my place here!...I've got to graduate!...I've got to get a job!...Mother's starving...if I don't...if I'm kicked out...what'll become of us?!...

FIRST STUDENT

(Slowly, sweetly, without raising his voice)

Shut up, you damn fool!...Who do you think cares whether you starve or not?

Second Student

(With hysterical bravado)

Shut up, all of you! Sure, it's a death sentence for us. But men don't whine before an execution. If *they* want to kick us out, let's meet it proudly...

(His voice breaks.)

...bravely...

Communist Student

(With a deadly ominous calm)

A fine speech—at a fine time. Rest assured it will be appreciated.

(COMRADE SONIA enters briskly, through archway, followed by PAVEL SYEROV.)

Comrade Sonia

Well, well, well! What's going on around here?

(No one answers. A cringing uncomfortable silence.)

Surely, you're not moping about because of such a little matter as the purging?

(Walks to Second Girl and slaps her affectionately on the shoulder)

What's the matter, dear? As a member in good standing of my Marxist Club, you know you have nothing to fear. Comrade Sonia is your friend. Comrade Sonia is everybody's friend!

First Girl

(Timidly)

Comrade Sonia...you're a member of the purging committee...you can tell me if...

Comrade Sonia

(Freezing, her manner officious)

I'm sorry. I do not discuss my official duty in private.

First Girl

(To Syerov)

Comrade Syerov, can you tell us when the list will come out...I mean, those expelled...I mean...

Syerov

(Striking an expansive, oratorical attitude)

Now let's get this clear about the purging, Comrades. No one will be expelled, except those of undesirable social origin, such as children of former bourgeois. Science is a weapon of class struggle. Proletarian schools are for the proletariat. We shall not educate our class enemies. This purging has been conducted strictly and solely on the basis of your social origin. Children of true proletarians among you have nothing to fear. That's all. It's very simple.

Fourth Student

Comrade Syerov, my social origin is above reproach. My father was a peasant, straight from the plow!

First Student

My pedigree's above reproach too. My parents were a peasant woman and two workers!

First Girl

(Hysterically)

Comrade Syerov... I... I... my father, he owned a grocery store before... before the revolution... but... but it's been nationalized... and my father's dead... and I... I'm a true proletarian in spirit... and... and I can't lose my place here... I...

(Breaks down into sobs. SYEROV turns away indifferently. The others are obviously sympathetic.)

Syerov

(With indignation)

I am ashamed of you, Comrades, if you feel any mawkish sympathy with the bourgeois in our midst, and their petty personal tragedies. We have outgrown the slobbering sentimentality and egotism of the bourgeois who whined for a personal career. We must remember that our sole aim and purpose in the Red Technological Institute is to become great engineers in the service of the Proletarian State. Such is our duty to Society! All of us exist only for the sake of society. Isn't that true, Comrades?

(A chorus of timid, half-hearted, eagerly obsequious voices answers hurriedly)

Students

Yes... of course... certainly... yes, Comrade Syerov... of course, Comrade Syerov... obviously... yes, Comrade Syerov!

Kira

(Offstage)

Oh rubbish, Comrade Syerov!

(She enters from corridor Right.)

First Student

(Applauding)

Good for you, Kira!

SYEROV

(Taken aback)

I beg your pardon, Comrade Argounova, what did you say?

KIRA

I said "No, Comrade Syerov"...I don't exist only for the sake of society.

SYEROV

Do you realize...

KIRA

No, I *don't* realize. What is society?

SYEROV

That's a perfectly childish question!

KIRA

(Deliberately naive)

But I don't understand it. Now for whom is it that I must exist? For you?

SYEROV

Certainly not.

KIRA

For Comrade Sonia here?

SYEROV

You're being perfectly ridiculous and...

KIRA

(Pointing at Fourth Student)

For that little runt over there?

SYEROV

Society, Comrade Argounova, is a stupendous whole!

KIRA

If you write a whole line of zeroes, it's still—nothing.

COMRADE SONIA

May I ask what you're doing here in our Red Technological Institute?

KIRA

Did it ever occur to you that I may be here for the very unusual, unnatural reason of wanting to learn a work I like only because I like it? If that's a great crime—go ahead, expel me for it. I know you will, anyway.

COMRADE SONIA

(Furiously)

Well, what can one expect from the daughter of an ex-factory owner! But we shall see what we shall see, and we don't have long to wait. When the purging list comes out, you'll find your beautiful white neck in a...

ANDREI

(Entering, quietly, with complete authority)

Leave her alone, Sonia.

COMRADE SONIA

Comrade Taganov, I demand this woman's arrest!

ANDREI

(Without moving or changing his voice)

I said leave her alone.

COMRADE SONIA

Look here, Taganov, do you think it's quite right for you, *in your position*, to tolerate such speeches as Comrade Argounova spouts here, and to take her side, and...

ANDREI

If you have any complaints to make about my conduct, you may report it to the Party and ask for my dismissal.

SYEROV

(With over-exaggerated enthusiasm)

Why, Comrade Sonia! How *can* you? We all know that Comrade Taganov is our most valuable worker, Party member since 1915, hero of the civil war! We cannot doubt his loyalty—even if some of his actions do seem *strange* at times.

(ANDREI ignores them and leads KIRA away from them, downstage.)

COMRADE SONIA

(Pointing at them venomously)

Look at them! The head of the G.P.U. detail and his best friend—the most insolent individualist we've got! Damn if I know what he sees in her!

SYEROV

Why, it's obvious.

COMRADE SONIA

Oh, no, not him! He's the kind of a saint that sleeps with red flags!

ANDREI

(To Kira, gently)
You shouldn't speak like that, Kira. Not here.

KIRA

And you shouldn't defend me, Andrei. Not here.

ANDREI

I know I shouldn't.

KIRA

Then why do you?

ANDREI

Because I think we're friends. Though don't ask me why we are, because I don't know that myself. We can never agree on anything. There isn't a thing in the world that we believe in common. Yet we meet here, and we talk, and we're always together. Don't ask me why.

KIRA

I know why. That's because we have the same root in both of us.

ANDREI

The same root? I, an ex-factory worker and you, the daughter of...

KIRA

Oh, stop being Marxist for five minutes! We have the same root. We both believe in life. It's a rare talent and it can't be taught. And it can't be explained to those in whom that word—life— doesn't awaken the kind of feeling that a temple does, or a military march. We both believe in it. But you want to fight for it, to kill for it, even to die—for life. I only want to live it.

(The door Center opens. A brusque young man with a list in his hand comes out hurriedly, ignoring the eager crowd that surges toward him. He posts the list on a blackboard on the wall, in a tense silence, and exits hastily. The crowd swarms to read the list, pushing one another frantically. KIRA shudders, makes a step forward and stops, controlling herself deliberately.)

FIRST STUDENT

(At the blackboard, pushing the crowd back)

Stand back, Comrades! Not all at once. I'll read the list aloud.
(Reading)

Citizens expelled from the Technological Institute of Petrograd as socially unde-sirable elements! Abankov, Ivan!...Avdeev, Sergei!...Avilova, Maria!...[5] (Etc.)

SYEROV

(To Sonia, uncomfortably, while the reading continues)

Come on, Sonia. Let's go. Your Marxist Club is in session, waiting for us.

COMRADE SONIA

(Looking in Kira's direction)

Wait a minute, there's something I want to see.

FIRST STUDENT

Akimova, Vera!
(A woman's scream rings out from the cluster of students, and the sound of a body falling; the FIRST GIRL has fainted.)

VOICES IN THE CROWD

Call the nurse!...Get her out of here!...Get some water!...Don't tramp on her, Comrades!...
(TWO BOYS carry the First Girl out. There are low moans, short, bitter gasps in the crowd as the FIRST STUDENT calls out their names, a few brusque, half-audible words: "Well, that's that!," "Oh, I knew it!," "Oh, God!," "Well, Comrades..." etc. STUDENTS leave the board, one by one, and wander away, some smiling cheerfully, sighing with relief, the majority haggard, white-faced, moving automatically in a stupor of despair.)

SECOND GIRL

(Jubilant)

My letter's past! I'm left! I'm left! Oh, thank God!
(Seeing the condemning stare of Comrade Sonia)

Oh, I beg your pardon! I didn't mean that!
(Runs away hurriedly)

FIRST STUDENT

Annisov, Vladimir!...Ar...
(Stops suddenly. With a mighty effort, in a dull, unnaturally steady voice.)

---

[5] The next name called is Akimova, so Avdeev and Avilova seem to be out of alphabetical order. Shoshana Milgram informed me, however, that in Russian these names are where they belong.

Arbatov, Stepan…Didn't I tell you? I'm kicked out. Well, long live the Dictatorship of the Proletariat!…Arbenkov, Nikolai!…

COMRADE SONIA

(To Syerov, with the best coquetry she can muster)

How about a little celebration tonight, Pavel? At my place? Just the two of us?

SYEROV

(Brusquely)

Sorry. Can't. Have a Club meeting tonight. Some other time.

FIRST STUDENT

Argounova, Kira!

(KIRA stands motionless; there is no cry, no sound or movement from her; only the sudden rigidity of her whole body shows that she had heard. ANDREI steps aside, watching her tensely. COMRADE SONIA chuckles loudly.)

FIRST STUDENT

(Ferociously, to Sonia and Syerov)

Oh, you God damned swine!

(Exits furiously)

(The STUDENTS surge toward the list. During the following scene, they drift off one by one, and others come to read the list.)

COMRADE SONIA

Well, Comrade Argounova, you didn't expect it, did you?

(KIRA does not move or look at her.)

Your dear friend Comrade Taganov was on the purging committee, you know, but he didn't lift a finger to help you.

KIRA

(Turning to her slowly)

I didn't expect him to.

SYEROV

(Uneasily)

Come on, Sonia, the Club is waiting.

(SYEROV and SONIA exit. KIRA turns slowly toward Andrei. He does not move. She makes an effort and smiles at him cheerfully.)

KIRA

It's all right, Andrei. I know you couldn't help it.

ANDREI

I'd give you my place—if I could.

KIRA

Oh, it's all right...Well...I guess I won't be a builder after all...I guess I won't build any aluminum bridges...

(She tries to laugh.)

It's all right, because everybody always told me one can't build a bridge of aluminum anyway.

ANDREI

Kira, I've fought in the Red Army. I've watched men being executed by the G.P.U. squads. But...but this is the hardest thing I've ever had to do.

KIRA

Do you know that that's exactly why I like you?

ANDREI

What?

KIRA

That you didn't try to help me and make an exception for me...And, Andrei, this doesn't mean that we won't see each other any more, does it?

ANDREI

(Taking her hand in both of his)

It doesn't, Kira, if you...

KIRA

Well, then, it doesn't.

ANDREI

Will you let me come to your house now?

KIRA

(Too frightened by the simple question)

No!...Oh, no, Andrei...

(Nervously, hurriedly)

You know that you promised me long ago never to call at my house. My...my parents would...they'd be frightened, you know what they are, and they'd never understand my friendship with a Communist. You must forgive them.

ANDREI

But...

KIRA

No!...Please, Andrei, please promise me that you'll never come to my house!

ANDREI

Why, certainly, I promise, if you prefer it. But will you call on me?

KIRA

Of course. You know I will. It's funny, but you, of all people, are the only real friend I have.

ANDREI

If you'll need a job now, I can arrange it for you.

KIRA

Thank you, Andrei. I'll need it.

ANDREI

I don't want to lose sight of you now.

KIRA

(Pointing at the board, defiantly)

Oh, that...Don't worry about that. I'm not finished. I'm not afraid. I'll be afraid only on a day that will never come: the day when I give up!

(LEO enters through archway; his face is set, grim. KIRA stops short.)

LEO

Allo, Kira.

KIRA

(A little nervously)

Good evening, Leo...This is Andrei Taganov—Leo Kovalensky.

(The two men shake hands, eyeing each other coldly.)

LEO

(To Kira)

I thought I'd drop in for you on my way home from the University.

ANDREI

(To Leo)

Haven't I met you before?

LEO

I don't think so.

ANDREI

Wasn't your father Admiral Kovalensky, executed six months ago?

LEO

Yes.
(Looking at Andrei closely)
I remember now; I saw you at the G.P.U.

ANDREI

When you surrendered yourself two weeks after his execution.

LEO

Kind of you to remind me.

ANDREI

You were released, weren't you?

LEO

Sure. To have every stray Communist stare at me as if you had it branded on my forehead; son of Admiral Kovalensky, executed for...

KIRA

Leo, please!

LEO

...and to have me kicked out of the University for the same crime of having been born!

KIRA

Leo! You...you're expelled?

LEO

(Nods)
What could you expect?...And yourself?
(She points silently at list on board.)
On the list?
(She nods. LEO turns to Andrei.)
I hope, Comrade Taganov, that you're enjoying this!
(To Kira)
Come on, Kira. Let's go.

KIRA

Andrei, I...I...

ANDREI

It's all right, Kira. I understand.

(KIRA and LEO turn to go.)

CURTAIN

SCENE 3

Same evening. Leo's home. A room that represents a visual illustration of the revolution, combining the luxury of the old with the misery of the new. The room, a former bedroom, had obviously been beautiful once; it is done in a graceful, subdued color-scheme of gray, silver, and black; a rich gray carpet, now spotted and bald-patched; a wide bed with a faded silver spread; silvery-gray curtains at the two tall windows, Center, and at the two doors: Right and Left; a rich, silver-maple wardrobe; a black onyx fireplace, downstage, Right; graceful chairs upholstered in gray satin, now split and spotted. The new order of things is evidenced by a crude old kitchen table, cluttered with old dishes, soot-blackened pans, paper sacks and a Primus; a "Bourgeoise"—an old, rusty, square iron stove at the fireplace, with long black pipes rising high and turning at a straight angle to disappear in a hole cut over the fireplace; an old tin can is suspended on wires from the pipe joint to gather dripping soot; a smaller table with tiny glass tubes and a tin of saccharine crystals on it;[6] a profusion of books, papers, Kira's blue-prints, scattered everywhere for lack of storage space. The room is now bedroom, dining room, study, and kitchen combined. It is dirty, badly neglected, desolate.

At curtain rise, the stage is empty, dark. Bands of light show under the two doors. The strains of Chopin's Valse #2, played expertly on the piano, come from behind the door Right.

A doorbell rings offstage, Left. Steps are heard approaching. The door Left is thrown open. CITIZEN LAVROVA enters and presses a button, lighting the room. She is followed by GALINA PETROVNA. LAVROVA is a plain, thin, young girl, in a filthy, faded kimono. GALINA PETROVNA is a tall, dried-out, domineering woman in her fifties, an ex-grande-dame, in spite of her ancient bedraggled clothes; when she speaks, she uses her hands a great deal, with graceful, studied movements, as if drawing attention to them deliberately; her hands are swollen, purple, though they had obviously been beautiful once.

---

[6] In the novel, Kira's family (not Kira and Leo, as in this scene) try to make money by packaging saccharine for someone else who produces it.

LAVROVA

You can wait here, Citizen. They ain't home yet.

GALINA PETROVNA

(Sitting down, unbuttoning her coat)
Can you tell me what time Kira will be back?

LAVROVA

How should I know?

GALINA PETROVNA

You're the new tenant, I believe?

LAVROVA

Yeah.
(Reaches into the pocket of her kimono for a handful of sunflower seeds and offers them to Galina Petrovna.)
Want some sunflower seeds?

GALINA PETROVNA

(With indignation)
No, indeed, thank you.

LAVROVA

(Chewing the seeds and spitting the shells out)
And a fine joint this is, let me tell you.
(Points at door Right)
That damn piano in there going all day long. An old maid lives there, a Countess or something. And your friends in here—a fine couple of bourgeois. Citizen Argounova's parents owned a factory before the revolution, a textile factory, the bastards!

GALINA PETROVNA

My dear young lady, I happen to be Citizen Argounova's mother.

LAVROVA

(Laughs loudly)
Well, that's a good one!
(The music stops abruptly. OLGA IVANOVNA enters brusquely from door Right. She is a tall, homely, anemic spinster in her thirties, with an old-fashioned hairdress, with shabby, painfully neat clothes, pathetic in their obvious attempt at gentility.)

Olga Ivanovna

Oh, good evening, Galina Petrovna.

Galina Petrovna

Good evening.

Olga Ivanovna

(To Lavrova)
So you're home, Citizen Lavrova? Have you taken my hair brush again?

Lavrova

Aw, stingy, aren't you, of a measly hair brush!

Olga Ivanovna

How many times do I have to ask you not to touch anything in my room when I'm out?

Lavrova

What are you gonna do about it? Report me?

Olga Ivanovna

Kindly return it to me.

Lavrova

Oh, hell!
(Exits Left and we hear her rummaging through her room, throwing things aside violently.)

Galina Petrovna

You were playing beautifully, Olga Ivanovna.

Olga Ivanovna

Oh, thank you. What other consolation is there, these days, but music? Music and prayer. People have forgotten the simple faith, that's why we're all suffering.

Galina Petrovna

(Sighs; takes a small nail buffer from her bag and busies herself polishing her nails, while she goes on talking.)
That was Chopin, wasn't it? Just like in the old days? That valse reminded me of the night when I almost lost my necklace. I was dancing, the clasp broke, it was a ruby necklace... I never wore any jewelry but diamonds and rubies...

Olga Ivanovna

Mother never let me wear jewels, I was too young...in those days. But I had a string of pearls grandmother gave me...I sold that...But I kept the piano...I think I'd die if I had to give up the piano.

Lavrova

(Rushing in with the brush in her hand)

Here's your damn brush! Had to wreck the room to find it.

Olga Ivanovna

May I mention another matter, Citizen Lavrova? Would you be so kind as to clean the bathroom after you leave it? That bathroom is a disgrace. It...

Lavrova

Aw, clean it yourself if you're so damn bourgeois about your bathroom! I ain't got time. I gotta lecture to prepare. I'm gonna give a lecture at the Educational Club of Revolutionary Sciences for our less enlightened comrades. Say, maybe you can help me. You know this damn German history. What century did they hang Robespierre in? Or was that France? Or did they hang him?

Olga Ivanovna

I am sorry, Citizen, I haven't the time to assist you.

(Turns and exits with dignity. The valse starts again.)

Lavrova

The lazy prehistorical fossil!

Galina Petrovna

Young lady, is that a way to speak about your elders?

Lavrova

Leave me alone; I've had enough of your type of...

(KIRA and LEO enter, Left)

Kira

(Stops at seeing Galina Petrovna)

Oh!...

(Indifferently)

Good evening, mother.

Leo

How do you do, Galina Petrovna?

GALINA PETROVNA

Good evening, children.

KIRA

(To Lavrova)

What are you doing in our room again? Get out of here!

LAVROVA

Hell, you'd think you owned the house!

(Exits Left, slamming the door. KIRA takes off her coat and hat.)

GALINA PETROVNA

My word, what an uncivil tenant you have!

LEO

(Removing his coat)

Can't help it. She was put in here forcibly by the House Manager. Now we have just this one room left. We sued in court to have her moved, but...

(Shrugs)

Well, she's a member of the Communist Union of Youth and we...you know what we are.

GALINA PETROVNA

Such times, the Lord help us!...We've had a tenant forced on us and he stole our stove and we can't get it back. And the cold these days! Look at what it's done to my hands!

(Exhibits her hands gracefully)

You know, Leo, I used to have the most beautiful hands in St. Petersburg. There was even a poem written about them, it was called "Champagne and Galina's Hands."

(Looks at her hands critically)

I do think they've changed—a little. But I'm taking good care of them. No matter what happens, I'll never neglect my hands.

KIRA

How is father? And Lydia?

GALINA PETROVNA

Oh...They're fine, thank you, only...only...I just dropped in to...to ask you...

(Hesitates)

Of course, I never would, for myself, but your father, Kira, he's not so well and...and...

KIRA

What is it, mother?

GALINA PETROVNA

(Bluntly, bravely, awed by the immensity of her request)

I wonder if I could borrow two rubles!

LEO

(Looks at her with a bitter little smile, slowly puts his hand in his pocket and throws a few coins down on the table. Softly, without reproach.)

That's all.

GALINA PETROVNA

(Appalled)

All?

LEO

All we have left. Let's see...seventy-six kopeks.

(Pushing half the coins toward her)

Take forty. We'll manage.

GALINA PETROVNA

No! Lord, no! I couldn't!

LEO

(Without any emotion)

Well, what are you going to do? Starve on the street? I saw a woman on the street yesterday, she fell in the gutter, she was dead, from hunger...

(GALINA PETROVNA stares at him miserably.)

Take it. We have some more coming tomorrow for this saccharine.

GALINA PETROVNA

(Gathering the coins avidly)

Thank you, Leo. You're a wonderful boy, Leo...you're like a real son...I wish...I wish you two would...Why don't you and Kira get married?

KIRA

Mother, we've agreed not to discuss that long ago.

GALINA PETROVNA

(With resignation)

Oh, well, it's your business…Of course, you've never listened to your elders. A stubborn brat, that's all you've ever been…Oh, well, things aren't what they were ten years ago…I'll return the money as soon as I can, Leo.

LEO

Don't worry about it, Galina Petrovna. We won't need it.

GALINA PETROVNA

I didn't realize things were that bad with you. How did you ever lose that grand job you had, Leo, translating books?

LEO

Why bring that up? I lost it. That's all.

(Coughs. Paces up and down the room nervously.)

I lost it because I refused to work without pay every night for "Social Activity," as they call it, to prove my social enthusiasm, or some damn thing. It was supposed to be voluntary work. It *was* voluntary. I only lost my job for refusing to volunteer!

GALINA PETROVNA

I can't say that I blame you. As for me, I'd rather starve than take any Soviet job. After all, there is such a thing as pride…But since you've compromised already, how about that position on a magazine someone promised you?

LEO

The boss's cousin got it.

GALINA PETROVNA

And that Soviet office?

KIRA

The manager asked a hundred rubles for the job.

GALINA PETROVNA

How about the teaching of foreign languages you were going to do?

LEO

Well, the school said I couldn't work there unless I belonged to the Pedagogues Union. The Union said I couldn't join unless I was working.

(Coughs)

GALINA PETROVNA

You better do something about that cough of yours, Leo.

LEO

Oh, that's nothing. Just a little cold I caught working in caissons on a river bottom...Don't worry about us. We're packing this saccharine now for a speculator. Doesn't pay much, but we could get along on it, if they hadn't raised the rent.

GALINA PETROVNA

(Horrified)

They raised your rent?

KIRA

Sure. Because we're unemployed.

GALINA PETROVNA

But you're both students and...

LEO

Not any more.

GALINA PETROVNA

What?! You mean...the purging? You...you're not...

KIRA

Yes. Expelled. Kicked out. Both of us.

GALINA PETROVNA

Oh, my poor children! My poor dear children! Those rotten swine...

KIRA

(Brusquely)

Please, mother. It doesn't matter. Forget about it.

GALINA PETROVNA

Maybe...maybe something can be done. Could you appeal or...

(KIRA shakes her head.)

But what are you going to do?

LEO

Look for work.

KIRA

Andrei Taganov promised to help me get a job.

LEO

I wish you wouldn't accept favors from a Communist.

KIRA

But he's my friend, Leo, and I like him.

(To Galina Petrovna)

Mother, if Andrei should telephone me at your house, please be sure to let him understand that I'm living there, with you.

GALINA PETROVNA

Well, what's that? Why?

KIRA

Because I've never told him...about Leo. I don't want to tell him. I can't bring him here. Leo won't...

LEO

I won't have him here. I don't mind if Kira wants a Communist for a friend, it's her business, but if he came here...well, I couldn't be polite to one of them.

KIRA

Besides, he's a G.P.U. man. And...well, you know Leo's past...It would be dangerous, he'd suspect Leo without any reason, as they always do.

GALINA PETROVNA

Your Andrei isn't getting jealous, is he?

KIRA

Oh, mother, of course not. He's just a friend.

GALINA PETROVNA

I certainly wouldn't be friendly with a Communist if I were you...But then I've never been able to understand you, anyway. I'll tell him anything you wish, I don't care...

(Rising)

Well, I have to go. Your father and sister haven't eaten anything since morning...Thank you, children. I'll return it as soon as I can.

KIRA

Good night, mother.

LEO

Good night, Galina Petrovna.

(GALINA PETROVNA exits. KIRA and LEO stand looking at each other silently.)

KIRA

(With an effort to sound gay)

Sit down, dear. Rest. I'll fix us some dinner.

> (She walks to kitchen table, tries to light the Primus. She pumps the handle furiously, but it doesn't work. Helplessly.)

The Primus is stuck again. We'll have to light the stove.

> (LEO walks to stove, kneels down, slips tiny logs and crumpled newspapers into it, strikes a match. The wood doesn't light; gusts of smoke blow back into the room; LEO blows on them desperately, coughing.)

KIRA

Really, Leo, you should see a doctor about that cough.

LEO

Oh, that's nothing. We can't waste the little money we have on doctors for a silly cold.

> (KIRA looks through the bags on the kitchen table, finds most of them empty, except one small bag of millet; she looks at it closely, smells it, puts it aside, searches frantically through the others; then picks up the millet bag again.)

KIRA

There's nothing left but this millet here and…and I'm afraid it's slightly mildewed…

(LEO shrugs.)

I'll cook it anyway. We have to eat something.

> (The wood catches fire at last. LEO rises. KIRA empties the millet bag into a pan, pours water from a pitcher and puts the pan on the stove. LEO stands at the fireplace, his back to her, his head in his arms on the mantelpiece. Then he whirls toward her suddenly.)

LEO

(Fiercely)

Let's borrow some vodka from our good neighbor Citizen Lavrova, and let's drink, drink and to hell with all of it!

KIRA

Leo!

LEO

Don't stare at me like that!…It's a good old custom to drink at births, and weddings and funerals…Well, we weren't born together, Comrade Argounova.

And we've never had a wedding, Comrade Argounova. But we might yet see the other...We might...yet...the other...Kira...

(Falls down on chair. She rushes to him, kneels by his side.)

KIRA

Leo...dearest...don't...Don't!...We have to think clearly now...We can't give up...You must spare yourself.

LEO

For what?

KIRA

For...

LEO

What is there left to us? Saccharine as a career and this Primus here as an inspiration! And now—not even a future.

KIRA

There's always a future.

LEO

For the aluminum bridge?

KIRA

It doesn't matter, Leo, as long as we don't give up.

LEO

What is there to give up now, that they haven't taken already?

KIRA

(Very simply)
You.

LEO

(Looks at her, smiles slowly)
You'd be better off without me.

KIRA

(Smiling)
Do you want me to leave you?

LEO

(Drawing her into his arms)

Would you?

(She laughs happily, her head buried on his shoulder.)

Darling, do you know that you're my worst enemy?

KIRA

Why?

LEO

Because I still have a reason for living.

KIRA

(Looks at him, then laughs softly, happily)

Did they throw me out of the Institute today? Funny, I seem to have forgotten all about it.

LEO

Don't be so happy. Don't be glad if I'm fool enough to love you with every living breath of mine when we're trapped in an age that gives us no right to breathe. Sometimes, I almost wish I didn't have you. You are that which I've lost long ago. But I'm trying to hold on to it, to that which you think I am, which I know I was, even though I can't hold on much longer. And, that's all I have to offer you.

KIRA

And that, Leo, is what they'll never take away from us.

LEO

Maybe.

(Walks to stove, sits down wearily)

KIRA

(Sitting down at his feet)

Listen, dear, let's forget all about today, about that purging. We're not finished. We can still fight...When I saw you for the first time, Leo, when I went with you, it was because...because I knew, then, that you're everything I want of life, everything they won't let me have today. And I won't let them break you.

LEO

What can you do?

KIRA

I'll get a job, and we'll work very hard, and try to save money, and then...We're still young, we're still alive, so much is still possible! We'll find some way to...to go abroad.

LEO

Abroad...Such a place does exist somewhere, doesn't it?...Abroad...

KIRA

It won't be too late. We'll go to school—there. Until then—don't think of anything. Try not to think.

LEO

I'll think of you. I'll get a job, I'll attend all their Clubs, all their meetings, I'll say all they want me to say, I'll talk of my great devotion to the proletarian cause. But I'll be thinking of you, working for you. Then I won't feel like a traitor.

KIRA

Leo, there's only one thing that matters and that we'll remember. I don't care what life is to be nor what it does to us. But it won't break us. That's the only banner we can hold against theirs. We'll fight it all, Leo: those millions, and our country and our century!

LEO

(Without much hope)

We'll try.

CURTAIN

SCENE 4

Four months later. Fall of 1924. Late afternoon. An office in the "House of the Peasant." A large room formerly part of a private mansion. Only the flowered walls, tall doors and windows, and carved marble columns remain of its former splendor; the rest is of recent origin: a low unpainted wooden railing separating the office proper from a small anteroom before entrance door Right, battered desks, rickety chairs, file cabinets, telephones, an old typewriter, the usual amount of red posters, slogans and pictures of proletarian leaders on the walls. A door marked "Comrade Voronov" in Center wall Left. Two windows in wall Left; a heavy rain is pounding the windows.

As the curtain rises the office work is in full swing. A young GIRL is battering a typewriter noisily; two others are busy at filing cabinets; a young MAN is working at a desk. KIRA stands before a desk, counting a tall pile of pamphlets in red paper covers. She wears an old faded patched black dress; her face is gaunt, paler than before; her manner is tense, nervous, barely disguising a consuming anxiety. COMRADE BITIUK, the office manager, a tall, thin, military looking woman, is gushing loudly into a telephone.

COMRADE BITIUK

...yes, yes, Comrade, it's all arranged. At one o'clock the Comrades peasants of the Siberian delegation go to the Museum of the Revolution. At three o'clock they visit our Marxist Club. At five o'clock they are expected at the circle of the Pioneers where there will be a display of physical culture drills by the dear little tots...yes, Comrade we have arranged everything. The House of the Peasant is the heart of a gigantic net that pours the light of the new proletarian culture into the darkest corners of our villages!...Goodbye Comrade.

(Hangs up, whirls around in her chair, snapping a military command)

Comrade Argounova! Do you have the requisition for the special lecture for the Comrades of the Siberian delegation?

KIRA

No, Comrade Bitiuk.

COMRADE BITIUK

Where is it?

KIRA

In Comrade Voronov's office. He hasn't signed it yet.

COMRADE BITIUK

Some people do not realize the tremendous cultural importance of the work we are doing!

COMMUNIST GIRL

(Suavely, but with unmistakable menace)

What was that, Comrade Bitiuk?

COMRADE BITIUK

(Hastily)

Of course I didn't mean to criticize our chief, Comrade Voronov. I meant you, Comrade Argounova. You do not show sufficient interest in your work and pro-letarian consciousness. That's what happens when one has to employ bourgeois who have Communist friends...Of course I didn't mean to criticize Comrade Taganov. See that you do justice to his recommendation in the future, Comrade Argounova.

KIRA

Yes, Comrade Bitiuk.

(Telephone rings)

COMRADE BITIUK

(Picking up receiver)

Allo…Yes, speaking…Oh, yes, Comrade. The Comrade peasants of the Ukranian delegation are expected at a lecture on "The Clamping of the Red City and Village"…Yes, the lecture…

(A bearded, ragged PEASANT has entered from door Right during her speech and stands timidly, expectantly crumpling his fur cap in one hand, scratching his head with the other. COMRADE BITIUK waves to Kira.)

Comrade Argounova, take care of the comrade peasant!

COMRADE BITIUK	(KIRA approaches the Peasant, her
(Continues on telephone)	manner automatically gushing, officious,
The lecture is all ready but you can	a good imitation of Comrade Bitiuk.)
have a choice of subjects: either that	KIRA
or "The Work Bench and the Plow"	What can I do for you, Comrade?
…or else "Marxism in City and	PEASANT
Village"…or "Leninism in Field	(Timidly, uncertainly)
and Factory"…Fine…Goodbye	Well…you see Comrade…as how that
Comrade.	grain matter…

KIRA

What delegation are you from, Comrade?

PEASANT

Well, we came from Saratov and…

KIRA

Oh yes, it's all arranged. At five o'clock there's an excursion for the comrades of your delegation through the Winter Palace where you can see how the Czar lived…an easy visualized lesson in class tyranny—and then…

PEASANT

Now about that grain shortage matter, Comrade…

KIRA

Then, after the excursion we have a special lecturer for you on "The Doom of Capitalism." It's all arranged.

PEASANT

That's fine, Comrade. But you see as how about that shortage, they said they'll send a punitive squad to our village and we can't…

KIRA

Now you must remember, Comrade, that the most important thing is the proper revolutionary ideology. You must attend these lectures and…

PEASANT

As God is my witness, we can't deliver that grain. May God strike me on this spot, Comrade, we can't. There ain't none to deliver. Take my own family for instance...

KIRA

You better hurry now, Comrade, or you'll be late for the excursion.

PEASANT

(Looking around helplessly, totally bewildered)

Well, I...I thought this here was the "House of the Peasant" and I thought as how you could help and...

KIRA

Of course, Comrade.

(Recites as a well memorized lesson)

The House of the Peasant is the heart of a gigantic net that pours the light of the new proletarian culture into the darkest corners of our villages. You just attend the lectures, Comrade, and they'll explain it all to you. Good day, Comrade.

(She returns to her desk. The PEASANT exits dazedly.)

COMRADE BITIUK

Comrade Argounova! Come here!

KIRA

(Approaching her)

Yes, Comrade Bitiuk?

COMRADE BITIUK

Comrade Argounova, this is no way to handle a situation such as this. If a citizen shows signs of a counterrevolutionary deviation, you must remind him that we're living in a temporary period of...

KIRA

(Obediently)

...State Construction.

COMRADE BITIUK

Precisely. And that we all must sacrifice and bear hardships patiently for the sake of...

KIRA

...the great Worker Peasant Collective.

COMRADE BITIUK

That's right. And that all these hardships are caused by...

KIRA

(Uncertainly)

...State Construction?

COMRADE BITIUK

(Indignantly)

Certainly not! By...

COMMUNIST GIRL

(Hurriedly)

...by the spineless socialists of the foreign countries who sold out to their bourgeois masters and did not join us in a World Soviet Revolution!

COMRADE BITIUK

Exactly! What's the matter, Comrade Argounova? Have you neglected your social studies?

KIRA

No, Comrade Bitiuk.

COMRADE BITIUK

Well, you'll have to do better than that! What's the matter with you lately? You tramp around like a ghost. You pay no attention to your work. You...

KIRA

I...I have some trouble...at home, Comrade Bitiuk.

COMRADE BITIUK

Personal trouble is no concern of ours. Your public work comes first. I understand you've gone so far as to miss the last session of our Marxist Club. You are actually neglecting your Social Activity!

KIRA

I...I try my best not to, Comrade Bitiuk. I attended a demonstration yesterday. I gave free lessons at our school Tuesday. I read a thesis at the Marxist Club Saturday. I didn't miss a single session but that last one...and that was because...because...

COMRADE BITIUK

Well?

KIRA

You see...there's someone at home...my...someone very dear to me. He's ill. Dangerously ill. I had to...

COMRADE BITIUK

So a private illness keeps you away from your social duties? A fine example of bourgeois psychology! Well let me tell you: there's a purging coming here, a reduction of staffs, and you know what awaits those who are not socially minded. Friends of Comrade Taganov or no friends of Comrade Taganov!

KIRA

But...

COMRADE BITIUK

That's all!

> (KIRA returns to her desk meekly, head bowed.)

CLERK

> (YOUNG GIRL sitting at the next desk bends over to Kira and whispers sympathetically.)

Any luck at that last hospital?

KIRA

The doctor in charge wouldn't even see him.

> (They go on working, talking in low voices.)

CLERK

How about that friend of mine I gave you a letter to?

KIRA

He said they had hundreds on their waiting list. Trade Union members. They couldn't even register him.

CLERK

Did you ever think of a private sanatorium? There are some.

> (KIRA shrugs hopelessly.)

'Smatter? Money?

KIRA

(Fiercely)

Money! And *what* money! Do you know how much it would cost?

CLERK

(Sighing)

That's too bad. What are you gonna do?

KIRA

I'll get him to a sanatorium. I'll get the money if I have to murder for it!

CLERK

How about Comrade Taganov? He got you this job. Maybe he could...

KIRA

(On the breaking point)

Oh forget Comrade Taganov!

(She continues counting the pamphlets—looks at Comrade Voronov's door. Hesitates. Drops the books and walks resolutely to the door. Knocks. An imposing SECRETARY opens. She whispers to him.)

SECRETARY

(Loudly)

No, Comrade, impossible!

(Slams door. She returns to her desk.)

(PAVEL SYEROV enters from door Right, swings the gate in the railing open and walks familiarly to Comrade Bitiuk's desk.)

SYEROV

(Cheerfully slapping her shoulder)

Good afternoon, Comrade Bitiuk! Busy as ever! More workers like you is what we need!

COMRADE BITIUK

(Sweet as sugar)

Oh, how do you do, Comrade Syerov. What can I do for you today?

SYEROV

We have a meeting of the Railroad Workers Union Club tomorrow—I'm secretary, you know— and I thought it would be a good idea if we could have a peasant delegation there, you know, real peasants from the soil, and we'll talk about Class Solidarity.

COMRADE BITIUK

What a sweet idea! Certainly, Comrade Syerov, certainly, we'll arrange it.

(Makes note on pad)

SYEROV

The meeting's for five o'clock.

(COMRADE SONIA rushes in from door Right.)

COMRADE SONIA

Ah, Pavel, there you are! They told me at your club that I'll find you here.

SYEROV

(Far from pleasantly)

Oh...how do you do, Sonia.

COMRADE SONIA

It's been ages and ages since I saw you last!

(With flatfooted coquetry)

You're not avoiding me, are you, bad boy?

SYEROV

Of course not, Sonia, my pal. But such a busy active person as you are...

COMRADE SONIA

You just wait for me a minute. I have some business here and then we can go together.

SYEROV

I'd love nothing better, but sorry, pal, have to run, urgent business. Special duty above personal pleasure, you know. So long!

(Exits hurriedly)

(COMRADE SONIA looks after him dejectedly, frowning.)

COMRADE BITIUK

What can I do for you, Comrade Sonia?

COMRADE SONIA

(Imperiously)

We need five hundred copies of the "ABC of Communism"[7] for our Club of Women Houseworkers, all peasant women, from the plow, you know, I'm honorary chairman, send the books to the club office, not later than tomorrow afternoon!

COMRADE BITIUK

Right, Comrade Sonia.

(Whirling in her chair)

Comrade Argounova! Five hundred copies of the "ABC of Communism" for the Club of Women Houseworkers!

---

[7] An elementary textbook of Soviet Communism, written by Nikolai Bukharin and Yevgeni Preobrazhensky, and published in 1920.

KIRA

(Making a note)

Yes, Comrade Bitiuk.

COMRADE SONIA

(Bursts out laughing)

Well, well, well! A loyal citizen like Comrade Argounova in the Red House of the Peasant!

COMRADE BITIUK

(Whispering nervously into Sonia's ear)

I know, I know, Comrade. But it's not my fault. You see how it is: Comrade Taganov of the G.P.U. got her the job. I couldn't help it, please don't doubt my loyalty, I'll rectify the matter at the next purging!

COMRADE SONIA

Don't worry, I understand.

(Walks through partition to Kira's desk)

Well how are you, Comrade Argounova?

KIRA

(Coldly)

How do you do.

COMRADE SONIA

Working in the House of the Peasant only because *you* like the work? Or have you changed your mind?

KIRA

(With an effort, in a dull unnatural voice)

I don't know what you're talking about. My ideology is above reproach. I'm very active socially.

COMRADE SONIA

So? You are, are you? We know you bourgeois. All you're active for is to keep your measly jobs. You're not fooling anyone. By the way, we don't see you with Comrade Taganov anymore. You two haven't quarreled, have you?

KIRA

No.

COMRADE SONIA

He hasn't deserted you by any chance, has he? And it was such a lovely friendship!

(Turns to go)

KIRA

Comrade Sonia?

COMRADE SONIA

Yes?

KIRA

Does Comrade Taganov still attend lectures at the Institute?

COMRADE SONIA

Certainly. And it will do him good in the Party if he's not seen with a woman of your social origin!

    (Exits)

    (KIRA stands looking after her helplessly.)

CLERK

    (In a whisper)

What's the matter? Has Comrade Taganov...

KIRA

    (Desperately)

He refuses to see me! I don't know what happened. He won't answer his telephone. He missed his last date with me. We used to be such good friends...all summer long...Then suddenly...I can't understand it!

CLERK

But what on earth...

KIRA

I don't know! And now, now of all times, when I need him so badly, when he could...

    (Checks herself abruptly; continues stacking the pamphlets fiercely)

    (LEO enters from door Right. He's wearing old ragged rain-soaked clothes, a short patched jacket, a cap, a scarf wound around his neck; he is pale, gaunt, exhausted; his clothes and hands are smeared with mud.)

    (KIRA jumps up when she sees him and rushes to railing.)

LEO

    (Weary)

Allo, Kira...I couldn't get away sooner.

KIRA

    (Staring at him, terrified)

Is it...is it awfully hard work, Leo?

LEO

No, it's all right. Don't worry. Did you get the bread?

KIRA

(Trying to hide the despair in her voice)

No. I couldn't. I...we had a mass meeting to attend during the lunch hour and I couldn't stand in line for the bread. I...

LEO

(Coughing)

That's all right. I'll get along without it.

KIRA

(Producing a little hunk of bread wrapped in paper from her pocket)

Here, a girl gave me that, take it, it's better than nothing.

LEO

(Pushing the bread aside)

No. I'm not hungry. Eat it yourself. You need it.

KIRA

I don't! I'm not hungry at all. Please, Leo...you...you haven't eaten anything today, and...

LEO

A fellow on the gang gave me a piece of dried fish. So really, I'm not hungry. I only came because you told me to.

KIRA

Leo, please I...

COMRADE BITIUK

(Sternly)

What is this, Comrade Argounova? Personal visitors during business hours?

KIRA

Comrade Bitiuk, I...

COMRADE BITIUK

Go back to your desk!

(To Leo)

Out of here, Citizen! This is a business office, not a restaurant!

LEO

(To Kira)

It's all right, dear. Don't worry. I'll see you later.
(Exits)
(KIRA stands staring at the bread in her hand.)

COMRADE BITIUK

What does this mean, Comrade Argounova?

KIRA

That's...that's a friend of mine...we...he had nothing to eat in the house, and he's working just around the corner on a gang repairing the street, and I told him to come here after lunch hour. I thought I'd get my bread ration today, but...

COMRADE BITIUK

Hereafter, Comrade Argounova, you will kindly refrain from inviting guests to your place of business. You have more important duties to attend to.

(KIRA returns to her desk, picks up her pamphlets, looks at Comrade Voronov's door. Telephone rings.)

COMRADE BITIUK
(Picking up receiver)
Allo...oh yes, Comrade...
the club meeting will be at eight
o'clock tonight and the guest
speaker will give a lecture on
"Capitalistic Exploitation"...
yes indeed...after that there
will be communal singing of the
Internationale and all the Red
songs...yes...goodbye
Comrade...
(Hangs up)

(Telephone rings)

(KIRA rises resolutely, walks to
Comrade Voronov's door, knocks.
SECRETARY throws it open.)
KIRA
Comrade, could I please...

SECRETARY
No! How many times do I have to tell you?
Comrade Voronov can't see you!
(Slams door)
(She returns slowly to her desk.)

COMRADE BITIUK

(Picking up receiver)

Allo...yes...*what?*!...I didn't know, I assure you Comrade. I'm so sorry!...I certainly shan't allow it!
(Hangs up)
(Calls)
Comrade Argounova!

KIRA

(Approaching her)

Yes, Comrade Bitiuk?

COMRADE BITIUK

What's this I hear? Comrade Voronov's secretary complains that you've been pestering him for two days trying to see Comrade Voronov! The presumption! Do you think our chief has time to see every stray clerk in the place? Going over my head, are you? What are you after?

KIRA

(Gathering her courage)

Comrade Bitiuk, it's very important, I have a favor to ask. Could you...

COMRADE BITIUK

Well?

KIRA

Comrade Bitiuk, could I please have an advance of my salary for six months?

COMRADE BITIUK

(Gasps)

Well! Lost your mind, have you?

KIRA

(Desperately trying to control herself)

Please listen! Please let me explain! It's...my friend, the one you saw here. He's dangerously ill. He...he has tuberculosis.

COMRADE BITIUK

(The word makes no impression on her whatever.)

Well? What of it?

KIRA

I've got to have money to send him to a private sanatorium in the Crimea. It's the only thing that can save him. The doctor said another winter in Petrograd would be fatal. You've seen what kind of work he is doing—it will kill him...please let me have the advance! It will be just enough to start him off.

COMRADE BITIUK

Why a private sanatorium? There are State sanatoriums, free for all Trade Union members.

KIRA

But he's not a Trade Union member.

COMRADE BITIUK

So? A bourgeois, is he? And you expect us to help him? The sooner all the members of his class are liquidated—the better. As to that advance, how can you be sure that you'll be working here another month, let alone six? Don't let me hear another word about it!

(KIRA returns to her desk. A sharp bell rings loudly somewhere in the building. The entire office is jerked into hectic activity as if by an explosion. Desks are slammed, typewriters pushed aside, hands reach hurriedly for hats and coats, all eager to get out first.)

COMRADE BITIUK

I shall remind you once more, Comrades, that you have just barely time for dinner. At seven o'clock you are to attend the Mass Meeting at the Palace of Labor in honor of the visiting delegation of the English Trade Unions. If any of you are absent, the names will be reported to me. I do not have to explain the consequences... Goodnight, Comrades.

(Exits)

(The others hurry out one by one, KIRA lags behind.)

CLERK

(On her way out)

Aren't you going, Comrade Argounova?

KIRA

I... I think I'll wait a few minutes.

CLERK

(Glances significantly with understanding at Comrade Voronov's door, then at Kira)

Well... good luck, Comrade!

(Exits)

(KIRA stands waiting anxiously, her eyes on the door. The door is thrown open. She jumps forward eagerly but it's only the Secretary. He crosses hurriedly to door Right without paying any attention to her and exits. COMRADE VORONOV enters from door Left. He is an imposing, middle-aged gentleman, immaculately dressed, thoroughly conscious of his position and authority. He's on his way out when KIRA stops him.)

KIRA

Comrade Voronov! May I speak to you, *please*?

VORONOV

(Stopping, annoyed)

Oh, it's you, Comrade Argounov! I believe my secretary has made it clear that...

KIRA

I know. But *I've got* to speak to you. It's...it's a matter of life and death. Please! Just a few minutes!

VORONOV

(Impatiently, glancing at his wristwatch)

Well, what is it, what is it?

KIRA

Comrade Voronov, there's a man and...and I love him. And he's going to die. He has consumption. You know what that means here, in Petrograd. I have to send him south. To a sanatorium in the Crimea.

VORONOV

My dear, what has that to do with me?

KIRA

I've tried every hospital in town. I've spent nights waiting in line. The sanatoriums are overcrowded. They won't even register him. But you can, in your position, you can arrange a place for him.

VORONOV

He'll have to wait his turn.

KIRA

But he can't wait! And they won't even register him. He's not a Trade Union member.

VORONOV

Oh...I'm afraid there's nothing I can do.

KIRA

Comrade Voronov, don't you see? I love him. And they will let him die because they didn't write his name on a piece of paper with many other names and call it membership in a Trade Union. It's only paper, you know. And something we think. But the other—the illness—the death in your body—that's real, Comrade Voronov. You can't stop that. You don't ask questions about that.

VORONOV

(Indignantly)

Do you know what you're saying?

KIRA

Comrade Voronov, I know they are important, these things, money, and the unions, and those papers, and all. And if one has to sacrifice and suffer for them, I don't mind. I don't mind if I have to work every hour of the day. I don't mind if I have to pretend to lie, lie, lie all the time...

VORONOV

What?!

KIRA

Oh forgive me! Don't pay any attention! I...I don't know what I'm saying. Perhaps I haven't always understood you, and all those things, but I can be obedient and learn. Only—only when it comes to life itself, Comrade Voronov, then we have to be serious, don't we? We can't let those things take life.

VORONOV

(Glancing at his wristwatch)
My dear, I'm really in a hurry and...

KIRA

(Stopping him)
Wait! Please think of it, Comrade Voronov! One signature of your hand—and he can go to a sanatorium, and he doesn't have to die. I love him. We all have to suffer. We all have things we want taken away from us. It's all right. But—because we are living creatures—there's something in each of us, something like the very heart of life condensed—and that shouldn't be touched. You understand, don't you? Well, he is that to me, and you can't take him from me, because you can't let me stand here, and look at you and talk, and breathe, and move, and then tell me you'll take him—we're not insane—both of us, are we, Comrade Voronov?

VORONOV

(Looks at her for a second, then says slowly, coldly, distinctly)
One hundred thousand workers died in the civil war. Why—in the face of the Union of Socialist Soviet Republics—can't one aristocrat die?[8]

(KIRA stands frozen, her eyes wide, incredulous, staring at him. He turns and exits through door Right.)

CURTAIN

---

[8] This line is taken straight from the novel, where it is spoken by a Commissar who knows of Leo's aristocratic background. It is unlikely Voronov knows of this.

SCENE 5

Same evening. Andrei's home. A strange room, former Palace Pavilion, with nothing remaining of its past Rococo splendor but the walls, ceiling, and fireplace. The walls are covered with white and silver brocade; a row of marble cupids encircles the cornice; the fireplace, Center back, is surmounted by a marble Leda reclining in the white wings of a swan; the ceiling is painted as a blue sky with pale pink clouds and white doves. The present furnishings of the room are as startling a contrast as can be imagined: a narrow iron cot with a coarse grey blanket, an unpainted kitchen table loaded with books in bright red covers, a telephone, a few rickety chairs, old boxes, serving as chests of drawers and bookcases, a few posters of Red Army soldiers and airplanes, tacked on the walls to conceal—partially—long splits in the brocade. Large tall windows in wall Left, archway leading into a dark little hall before entrance door, Right.

The curtain rises to disclose Andrei and Pavel Syerov. ANDREI is in shirt sleeves, SYEROV has his overcoat on and his hat by his side.

ANDREI

I'm warning you for your own good. And the next time it won't be in private. You'll find yourself called to the office at the Institute.

SYEROV

But, Andrei, whoever told you . . .

ANDREI

The Transport Section of the G.P.U. reported it to me. You're a student of the Technological Institute and it comes under my department. In the first place, since you haven't graduated yet, I don't see what business you have with the Railroad Workers Club.

SYEROV

But, Andrei! Purely in the spirit of social activity! I'm just doing my proletarian duty and organizing a little political education for the workers. I'll have a job at the Railroad, you know, as soon as I graduate.

ANDREI

Purely in the spirit of social duty?

SYEROV

Andrei my pal! Surely you're not accusing me of any personal motives!

ANDREI

See that you don't give me grounds to.

SYEROV

Andrei! You can't suspect me. Aren't we old friends? Haven't we fought in the trenches together, under the Red flag, you and I, shoulder to shoulder.

ANDREI

(Slowly)

Yes. We have. For the freedom and the glory of all mankind. And sometimes I wonder if we got what we were fighting for.

SYEROV

Andrei!

ANDREI

To make all men free and strong and proud! Well, you don't go about it by herding people into clubs and deducting club dues before the workers get paid. I have a report here on a family of six that's had nothing to eat but millet for two weeks.

SYEROV

But...

ANDREI

...while you're organizing a club to show your activity to a certain powerful friend of yours, so he'll give you the job when the time comes.

SYEROV

But, Andrei, clubs are organized everywhere. You don't talk like a member of the Party.

ANDREI

I belong to a Party that promised to feed the people.

SYEROV

But they need the club! Their ideology...

ANDREI

Damn their ideology!

SYEROV

What?!

ANDREI

You heard me. Set an example for them of what a Party man should be—and the ideology will take care of itself, even if they can't define Leninism.

SYEROV

But, Andrei, am I not setting an example of social activity...

ANDREI

Take that coat off.

SYEROV

(Bewildered)

Huh?

ANDREI

I said take that coat off.

(SYEROV obeys, puzzled; he reveals a flashy, gaudy obviously new sweater.)

Germany or Latvia?

SYEROV

What are you talking about?

ANDREI

The sweater. That wasn't made in Russia, was it?

SYEROV

(Nervous, flustered)

Well...you see...it was like this...

ANDREI

That came from abroad. From a speculator. The Party is fighting speculators to the death, but they have a way of slipping by at railroad stations...haven't they?

SYEROV

Andrei...I...you see...

ANDREI

Yes, I see. And I don't want to see any more of it. I don't want any explanations. You've been warned. Watch your step at that club of yours. Good night. I have a lot of work to do.

SYEROV

(Rising, putting his coat on)

Well, pal, I'm not one to criticize a valuable Party worker like you. But, you know, as Comrade Lenin said, a Communist must be adaptable to reality. Idealism is a good thing in the proper amount. Too much of it is like too much of a good old wine: one's liable to lose one's head.

ANDREI

What are you talking about?

SYEROV

Oh, idealism in general. And some idealists in particular who pick on Party comrades, but go mushy over aristocratic ladies.

ANDREI

(Rising)

What?

SYEROV

Take a certain citizen, Kira Argounova, for instance. Her closest friend, so I'm told, is one Leo Kovalensky, son of an admiral, executed for counterrevolution. A fine employee to force upon the House of the Peasant.

ANDREI

(Quietly)

Get out of here.

SYEROV

Oh, no ill feeling, pal, no ill feeling. I'm merely...

(A knock on the door)

Come in.

(KIRA enters. Stops uncertainly in the archway. ANDREI stares at her, startled.)

ANDREI

Good evening, Kira.

KIRA

Good evening.

SYEROV

Well, well, well! Comrade Argounova is a better friend of yours than I thought!

(Angry movement from ANDREI)

Oh, I'm going, I'm going. I wouldn't intrude for a minute—under the circumstances. So long, pal!

> (Exits)

ANDREI

Take your coat off, Kira. Sit down.

> (She obeys hesitantly. He watches her intently. He speaks with an effort, obviously ill at ease.)

How have you been, Kira. You look tired.

KIRA

I am a little tired.

ANDREI

How is your job?

KIRA

Not for long, I'm afraid. There's a purging coming.

ANDREI

I'll see what I can do about that.

KIRA

> (Wearily, indifferently)

Thank you. But I don't know whether it matters now.

ANDREI

Don't be afraid of them.

> (Silence)

How is your family?

KIRA

They are fine, thank you.

> (Silence)

Andrei, if I make you uncomfortable, I'll go.

ANDREI

No! Don't go. Please don't go.

> (Tries to laugh)

Make me uncomfortable? What makes you say that? I'm just...just a little embarrassed...This room of mine...it's in no condition to receive such a guest.

KIRA

(Looking around her)

It's a funny room.

ANDREI

It's a former palace of some kind. I understand it used to be some grand duke's love nest. The Party club has the building now and they let me have this. Rooms are so hard to get these days.

KIRA

Yes.

ANDREI

I really don't mind it. You see, I've never had time to care where I lived or how.

KIRA

Have you been very busy, Andrei?

ANDREI

Yes. At the G.P.U. Day and night. Searches. Arrests...I don't like searches.

KIRA

Do you like arrests?

ANDREI

I don't mind, when it's necessary.

KIRA

Andrei, why doesn't your Party believe in the right to live while one is not killed?

ANDREI

In our fight, Kira, there is no neutrality.

KIRA

You have a right to kill, as all fighters have. But no one before you has ever thought of forbidding life to those still living.

ANDREI

What's the matter, Kira? I've never seen you frightened before. If you're worried about that purging...you know I'll always help you. I make more money than I can spend on myself, anyway.

KIRA

(Suddenly alert)

You...what?

ANDREI

Oh, of course. My salary is much more than I need. So that if you ever need anything...

KIRA

(Resolutely)

Andrei, there's something I wanted to ask you.

ANDREI

Certainly. Anything. Will you also let me ask you something I've wanted to know?

KIRA

What is it?

ANDREI

That Leo Kovalensky, is he a good friend of yours?

KIRA

Why?

ANDREI

Of course I don't presume to criticize your friends, but I wanted to warn you. He's not the type of friend you should have. It's dangerous, Kira. With your own difficult social position, to have that notorious young counterrevolutionist around...

KIRA

Andrei, you know how I feel about that.

ANDREI

It's not only that. I don't like him. I don't trust that type of man. An arrogant egotist who...

KIRA

Oh forget about it, Andrei. He's...he's only an acquaintance of mine.

ANDREI

Well, just be careful, for your own sake...Now what was it you wanted to ask me?

KIRA

(Without looking at him)

Oh...nothing.

(With sudden resolution)

Andrei, what have I done? Why have you been avoiding me?

(He doesn't answer.)

(Pause)

ANDREI

(Brusquely)

Why did you come here?

KIRA

It's been such a long time since I saw you last.

ANDREI

Two months, day after tomorrow.

KIRA

I came because I thought...because I thought maybe you wanted to see me.

ANDREI

I didn't want to see you.

(She rises.)

Don't go, Kira.

KIRA

Andrei, I don't understand!

ANDREI

(Rises, stands facing her. His voice is flat, harsh as an insult.)

I didn't want you to understand. I didn't want you to know. But if you want to hear it—you'll hear it. I never wanted to see you again. Because...because I love you.

(Her hands fall limply. She stares at him unable to speak.)

Don't say it. I know what you're going to say. I've said it to myself again and again and again. But it's useless. I know I should be ashamed, and I am, but it's useless. I know that you liked me, and trusted me, because we were friends. It was beautiful and rare, and I've destroyed it, and you have every right to despise me.

KIRA

(Almost a whisper)

Andrei...don't...

ANDREI

When you came in, I thought: "Send her away." But I knew that if you went away, I'd run after you. I thought: "I won't say a word." But I knew that you'd know it before you left. I love you. I know you'd think kindlier of me if I said I hate you.

KIRA

Andrei...I...

ANDREI

You shouldn't have come here. I'm not your friend. I don't care if I hurt you. All you are to me is only this: I want you.

KIRA

Andrei...I didn't know...

ANDREI

I didn't want you to know. I tried to stay away from you. To break it...You don't know what it's done to me. I've never wanted anything in my life. I've taught myself to have no desires. It's some kind of revenge, perhaps. Every living wish I ever could have had is now in one. I want you. You're everything I've always expected to hate. But I want you. I'd give everything I have—everything I could ever have—Kira—for something you can't give me!

KIRA

(Her eyes open wide to a sudden thought. She whispers.)

What did you say?

ANDREI

Everything I have for something you can't...

KIRA

Andrei...I better go...I better go now...

ANDREI

(Looking at her, his voice suddenly very soft and low, with a new hope)

Or is it something you...can...Kira?

KIRA

(She is pressed to the wall, cornered, as he approaches her. Her body rises slowly against the wall, to her full height, her head thrown back. She throws at him, madly, defiantly.)

I can! I love you!

ANDREI

Kira...!

KIRA

(Hysterically)

I can! I can do anything! I love you!...Anything! Everything I have for something you alone can give me!

(She's in his arms. He kisses her. Her head falls back. She screams, a wild cry of sheer despair.)

Andrei! No one must know about this! No one must know!

CURTAIN

ACT 2

SCENE 1

Eight months later. Summer of 1925.

Leo's home—same home we have seen before in the same desolate state. A late afternoon sunshine streams in through the windows.

As curtain rises KIRA is sitting in an armchair, her legs thrown over the arm, smoking. GALINA PETROVNA, as ragged as ever, with a bundle in her lap, sits polishing her nails, watching Kira with obvious disapproval.

Galina Petrovna

It's insanity, Kira, sheer insanity! In the first place, they won't give it to you. You have no reason to show why you want to go abroad.

Kira

I'll try anyway.

Galina Petrovna

And even if you do get the foreign passport—then what? No foreign country will admit a Russian, and I can't say that I blame them.

Kira

I'll think of that later.

Galina Petrovna

What will Leo say?

Kira

He's been dreaming of it for seven years. As soon as he comes back, we'll both apply for foreign passports.

Galina Petrovna

When's he coming back?

Kira

Today.

Galina Petrovna

What?

KIRA

He was to be back yesterday. But the train's late. No one knows when it will arrive. Perhaps any minute now.

GALINA PETROVNA

And he's well? Completely cured?

KIRA

Yes. The doctors said so.

GALINA PETROVNA

Isn't it wonderful! Ah, the Crimea is a paradise! The lucky boy! Eight months of sunshine and rest. A miracle these days.

KIRA

(Without looking at her)

Yes.

GALINA PETROVNA

You know, the most wonderful thing about it all is Leo's aunt in Berlin. There is an example of family loyalty! Helping you both like that, sending you all that money all winter long. She saved Leo's life.

KIRA

(A barely disguised anxiety in her voice)

Mother, when you see Leo, will you remember never to mention it? His aunt's help, I mean. He's so sensitive about being under obligation to her like that, and we must be careful not to remind him of it.

GALINA PETROVNA

Certainly, I understand.

(OLGA IVANOVNA enters briskly from door Right. Her long hair is undone, hanging over her shoulders; she has a hairbrush in her hand.)

OLGA IVANOVNA

(Crossing room swiftly to door Left)

Excuse me, please.

(Knocks at door)

Citizen Lavrova!

LAVROVA'S VOICE

(Offstage)

Yeah?

Olga Ivanovna

Come here, please!

Lavrova

(Throwing door open)

Well, what'd you want?

Olga Ivanovna

Citizen Lavrova, have you taken my bottle of eau de cologne?

Lavrova

Well, what of it? You think you're the only one who can stink nice?

Olga Ivanovna

Kindly return it to me.

Lavrova

Aw, I just took a drop of it ...

(LAVROVA disappears and returns with the bottle.)

Here is your cologne, stingy. You had it hidden under your pillow, too.

Olga Ivanovna

Well, it is a rare treasure these days, and I'll have you understand ...

(LAVROVA exits, slamming the door. OLGA IVANOVNA turns to the others.)

Please excuse my appearance. I was brushing my hair and ...

Galina Petrovna

Oh, it's perfectly all right, Olga Ivanovna.

Olga Ivanovna

No matter what happens, I always brush my hair for half an hour each day, and practice my piano for two hours.

Galina Petrovna

That's very sensible. Just like I never neglect my hands. And I do enjoy your music so much! Won't you play for us today?

Olga Ivanovna

No, I'm sorry, you'll excuse me please? I have to practice the Internationale today. I'm working as accompanist in a Worker's Club. And it's required.

GALINA PETROVNA

Well, I'm glad to hear that you've taken a sensible attitude about working, as we all should.

OLGA IVANOVNA

(Looks at her surprised)

We all have our cross to bear. These are hard days...But I had a vision again, a call from above. And the voice said that this is the reign of the Anti-Christ. I know. It has been revealed to me.

GALINA PETROVNA

Really, Olga Ivanovna, I wouldn't...

OLGA IVANOVNA

Men have forgotten the simple faith. That's the trouble.

(Exits through door Right)

GALINA PETROVNA

There's an example of lacking in modern ideology...Really, Kira, I wish to God you'd give up that crazy notion about going abroad. What for? If Leo can't find a job, his aunt can still help you and...

KIRA

Mother, why argue about it?

GALINA PETROVNA

After all, what's wrong with this country? There are so many opportunities here for everyone.

KIRA

So many...what?

GALINA PETROVNA

Well, look at me, for instance. I have a fine job teaching sewing in a Worker's school. An important practical subject for our little future citizens. Of course you understand I'm not going Red, but I do think that all of us, the intelligentsia, must help to enlighten our less fortunate brothers. And the food rations at the school are excellent: Two pounds of millet last week!

KIRA

(Indifferently)

That's nice.

GALINA PETROVNA

And I've been elected Assistant Secretary of our Teacher's Council. Really, the Soviets do appreciate qualities of leadership. It is most gratifying. If only you could drop your arrogant independence, and come down to earth! We all have to compromise, you know.

KIRA

Mother, you didn't come here just to argue with me, did you?

GALINA PETROVNA

Well, no...as a matter of fact, I...I just dropped in to...to show you something, see if you like it...maybe you'll want to...buy it.

KIRA

To *buy* it? What is it?

> (GALINA PETROVNA unwraps her bundle hurriedly and holds high in her outstretched arms a plain old fashioned wedding gown of flowing white lace.)
>
> (KIRA gasps.)

Why, Mother! Your wedding gown!

GALINA PETROVNA

(Hurriedly, nervously, hiding her embarrassment)

You see, it's because of the school. Your father needs new shoes, the cobblers refuse to mend his old ones, and I was going to buy them this month, but...but I got my wages at the school yesterday and they had deducted so much as my contribution to the Proletarian Society of Chemical Defense—and I didn't even know I was a member of it—that I haven't enough money left...you see, you could alter it nicely, the dress, it's good material, I've only worn it...once.

KIRA

Mother, you know very well that if you need anything...

GALINA PETROVNA

I know, child, I know, but I didn't feel I could ask you and I thought I'd rather...but then, if you don't like the dress, you don't have to...

KIRA

Yes. I like it. I'll buy it, Mother.

GALINA PETROVNA

You can alter it nicely for an evening gown. I really don't need it and I don't mind at all.

> (KIRA rises, gets her pocketbook, slips some bills into Galina Petrovna's hand.)

Why, Kira! Not all that! I didn't want that much. It isn't worth it.

KIRA

Of course it's worth it. And thank you so much.

GALINA PETROVNA

(Cramming the bills into her old bag with a frightened hurry)
Thank you, child.
(Rises)
Well, I'll have to be going. I'd love to wait for Leo, but it's getting late and your father is waiting. There's nothing but millet in the house.

KIRA

Goodbye, Mother.
(GALINA PETROVNA throws the door Left open and collides with LAVROVA who is hurrying in, a cup in her hand.)

LAVROVA

Look where you're going, you blind slob!

GALINA PETROVNA

(With obsequious cheerfulness)
I'm so sorry, Citizen! My, our modern youth has such high spirits!
(Exits)

LAVROVA

Citizen Argounova, can I borrow some lard?

KIRA

I have nothing but linseed oil. I can let you have some.

LAVROVA

Linseed oil? How can you eat that stinking stuff? Well, gimme half a cup.
(KIRA walks to kitchen table, pours oil from bottle.)
(LAVROVA falls down on a chair wearily.)
God, I'm tired! The University this morning, the Marxist Club at noon, the Leninist Circle at one, Demonstration Against Italian Fascism at two—and do my feet sweat!—Conference on French Imperialism at three-thirty...You can't say I ain't class-minded and socially active, you really can't.

KIRA

I never have.

LAVROVA

So the boy friend's coming back today?

KIRA

You've been eavesdropping again!

LAVROVA

Oh, don't be so damn bourgeois!... He won't like it, I bet.

KIRA

Like what?

LAVROVA

You and Comrade Taganov.

KIRA

What are you talking about?

LAVROVA

Oh, I hear things at the Party Club. Comrade Syerov said he'd seen you at a smart restaurant with Comrade Taganov three days ago.

KIRA

Any business of yours?

LAVROVA

Oh, I put two and two together. I've lost track of how many times this winter you've been away from home all night!

KIRA

Listen, you. You spread any more gossip around and I'll kill you as sure as I stand here. Then let your Party comrades try me for political assassination!

LAVROVA

(Frightened)
(Grabbing her cup)
I... I was only kidding, Citizen. I didn't mean any harm. Thanks for the oil...
(Doorbell rings offstage)
I'll answer it.
(Exits quickly, Left)
(Steps are approaching. LEO enters. He is wearing an old overcoat and carrying a suitcase. He looks tanned, healthier than before. KIRA stands, the back of her hand at her mouth, unable to move.)

LEO

Allo, Kira.

> (She doesn't kiss him. Her hands fall on his shoulders and she sags suddenly, her face sliding down his chest; he tries to lift her head; she presses her lips to his hand, her shoulders jerking, sobbing silently. He says tenderly.)

Kira, you little fool!

> (He laughs softly. He lifts her in his arms, carries her to the armchair and sits down, holding her on his lap, forcing her to kiss him.)

And that's the strong Kira who never cries. You shouldn't be so glad to see me, Kira...Stop it, Kira...My little fool...My dearest, dearest...

KIRA

> (Raising her head with a radiant smile, trying to get up)

Leo...you must take your coat off and...

LEO

Stay still...Was it terribly hard for you this winter?

KIRA

A little. But we don't have to talk about it. It's past. Do you cough any more, Leo?

LEO

No.

KIRA

And you're well? Quite, quite completely well? Free to live again?

LEO

I am well—yes. As to living again...

> (Shrugs)

KIRA

Leo, isn't the worst of it over? Aren't we ready now to begin...

LEO

Begin with what? I've nothing to bring back to you—but a healthy body.

KIRA

What else can I want?

LEO

Nothing else—from a gigolo.

KIRA

(Rising)

Leo!

LEO

Well, am I not one?

KIRA

Leo, don't you love me?

LEO

I love you. I love you too much. I wish I didn't. It would all be so simple if I didn't. But to love a woman and to see her dragging herself through this hell they call life here, and not to help her, but to let her drag you instead, when it's hard enough for her alone...Did you really think I'd bless this health you gave me back? I hate it. I hate it because you gave it back to me. And because I love you.

KIRA

(Anxiously)

Leo, that money wasn't...

LEO

I know. It wasn't yours. Your uncle's. What's the difference?

(Offstage OLGA IVANOVNA strikes up the Internationale. She plays hesitantly, stopping often, beginning over again, practicing. LEO rises.)

Write at once to your uncle in Budapest. Thank him and tell him not to send us money any longer. I'm well. We'll struggle on our own.

KIRA

(Without looking at him)

Yes, Leo.

(Turning to him sharply)

Leo, when you see my family, will you remember never to mention my uncle in Budapest and the money he sent us? You see, there's a family quarrel behind it, he left Russia before the war and my father forbade us ever to mention his name. Father would kill me if he knew I had accepted money from him.

LEO

I understand. But we'll have to start repaying him—if he's patient, for the devil alone knows how long it will take. However, I have a plan.

KIRA

A...plan? For what?

LEO

For making money. It's an offer that's been made to me and I've accepted.

KIRA

What? With whom?

LEO

I'm expecting them now. They'll be here any minute. It's a woman I met at the sanatorium—she was taking a rest cure for her nerves. Oh, she could afford it. She's living with a certain Morozov, a prosperous citizen who's assistant manager of the State Food Trust. A nice position.

KIRA

What do they want to do?

LEO

She'll explain it all to you. I don't know much about the details. It seems that her boyfriend has been looking for someone like me. I came back on the same train with her and she's gone to get Morozov.

KIRA

Leo, why start anything? I have other plans. We'll apply for foreign passports.

LEO

(Laughing)
Do you think they give passports to men with my record?

KIRA

We have to try.

LEO

(Indifferently)
Try it. They'll refuse anyway. In the meantime, I'll be making money. I've had enough of this.
(Notices an expensive wristwatch on her arm)
Where did that come from?

KIRA

(A little taken aback)
It's a present. From...Andrei Taganov.

LEO

Oh, really? So you're accepting presents from him?

KIRA

Why not, Leo? It was my birthday and I couldn't refuse it.

(The Internationale stops abruptly in the middle and we hear the piano cover being slammed down furiously.)

LEO

(Shrugging)

Oh, I don't mind. It's your business. Personally, I wouldn't feel comfortable wearing something paid for with G.P.U. money.

(Doorbell rings offstage)

Here they are now. I'll open the door.

(Exits)

(Voices are heard offstage, with a high, shrill feminine voice predominating, gushing loudly.)

ANTONINA PAVLOVNA

(Offstage)

And this is Leo, a dear, *dear* boy!

(The voices approach. ANTONINA PAVLOVNA enters, followed by LEO and MOROZOV. She's a stout woman in her forties, flashily expensively dressed. With obviously dyed red hair and too much makeup. MOROZOV is a heavy, middle-aged man, awkward and peasant-like in his manner, shrewd, sly, and obsequious.)

LEO

Kira, this is Antonina Pavlovna Platoshkina—Kira Alexandrovna Argounova.[9]

ANTONINA PAVLOVNA

(Studying Kira shrewdly, extending her hand in a grand manner, significantly)

Oh.

KIRA

(Coldly)

How do you do.

LEO

And Karp Karpovitch Morozov.

---

[9] A complete name in Russian consists of a first name followed by a patronymic and a last name (both of which are masculine or feminine). Kira's full name is Kira Alexandrovna Argounova (her father being Alexander Argounov); Leo's full name is Lev Sergueievitch Kovalensky (his father being Sergei Kovalensky—and note Leo's preference for the European version over the Russian "Lev"). Complete names are not provided for all characters.

KIRA

How do you do.

MOROZOV

(Shaking her hand lengthily, bowing low in a peasant manner)
Honored to meet you, Kira Alexandrovna, soul of mine.

LEO

Sit down, please. Take your coat off, Tonia.

(Helps her out of her coat)

ANTONINA PAVLOVNA

(Looking around)
Merciful heaven, what a place to live in, Leo! For a brilliant young man like you! Well, we'll remedy that quick enough. I promised that Koko would do a great deal for you. With his connections...!

(Imperiously to Morozov)
Won't you, Koko?

MOROZOV

(Settling down comfortably)
Sure thing, Tonia, soul of mine.

ANTONINA PAVLOVNA

Really, Leo, I'm so glad to be back. I'm sure the sanatorium lost all its charm without you.

(To Kira)
You know, he was the most charming person in that dull place and everybody admired him so much—oh, purely platonically, my dear, if you're worried.

KIRA

I'm not.

ANTONINA PAVLOVNA

(To Leo)
And you must realize, Leo, that it would be too much to expect of a woman if you asked her to abandon such a lovely friendship as ours.

MOROZOV

Friendship and business, I always say, that's a great combination. The only way to get along these days.

Antonina Pavlovna

Business! Why must you always think of business, Koko? Poor Koko! He's really very artistic at heart, you know, if one knows how to approach him. He even reads poetry. He really did appreciate that latest volume of verse by Valentina Sirkina, which I gave him. Have you read it, Leo?

Leo

No, I'm sorry. I don't read any of that new stuff.

Antonina Pavlovna

You must read it. It's magnificent. I'm sure you'll appreciate it. I know you're really romantic at heart. I wondered about it in the Crimea. I didn't see how you could remain so indifferent to its magic spell. I thought you were essentially unromantic. But of course I can understand the reason—now.

(Throws a swift glance at Kira)

Kira

(Brusquely)

What was the business offer you made to Leo?

Leo

(Reproachfully)

Kira!

Antonina Pavlovna

So you're always being held down to business, too, Leo? I felt that we had a lot in common...well, I'll let Koko explain it all to you. I have such a helpless, sentimental head, no good for business.

Morozov

(To Leo)

Well, Lev Sergueievitch, it's like this: we're planning a big business, a partner of mine and me. And, first of all, we got to have a private food store—for protection. Now a private trader is no easy title to bear these days. I couldn't take it upon myself, and my partner—he's a Communist, Party member, so he can't even think of it.

Leo

Well?

Morozov

Well, your part of it will be to get the store. We'll pay for it, but you gotta get the license in your name. You'll be the sole, official, registered owner—and you have no partners, if anyone asks you.

KIRA

(Nervously)

A store? What kind of a store?

MOROZOV

Just a little private food store—*officially*. Now that partner of mine, the Communist, he's got one of those big engineering positions with a railroad—and plenty of pull. All he's got to do is see that the food shipments for the State Co-operatives are damaged a wee bit—dropped accidentally, or dampened, or something—and see that they are pronounced worthless. That's all. The rest is simple. The shipment goes quietly to the basement of our little shop. Nothing suspicious in that—is there?—just supplies for the store. We break up the load and ship it to our own customers, private traders all over the country, reasonable and discreet, I have all the addresses.

KIRA

(Jumping up)

Leo! Are you insane?!

LEO

(Coldly)

Kira, please keep quiet.

KIRA

Leo! If that's a new way of committing suicide, there are much simpler ones!

ANTONINA PAVLOVNA

(Coldly)

Really, Kira Alexandrovna, you're unnecessarily tragic about it.

MOROZOV

(Soothingly)

Now, now, Kira Alexandrovna, soul of mine, there's nothing to be excited about. There's no danger. If anyone comes snooping around the store—well, we'll have some punk clerks there and he'll sell them half a pound of butter if they ask for it, and that's all we're doing, for all they know, retail trade—open and legal.

ANTONINA PAVLOVNA

And furthermore, if anything should go wrong, Syerov has...

KIRA

Who?!

MOROZOV

That's my partner—Pavel Syerov.

(KIRA gasps.)

Do you know him?

KIRA

Slightly.

MOROZOV

A brilliant young man.

(Looking around furtively, lowering his voice)

Yes, he has connections in the G.P.U. A powerful friend and protector. One of the heads. I'd be scared to mention the name.

LEO

Oh, we'll be safe from that quarter, if we have enough money.

MOROZOV

Money? Why, Lev Sergueievitch, soul of mine, we'll have so much money that you'll be rolling ten ruble bills to make cigarettes. We split it three ways, you understand: me, yourself, and Syerov. But then, you must remember that on the face of it you're the sole owner. It's your store, in your name. I have my position with the Food Trust to think about. If they learn I have a private store, they'll kick me out fast. And I gotta keep that job. You can see how useful it will be to us.

LEO

Don't worry. I'm not afraid.

(Offstage OLGA IVANOVNA starts practicing the Internationale again.)

MOROZOV

Then it's settled, eh? Why, pal, in a month from now, you won't believe you ever lived like this. You'll put some pretty clothes on Kira Alexandrovna, and a diamond bracelet or two, and then maybe a motor car and...

KIRA

Leo! Don't you see what they're doing? You're nothing but a living screen for them. They're investing money. You're investing your life!

LEO

I'm glad to find some use for it.

KIRA

Leo, listen to me! Don't you know that it's the firing squad for anyone caught in a crooked criminal speculation?

MOROZOV

Kira Alexandrovna, why use such strong names for a simple business proposition which is perfectly permissible and almost legal and...

LEO

(To Morozov)

You keep quiet!

(To Kira)

Listen, Kira, I know that this is as rotten and crooked a deal as could be made. And I know I am taking a chance on my life. And I still want to do it. You understand?

KIRA

Even if I begged you not to?

LEO

Nothing you can say will change things. Do you think I'll spend the rest of my life crawling, begging for a job, dying slowly? So they shoot speculators? Why don't they give us a chance at something else? What is there left to me? I'm not risking much when I risk my life.

MOROZOV

(With admiration)

Lev Sergueievitch, soul of mine, how you can talk!

(The Internationale breaks off suddenly on a furious explosion, as if two fists had struck the keys viciously. There is a pause. Then Tchaikovsky's "Autumn Song" is heard, played with a quiet despair.)

LEO

You two can go now. I'll see you tomorrow, Morozov, and we'll settle everything.

ANTONINA PAVLOVNA

(Rising with dignity)

Indeed, Leo, I'm surprised! If you let yourself be influenced and do not seem to be grateful...

LEO

Who's to be grateful? You need me and I need you. It's a business deal.

MOROZOV

(Rising)

Sure, sure, that's what it is. It's all right, Tonia, soul of mine, you come along now and we'll settle all the details tomorrow.

(ANTONINA PAVLOVNA exits without looking at Kira.)

(MOROZOV shakes hands with Leo at the door.)

Thank you, Lev Sergueievitch. You won't regret it. I'll take you to meet Pavel Syerov tomorrow.

(Bows low to Kira and exits)

LEO

(Sharply)

Kira, we won't argue about it any more.

KIRA

There's only one thing, Leo, and I couldn't say it before them. You said you had nothing left in life. I thought you had...me.

LEO

I haven't forgotten it. And that's one of the reasons for what I'm doing. Do you think I'm going to live off you for the rest of my days? Do you think I'm going to stand by and watch you slaving in a Soviet office? You poor little fool! You don't know what life can be. You've never seen it. But you're going to see it. And I'm going to see it before they finish me.

(She leans helplessly against the table, sagging.)

Listen, if I knew for certain that it's the firing squad in six months—I'd still do it!

CURTAIN

SCENE 2

Three weeks later. Andrei's room. Evening.

At curtain rise ANDREI is sitting on a table, a telephone receiver in his hand, speaking into phone with a barely restrained fury.

ANDREI

...yes, I'm going to arrest him. I've reported the case already and I have the order. Savinsky is a speculator and you know it...Yes, we have the proof. Smuggling foreign dress goods from Riga...What of it?...I said what if he is your friend? A Party member shouldn't have such friends...Thank you, I know you could, but I don't need any favors from you...Did you ever walk on the street, Comrade? Did you see what men wear, what they eat? Then did you see the limousines speeding by? Did you wonder who's riding in them?...To hell with your temporary period of State Construction!...All right, call me a Trotskyist[10]...All right, try to have me thrown out of the Party...Yes, damn

---

[10]The typescripts usually (but not consistently) have "Trotzky," "Trotzkiist," and so on; I have changed them to the now standard "Trotsky," "Trotskyist," and so on.

you, I'm going to arrest him...I said damn you!...And damn your kind of Party discipline!

> (Slams receiver down. Brushes his hair off his forehead with a weary movement. There is a knock on the door.)

Come in!

> (KIRA enters. ANDREI jumps up, stands still, looking at her happily, incredulously.)

Kira!

KIRA

Good evening, Andrei.

ANDREI

> (Seizing her violently, kissing her)

Kira...Kira, it's been such a long time!...What happened?...I...

KIRA

> (Answering his kiss with an effort, disengaging herself)

I couldn't come sooner.

ANDREI

But three weeks? Do you know it's been three weeks since I saw you last?

KIRA

I know.

ANDREI

I was worried. I was going to telephone your house and...

KIRA

No! Andrei! You promised never to do that! Never!

ANDREI

But surely your parents wouldn't mind a simple telephone call...

KIRA

No! Andrei, we must be careful. We must be careful. Particularly now.

ANDREI

Why particularly now?

KIRA

Oh, no more than usual. But you promised, remember, that no one would know. Even...even after it's ended.

ANDREI

Ended? What are you talking about?

KIRA

(Removes her coat; she is wearing a short dress of bright red crepe, with short sleeves, a patent leather belt, four buttons and a patent leather collar with a large leather bow.)

Andrei, I came to tell you that...

ANDREI

(Drawing her to him, looking at her with admiration)

My favorite dress!...Why do you look so...so much more grown up in a childish dress like that?...Was it your own idea, this leather bow...I love that bow...I've missed that dress so much—for three weeks!

KIRA

Andrei, I'm sorry, but I couldn't...I...

ANDREI

(Sitting down, his arms around her)

It's been torture. I waited here for you, day after day. I thought I'd go insane, without a word from you, without the right to call you, to hear your voice...Oh darling, I'm not reproaching you. Only why—all of a sudden—when all winter long you came here so often?

KIRA

Andrei, I wanted to tell you...I came to tell you...

ANDREI

Oh, forgive me!

(Reaches into his pocket and takes out a roll of bills)

It's been so long and you probably need it. Your family...

KIRA

(A little too violently, pushing the money back)

No, Andrei!...No, thank you...I don't need it. And...and I don't think I'll need it again.

ANDREI

But your family...

KIRA

You've given me enough for them already. All winter long...we...they will manage now...Please, Andrei! If...if I need it again, I'll tell you.

ANDREI

Promise?

KIRA

Yes...

ANDREI

(Drawing her to him)
You know, when you're here, it's worth all the torture, all the waiting.

KIRA

(Trying to laugh)
Why be so serious, Andrei? About a love affair like any other you've had, like any other you will have.

ANDREI

Kira! What are you saying?

KIRA

I...

ANDREI

Don't you know what you are to me?

KIRA

But...but you'll be tired of me some day...it will have to end some day...I don't want you to feel that...that you're tied to me, that you need me, that...

ANDREI

I need you more than anything on earth.

KIRA

(Resolutely)
Andrei, I wanted to tell you...I came to tell you that we can't go on like this!

ANDREI

(Calmly)
I know it. Will you marry me, Kira?

(She stares at him silently, helplessly.)
Kira, dearest, don't you see what we're doing? Why do we have to hide and lie? Why do I have to live in this agony of counting hours, days, weeks between our meetings?

KIRA

(Desperately)

Andrei, I can't...we can't...My...my family wouldn't allow it...And you...your Party would never permit you such a marriage. I can't stand in your way. Your work is your real life, your whole life.

ANDREI

Not any more, Kira.

KIRA

Andrei!

ANDREI

Don't you think I can see what's going on around us? Don't you think I see it, that betrayal of everything I've fought for all my life? I try not to see. I'm still fighting. But...Oh, don't let's talk about that...What's the matter, Kira? Why are you frightened?

KIRA

Andrei, I can't marry you.

ANDREI

All right, dear. We'll go on as we are. We'll keep it secret. I don't care—as long as I have you.

KIRA

But if we go on like this, it...it will be dangerous for you. I'm not...I'm not the kind of a...a mistress your Party would approve. And your work...

ANDREI

I couldn't hold on to my work another day if I didn't have you.

KIRA

Andrei, I'm no help to you.

(Desperately, breaking down)

And I don't want to hurt you. Oh Andrei, I don't want to hurt you!

ANDREI

Hurt me? You're the only one in this world who's helping me.

KIRA

How?

ANDREI

Because, no matter what happens, I still have you. Because, no matter what human wreckage I have to see around me, I still have you. And—in you—I still know what a human being can be.

KIRA

Andrei, are you sure you know me?

ANDREI

That's the only thing I'm sure of. That's the only thing I have left. My highest reverence—and my only one.

KIRA

Andrei, you must think...once in a while...that it's possible that we...we'll have to part. What if anything should happen to me?

ANDREI

Why think about it?

KIRA

But it's possible.

ANDREI

It's also possible for every one of us to have to face a death sentence some day. Does it mean that we have to prepare for it?...Don't let anything happen to you, dearest. You can't leave me now.

KIRA

(Dully)

No. I can't.

ANDREI

(Gathering her into his arms)

I wasn't complaining...I'm happy...happy that I have nothing left but you...

KIRA

(A desperate moan)

Andrei, don't say it! Please, please don't say it!

ANDREI

But you know it. I have nothing left but you...nothing...but you...

(His kiss silences her answer.)

CURTAIN

SCENE 3

Six months later. Winter of 1925. Syerov's home. Evening.

A large room, miscellaneously furnished with incongruous bits of furniture obviously looted from different places; some cheap, tasteless junk. Many revolutionary posters on the walls and pictures of Marx and Lenin prominently displayed. Entrance door in wall Center. Door into next room is wall Left.

As the curtain rises a noisy party is drawing to an end. About a dozen young COMMUNISTS, boys and girls, are relaxing, after an obvious overdose of drinking, all over the room, on chairs, tables, the bed, and the floor. A young GIRL lies sound asleep in a corner by a cuspidor. A great number of empty bottles are strewn everywhere; dishes of pastry on the floor, broken glasses, cigarette smoke.

KIRA and ANDREI are sitting aside downstage Right, the only sober ones among the guests; KIRA is wearing her red dress. COMRADE SONIA, in a stained, mussed "best" dress, with a faded rose on her shoulder, presides over the gathering.

FIRST BOY

(Sitting on the floor in a corner, mutters drunkenly to no one in particular, while no one is listening)

...and then I said, Comrades, said I, Leninism is Marxism adapted to Russian reality. Karl Marx, the great founder of Communism, believed that Socialism was to be the logical outcome of Capitalism in a country of highly developed Industrialism. But, said I...

FIRST GIRL

(Throwing a shoe at him)

Oh shut up!

(As the boy shuts up, SYEROV's voice is heard from the next room.)

SYEROV'S VOICE

(Offstage)

...but I know he's in! God damn it, I've got to speak to him! Tell the bastard that I...Oh, all right!

(Sound of receiver being slammed down violently. SYEROV enters from door Left, staggering, obviously drunk and furious.)

COMRADE SONIA

(In a low voice to Syerov)

You don't have to telephone while they're all here.

SYEROV

Hell, I've got to get that bastard. He's kept me waiting for two days. He...

COMRADE SONIA

Not now, Pavel, not *now*.
>(SYEROV staggers away from her, picks up an empty bottle, brandishes it in the air.)

SYEROV

A drink...who wants a drink...Doesn't anyone want a drink?

SECOND BOY

Hell, Pavel, your bottle's empty.

SYEROV

>(Holds the bottle up to the light, spits and throws the bottle away; waves his fist menacingly at the room)

So you think I haven't more? Think I'm a piker, don't you?...A measly piker that can't afford enough vodka at his own wedding?...Well I'll show you who can't afford things...I'll show you...

COMRADE SONIA

>(A warning command)

Pavel!

SYEROV

Shut up!
>(Fumbles in a box under a table and rises, swaying, brandishing a new, unopened bottle over his head)

I can't afford, can I?
>(Reels over second boy, giggles and swings the bottle in a huge circle over his head, bringing it down to smash against the bookcase. A GIRL screams.)

SECOND BOY	FIRST GIRL
You damn...	(Raising her skirt over drenched legs)
	My stockings, Pavel, my stockings!

THIRD BOY

>(Putting his arm around girl)

Never mind, sweetheart. Take 'em off.

SYEROV

So I can't afford it, can I?...Pavel Syerov can afford anything on this God damn earth!...He can buy you all, guts and souls!

ANDREI

(Calmly)

With what?

SYEROV

With...

COMRADE SONIA

Pavel!

SYEROV

Shut up! Even if you're my wife, shut up!
(To Andrei)
None of your business.

ANDREI

It's a nice party you've given us, Pavel. I hear it's not the first one. Must cost a lot of money. Doesn't it?

SYEROV

You bet it does. You couldn't afford it. None of you lousy punks here could afford it. But Pavel Syerov...

COMRADE SONIA

Pavel Syerov had better sit down.

SECOND BOY	FIRST BOY
(During preceding scene has crawled under the table and produced another bottle) Who wants a drink, Comrades?	...but I said, if the bourgeoisie is attuned to a high degree of class consciousness, then Nationalism becomes Imperialism...

SECOND GIRL

Me first, Grishka!

SECOND BOY

(Fills glasses, staggers to Andrei and Kira)
Another one, Comrades?

ANDREI

No, thank you.

FIRST BOY

...when dialectic materialism is opposed to philosophical Eclecticism and...

SECOND BOY

(Shoving a glass into his hand)
Here! Shut up!

FIRST BOY

...and bourgeois Opportunism turns into...
(Takes glass)
Thanks...into renegade Trotskyism...

SECOND GIRL

Well, here's to the newlyweds!

THIRD BOY

To Pavel Syerov and Comrade Sonia, our best Party Workers!

SECOND BOY

To a real revolutionary marriage.

SECOND GIRL

And may there be many little citizens of the U.S.S.R.

SYEROV

(Extending glass)
Gimme another one!

COMRADE SONIA

(Rises, takes him imperiously by the arm and leads him away from the
bottle)
You've had enough, Pavel.
(The others drink.)

FIRST GIRL

(Whispering to Second Girl)
I hear one little citizen is on its way already!

SECOND GIRL

Ssh!
(Looks cautiously at Comrade Sonia and Syerov, whispers)

Well, you know, Pavel never did like her, but when Comrade Sonia makes up her mind...It seems there was a party, two months ago, and he...

(Shrugs)

FIRST GIRL

Well, here's to the little citizen!

SYEROV

(Trying to disengage his arm from Comrade Sonia's firm grip)

Aw, come on now, Sonia, can't I have another drink? On our own wedding night?

COMRADE SONIA

No.

SYEROV

You can't treat me like that!...I'm a great man...You've married a great man...I'm going to make foreign capitalists look like mice...That's what: mice...

(Staggers away from her, stumbles over Third Boy's legs)

Beg your pardon.

(Looking at boy's boots)

Hell, what old junk you're wearing! Look at mine.

(Stretches out his leg in a shiny new boot)

THIRD BOY

(Awed)

God, Pavel! Foreign?

SYEROV

You bet. Three hundred and fifty rubles!

SECOND BOY

(Emptying his glass, reaching for his hat)

Well, folks, thanks for a swell party. I gotta be going. I gotta Marxist Club meeting first thing in the morning.

SECOND GIRL

(Fishing for her coat in a pile of coats in a corner)

I'm going with you. I got a thesis to write tonight—on "The Free Toil of the Proletariat."

THIRD BOY

(Helping himself to another drink)
That's what I say: free toil and free fun.

SECOND BOY AND SECOND GIRL

(At door)
So long, Comrades.
(No one pays any attention. The two exit.)

THIRD GIRL

(Slipping an arm around Syerov's shoulders)
That's a beautiful suit you have, Pavel.

SYEROV

You bet it is. Five hundred rubles. I'm the best dressed man in Leningrad.

THIRD GIRL

You sure are.

SYEROV

Well, what do you think? Think I'm going to be just another stray mongrel eating outta slop pails all his life?... I'll show you! I'm going to be the Capitalist of the whole world!

ANDREI

How?

COMRADE SONIA

Pavel, for God's sake!
(To Andrei)
Don't pay any attention to him, Comrade Taganov. He's drunk.

SYEROV

Who's drunk?
(Staggers at Andrei)
And as for you, Comrade Galahad,[11] or whatever it's called, let me tell you, you better keep your nose outta my affairs. See? You better come off your high perch. On accounta I got a friend who can cut your head off like that...

---

[11] In the novel, and in the later version of the play (see p. 159), Syerov calls Andrei Sir Galahad in a more suitable context, namely, when Andrei blackmails Syerov into releasing Leo on Kira's behalf: "Sir Galahad of the blackmail sword."

(Snaps his fingers)

...just like that.

ANDREI

(Calmly)

What's his name?

SYEROV

None of your damn business. He's in the G.P.U. too. Over you and over your boss. You lay off me, 'cause all I gotta do is say the word and...

ANDREI

And?

COMRADE SONIA

(Dragging Syerov away from Andrei and pushing him into a chair)

Sit down here and keep your mouth shut, you drunken fool!

(Laughter and approving cheers from the crowd)

ANDREI

(To Kira, in a low voice)

I'm sorry, Kira, I knew it would be like this. I had to come, but why did you want to go with me?

KIRA

I...I wanted to know why you had to come.

ANDREI

There's something I'm trying to find out.

KIRA

(Nervously)

What?

ANDREI

Kira, we've never discussed my work.

KIRA

I wish you'd take me home.

ANDREI

In just a little while. Do you mind?

First Boy

...and Socialism plus Electrification is Communism...

(SYEROV looks at his wristwatch, jumps up, and staggers out through door Left.)

Third Boy

(Throwing his arm about First Girl's waist)

Well, sweetheart, shall we be going?

First Girl

(Hesitating)

Yes...only...only I gotta go home. I got two books of Comrade Bucharin's to read for the speech I'm making at the...

Third Boy

Now, sweetheart, you're afraid of me, and that's bourgeois prejudice. You come home with me or else I'll tell everyone that you've got a bourgeois deviation.

First Girl

Oh, no, no! I...I'm not afraid! I'll go.

(They reach for their coats.)

Syerov's Voice

(Offstage)

Ring again, operator! I know he's in!

(Knock at entrance door)

Comrade Sonia

(Surprised)

Come in!

(ANTONINA PAVLOVNA in a resplendent evening gown enters followed by LEO, in dinner clothes. Both are obviously drunk, particularly Leo.)

Leo

Good evening. Where's Syerov? We thought we'd just drop in to congratulate.

(THIRD BOY and FIRST GIRL depart unnoticed.)

Kira

(She has jumped to her feet, terrified.)

Leo!

LEO

(Turning to her)
Well, what are *you* doing here? Oh, with Comrade Taganov, are you?

ANDREI

I didn't know you were a friend of Syerov's, Citizen Kovalensky.

KIRA

(Hurriedly)
I introduced Leo to him, at the Institute, a long time ago.

ANDREI

Oh, did you?

COMRADE SONIA

(On her feet, rudely, nervously)
Who asked you to come here?

ANTONINA PAVLOVNA

We were out at a smart casino, and Leo thought it would be nice to come over and congratulate you. Leo is such a dear boy.

LEO

At a smart casino is right. Lost five hundred rubles on the roulette.

KIRA

Leo! Again?

LEO

Why not? We don't have to worry if we lose a few hundred, do we, Tonia?

FIRST GIRL

(Drunkenly. Pointing at Leo.)
Who's the pretty gentleman? Seems I have seen him in every night club I've been to for the last two months!

LEO

Sure you have, sweetheart. And you'll see me in every new one they open for months and months to come, unless...unless you see me in a coffin with six little holes in my chest.

KIRA

Leo!

> (Sound of receiver being slammed offstage. SYEROV enters and stops short.)

LEO

Allo, Comrade! Congratulations! Hearty proletarian congratulations.

SYEROV

What are you doing here?

COMRADE SONIA

It was very nice of you to come, but the party is really over, and...and it's about time for all of us to be going to bed and...

ANTONINA PAVLOVNA

I told you we shouldn't have come, Leo.

LEO

Give me a drink, somebody.

> (No one moves. He helps himself.)

What are you all staring at me for? Afraid, are you?

> (Empties the glass in one swallow and laughs loudly)

Well, I'm not afraid! I'm the only one who's not afraid! I'm going to the firing squad some day! All of you are going to end at the firing squad! So live while you can, because there is no tomorrow, not for any of us!

KIRA

Leo! Leo, you promised me to stop it!

LEO

Why shouldn't I squander money? Why save? I may never need it. I've trembled over money long enough! Can't I throw it away if I want to—while I can? Why not have a good time, so that I won't have to think? Not to think, not to think at all!

KIRA

Leo!

LEO

Who are you to talk? What are you doing here? What are you doing running around to drunken parties with that damn Communist?

ANDREI

(To Leo)

And just what right have you to say with whom she may run around?

LEO

What right? I'll tell you what right. I'll...

KIRA

(Calmly, distinctly)

Leo, people are looking at you. Now what was it you wanted to say?

LEO

(Abruptly)

Nothing.

ANDREI

If you weren't drunk...

LEO

If I weren't drunk, you'd what? You seem sober. And yet not sober enough not to be playing a fool about a woman you have no right to approach!

ANDREI

Well, listen to me, you...

KIRA

(Loudly, firmly)

You better listen, Leo. Andrei finds this the proper time to tell you something.

LEO

What is it, Comrade G.P.U.?

ANDREI

Nothing.

(To Kira)

Come on, Kira, I'll take you home.

KIRA

Yes.

LEO

You're not taking her anywhere! You're...

Antonina Pavlovna

Yes, he is!

> (Wheels Leo about, nodding to Kira, signaling her to hurry. To Leo, in a whisper.)

Have you lost your head? Are you picking a fight with a G.P.U. agent?

Leo

All right. Let her go. Let her go with anyone she wants.

> (KIRA and ANDREI have picked up their hats and coats. COMRADE SONIA escorts them to the door. They exit, while the others...)

Third Girl

Well, this is one helluva party.

Syerov

Well, get out, all of you! Who's keeping you!

Comrade Sonia

Don't pay any attention to him. He's...

Antonina Pavlovna

Merciful heaven, Leo, I believe they're not at all glad that we came!

First Boy

> (Fishing his coat and hat out of a pile in the corner)

Well, I'm going...So long, Comrades. Thanks for the party.

> (SONIA bids the guests goodbye, as they file out one by one with drunken farewells, while SYEROV takes Leo and Antonina Pavlovna aside downstage.)

Syerov

> (In a low furious voice)

What on earth possessed you to come here? Don't you know it's dangerous?

Leo

Oh, don't be a damn coward!

Syerov

Well, maybe I am one. And maybe it would do you good to acquire some of the same quality!

Antonina Pavlovna

Now, now, Pavel. It's all right. We're going.

FIFTH BOY

(Shaking girl asleep in the corner)

Come on, Dashka. Wake up. Time to go home.

(She mumbles drunkenly. He exits practically carrying her out.)

SYEROV

(To Antonina Pavlovna in a low voice)

Listen, tell that hog Morozov to send the money. He's late again on the last deal. I told him I'm not to be kept waiting. I've been telephoning him, but...

ANTONINA PAVLOVNA

(Anxiously)

I'm so sorry, Pavel, dear boy, but Koko is out of town. Urgent business that...

SYEROV

Out of town, hell! He was in his office today. You just squandered my share again!

ANTONINA PAVLOVNA

He'll be back tomorrow, I'll tell him. I'll...Come on, Leo, we really must be going.

LEO

(Following her, somberly)

I wonder what she was doing here with Taganov...

SYEROV

(At the door)

And don't you dare show your faces here again!

(They exit. SONIA and SYEROV, left alone, look at each other and sigh with relief.)

COMRADE SONIA

Thank God! At last!

FIRST BOY

(From behind a chair in the corner)

...and if you take Fascism combined with capitalistic Economism...

COMRADE SONIA

(Wheeling upon him)

Oh, for God's sake!
> (Yanking him to his feet)

Get out of here!
> (Drags him to door)

First Boy

That's what you call the worst kind of Militarism...
> (SONIA throws him out and slams the door.)

Comrade Sonia

A fine bunch of friends!

Syerov

Whose friends? They're your friends as much as mine.

Comrade Sonia

What the hell did you have to invite Taganov for?

Syerov

Well, you know, one's got to be friendly. He could be dangerous.

Comrade Sonia

Yeah. That's just what he was doing, being dangerous. Snooping about... You'll have to be more cautious from now on, understand? You've got to hang on to Morozov. In the first place, I need a fur coat. And no rabbit fur, either. With the baby coming, I can't afford to catch a cold.

Syerov

Oh, damn you and your baby! It's hard enough to collect from that skunk Morozov. But I'm going to his house right now and I'll tell him a few things.

Comrade Sonia

Pavel! You can't do that!

Syerov

Oh, I can't, can I? You just see if I can't! That's just what I'm going to do! Out of town, is he? Stalling me off, is he, the damn crook? I'll show him! And if he won't open the door, I'll leave him a little love letter!

Comrade Sonia

Pavel, are you insane?

Syerov

> (Grabbing a piece of paper and scribbling hurriedly, giggling)

You just wait and see!

(Signs the note and holds it off admiringly)

That'll show him! Listen!

(Reads)

"Morozov, you God damn bastard! If you don't come across with what's due me, before tomorrow morning, you'll eat breakfast at the G.P.U., and you know what that means. Affectionately, Pavel Syerov."

COMRADE SONIA

(Horrified)

Pavel! You can't leave him a note like that!

SYEROV

Oh, can't I?

(Grabs his coat and hat)

COMRADE SONIA

Pavel! You're drunk! You don't know what you're doing when you're drunk!

SYEROV

You ought to know! Like that time, two months ago, when you dragged me into...And now the baby, and this, *this*! Oh, damn you all!

COMRADE SONIA

(Struggling with him)

Give me that note, you fool! Give me...

(He pushes her aside and she falls against a chair, as he exits, slamming the door.)

CURTAIN

SCENE 4

Same night. Restaurant.

Part of a large room, decorated in an attempt to imitate the modernistic style abroad. White clothed tables. An orchestra is playing Viennese Operettas, offstage.

At rise of curtain most of the tables are occupied. The guests are a flashy, well dressed, prosperous looking crowed, with portly profiteers, trim army officers and decollete'd women predominating. WAITERS in full dress clothes glide obsequiously among the tables, serving food and drinks—mainly drinks. A ragged old MAN circulates through the room, selling papers; he is tall, erect, obviously a nobleman, with the Cross of St. George in his lapel and an armless sleeve hanging at his left shoulder.

NEWS VENDOR

(Timidly)

Pravda...Krasnaya Gazeta...latest news, Citizens.

FIRST PROFITEER

(A fat gentleman in evening clothes, seated at a table with a lanky, shifty-eyed companion)

Listen, I'm telling you, white flour, genuine pre-war white flour, four hundred pounds—and no danger, the Commissar guarantees safe and secret delivery.

SECOND PROFITEER

Yeah, but where do I come in?

FIRST PROFITEER

Well, you can come in on the deal with diamonds. I know you have them, the ones you bought from that starving old fossil. Only—blue white, understand? No flaws.

SECOND PROFITEER

I've invested those in a little deal with Riga. They smuggle silk stockings, perfume, and sardines.

FIRST PROFITEER

(Overwhelmed)

No?! *Real* sardines?

SECOND PROFITEER

Sure. Real Norwegian sardines.

NEWS VENDOR

Pravda...Izvestia...

OFFICIAL

(A husky, middle-aged man, seated at a table with a very young girl, taking her hand softly)

Now listen, darling, all those childish doubts are outmoded bourgeois prejudice.

GIRL

(Jerking her hand away, hysterically)

No! I can't! I won't!

OFFICIAL

Well, what are you going to do? Starve all your life in a dinky office? A beautiful girl like you! Besides, I could dismiss you from the office, you know. There's a purging coming. And then what?...Oh, don't cry like an idiot! Go on, eat your steak. I could give you steaks like this every day!

THIRD PROFITEER

(At a table with two others, whispering confidentially)

Genuine American dollars and English pounds...Cash in advance...Well, this ain't a Government exchange, you gotta pay for it.

(A noisy, intoxicated OFFICER, at a table with TWO WOMEN, hurls a glass to the floor, laughing uproariously.)

WOMAN

Sasha, for God's sake, keep quiet!

OFFICER

(Roars)

Why should I keep quiet? I'm the boss! If they don't like it, I'll have them shot! All of them! Who the hell can tell *me* what to do?

(KIRA and ANDREI enter Left. A WAITER escorts them to a vacant table downstage Right. They sit down.)

ANDREI

What would you like, Kira?

KIRA

Some sherry, please.

ANDREI

A bottle of sherry.

(WAITER bows and exits.)

KIRA

Sorry, Andrei, to ask you to come here.

ANDREI

I don't mind, if you like it. Only it's the rendezvous of all the speculators in town.

KIRA

I like it because it looks like...like Europe. At least people try to be gay here. And the music...just like abroad. I had to get away from Syerov's. I couldn't stand it another minute.

ANDREI

I'm sorry, dear, to have taken you there. I'll never do it again. And, anyway, Syerov won't be throwing parties much longer.

KIRA

What...what do you mean?

ANDREI

That man's been spending too much money. One of these days I'll know exactly where he gets it.

KIRA

Well, he has a good position with a railroad.

ANDREI

Yes. Too good a position.
　　　(The WAITER brings a bottle with two glasses, pours, and exits.)
Kira, do you see him often?

KIRA

Whom? Syerov?

ANDREI

No. Leo Kovalensky.

KIRA

Don't you think you're being presumptuous?

ANDREI

Kira, of all your friends, he's the one...

KIRA

...whom you don't like. I know. Still, don't you think that you're mentioning it too often?

ANDREI

You're not interested in politics, are you?

KIRA

No. Why?

ANDREI

You've never wanted to sacrifice your life uselessly, to have years torn out of it, years of jail or exile. Have you?

KIRA

What are you driving at?

ANDREI

Keep away from Leo Kovalensky.
> (She stares at him, paralyzed, for a long moment.)

KIRA

> (With an effort)
What—do—you—mean—Andrei?

ANDREI

He owns a certain private food store, doesn't he?

KIRA

Are you being the G.P.U. agent with me and...

ANDREI

No, I'm not questioning you. I have nothing to learn from you. But I want to make sure that you don't let your name be implicated, by chance, in any way.

KIRA

Implicated—in what?

ANDREI

Kira, I'm not a G.P.U. agent—*with* you or *to* you.

NEWS VENDOR

> (At officer's table)
Latest news, Citizens.
> (The OFFICER empties a glass of liquor at the news vendor's face. One of the women screams.)

WOMAN

Sasha!
> (HEAD WAITER rushes to them.)

OFFICER

> (To Head Waiter)
Throw him out! Throw the bastard out! Czarist General, that's what he is!

Woman

God, what do you care, Sasha? The poor guy has a living to make.

Officer

Out with the bastard! Don't want his damn White snoot around!

> (The HEAD WAITER grabs the News Vendor. ANDREI rises slowly and walks to Officer's table.)

Andrei

(Calmly)

Leave him alone.

Officer

(Rising aggressively)

Huh? And who are you? Want your snoot smashed too?

Andrei

(To Head Waiter)

I said let him go.

> (HEAD WAITER releases the news vendor. ANDREI takes his wallet from his pocket and shows it to the Officer, open, showing a red card.)

Officer

(Sitting down, very much subdued)

Oh...G.P.U....Oh.

> (ANDREI turns away from him; OFFICER mutters under his breath.)

One of those mawkish idealists, eh?...A Trotskyist, I bet...Well, the Party will take care of you fine gentlemen, some day...

Andrei

(To News Vendor)

I'm sorry, Citizen.

News Vendor

(In a low voice)

Thank you, Citizen.

> (NEWS VENDOR moves away and presently leaves the room. ANDREI returns to his table, sits down wearily, empties his glass in one swallow. Looks at Kira.)

Andrei

And that, it seems, is what I've fought for all my life.

KIRA

When you've denied the best in men, Andrei, this is all that can survive.

ANDREI

(Abruptly)

Kira, would you like to go abroad?

KIRA

(Gasps)

What...what did you say?

ANDREI

(Eagerly)

Listen! It could be done. I could be sent there on some secret mission and you'd go as my secretary. Once across the border, we'll drop the mission, and our Red passports, and our names. We'll run away so far they'll never find us!

KIRA

(Aghast)

Do you know what you're saying?

ANDREI

I want to run away before I see too much of what I see here around us. To break with all of it at once, with my whole past. It would be like starting everything again, from a total void. But I'd have you. The rest doesn't matter.

KIRA

Andrei, you who were the best your Party had to offer the world, you...

ANDREI

Well, say it. Say I'm a traitor. Maybe I am. And maybe I've just stopped being one. Maybe I've been a traitor all these years, to something greater than what the Party ever offered the world.

KIRA

What?

ANDREI

That which you taught me.

KIRA

(Helplessly)

What did I teach you?

Andrei

When you've spent a whole life—as I have—where every hour had to have a reason in the service of others, and suddenly you discover what it is to feel things that have no reason but yourself and you see suddenly how sacred a reason that can be, so that you can't argue, you can't doubt, you can't fight it, and you know suddenly that a life is possible whose only justification is your own joy—then everything else suddenly seems very different to you.

Kira

(Desperately)

Andrei, I can't go abroad.

Andrei

Why?

Kira

Don't ask me why. But if you want to go alone...

Andrei

Let's forget it, Kira. I won't ask any questions. But as for my going alone—don't you really think you shouldn't say that?

Kira

Yes, let's forget it!

(Fills his glass, raises hers)

To your cause, Andrei.

Andrei

(Raising his glass)

No. To my highest reverence.

(They drink.)

(MOROZOV enters Left. He stands surveying the room anxiously. The THIRD PROFITEER notices him and waves a greeting. MOROZOV hurries to his table.)

Third Profiteer

Well, well, well! How are you, Morozov? What a pleasant surprise! Sit down.

(The other two at the table nod curtly, suspiciously.)

Morozov

(Sitting down)

Good evening, pal. I'm sure glad to find you here.

THIRD PROFITEER

Just the person I wanted to see. You're an old friend and I'll let you in on the greatest little deal you ever heard of! With your grand business, you certainly can afford it. Genuine American dollars and . . .

MOROZOV

My grand business be damned! Listen, pal, I'm in trouble.

THIRD PROFITEER

What's the matter?

MOROZOV

Tonia and that damned Leo Kovalensky have gone wild in the last few months, running around night clubs, drinking, spending more money than we make. Guess the money's gone to Kovalensky's head.

THIRD PROFITEER

Well?

MOROZOV

They've spent Syerov's share on the last deal and he's raising hell. I don't dare take any chances with him. I've tried to keep out of his way, till I raised the money, but he's left me a note—Lord Almighty, what a note! Here, see for yourself.
        (Takes note from his pocket and hands it to him)

THIRD PROFITEER

        (Reads it, shakes his head)
That's pretty bad. Sounds like trouble.

MOROZOV

        (Shoving the note back into his pocket)
Listen, pal, soul of mine, could you let me have a thousand for two days? You know I'll return it, I'm an honest man, I have a big payment coming day after tomorrow and . . .

THIRD PROFITEER

        (Freezing instantly)
Sorry. Can't be done.

MOROZOV

Listen, pal, you'd save my life. I gotta have . . .

THIRD PROFITEER

Impossible. Everything I got is tied up in foreign currency. Not a ruble on hand.

MOROZOV

(Rising, with a heavy sigh)

Well...I gotta raise the money by morning. Syerov will kill me.

THIRD PROFITEER

(Indifferently)

Good luck.

   (MOROZOV glances around and hurries to First Profiteer's table.)

MOROZOV

(Unctuously)

Good evening, pal, old pal of mine.

FIRST PROFITEER

(Abruptly)

Oh, it's you? Good evening. What do you want?

MOROZOV

(Sitting down)

So glad to see you again. It's been such a long time since I've had the pleasure.

FIRST PROFITEER

Skip it. What's on your mind?

MOROZOV

How you can talk!...Well,...as a matter of fact...I was just wondering if you could let me have a thousand for...

FIRST PROFITEER

Beat it. I'm not in the charity business.

MOROZOV

(Desperately)

Listen, soul of mine, I've gotta have it! To save my skin! You wouldn't want me to get thrown into the G.P.U., would you?

FIRST PROFITEER

To hell with you! G.P.U. is it? So you want to drag me into it along with you?

MOROZOV

(To Second Profiteer)

Citizen, could you maybe...

SECOND PROFITEER

Get out of here!

(MOROZOV rises, looks around desperately. Sees Kira and Andrei. His face melts into a wide smile and he hurries toward them.)

MOROZOV

Ah, good evening, Kira Alexandrovna, soul of mine!

KIRA

(Flustered, terrified)

Good evening.

MOROZOV

(Sitting down)

So glad to see you! Who's the gentleman friend, Kira Alexandrovna?

KIRA

(Rising)

Really, you'll have to excuse us, we were just ready to go...

ANDREI

(Watching her)

What's the matter, Kira?

(To Morozov)

Haven't I seen you at the Food Trust?

MOROZOV

(Beaming)

Sure thing. Karp Morozov, assistant manager. A great position as you can see.

(Winks significantly, extending his hand)

ANDREI

(Shaking hands)

My name's Andrei Taganov... What's the matter, Kira? Sit down.

(She sits down, watching them tensely.)

MOROZOV

Any friend of Kira Alexandrovna is a friend of mine. We're all of the same crowd, aren't we?

(Winks)

KIRA

I don't know what you're talking ab...

ANDREI

Certainly. We're all of the same crowd.

MOROZOV

A bright young man—aren't you?—as I can see. Making good money? Must be—to entertain charming young ladies in a place like this. What's your line?

KIRA

Comrade Taganov is...

ANDREI

(With a warning glance that paralyzes her)

I have a particular interest in speculations.

MOROZOV

Ssh! Not so loud! You must learn to be more cautious, young man. There are G.P.U. agents everywhere.

KIRA

Yes, we must be cautious, Comrade Morozov. You never can tell when you'll meet a G.P.U. agent.

ANDREI

Nonsense! You don't know any G.P.U. agents, *do you*, Kira?

KIRA

No...I...

MOROZOV

(Laughing uproariously)

Kira Alexandrovna and G.P.U. agents! That's a good one! Why, she's the greatest little counterrevolutionist we've got—as you must know.

ANDREI

I do.

MOROZOV

No danger of these new fangled ideas with her! Why, with her mother and father, and then Lev Sergueievitch...

ANDREI

Who?

MOROZOV

Leo Kovalensky, her dear friend...you know him, of course?

ANDREI

Yes, I know him.

MOROZOV

A good friend of the family, aren't you? How long have you known Kira Alexandrovna?

ANDREI

About two years.

MOROZOV

Oh, well, you're safe then.

KIRA

Really, Andrei, it's getting late and I'd like to go home.

ANDREI

In just a little while, Kira. You don't mind if I have a little talk with Comrade Morozov? Or do you?

KIRA

Why, no...no, of course not. Why should I?

ANDREI

I think Comrade Morozov and I can be of great help to each other.

MOROZOV

(Eagerly)

Sure. Sure, I knew it from the first. Tell me, what particular line of...er...speculation are you in?

ANDREI

I'm interested in *food products*, just now.

MOROZOV

Well, pal, just along my line.

(Drawing his chair closer to Andrei)

Listen, I can let you in on a little deal that's the biggest thing in this U.S.S.R. I'll give you a good rate of interest if you'll just let me have a thousand as down payment and...

KIRA

I assure you, Comrade Taganov is not interested.

ANDREI

Why, no, Kira, I'm greatly interested.

MOROZOV

You see, there's a Communist in it with me...Oh, don't be afraid, he's perfectly safe...Well, I owe him the thousand on the last deal, and he's mad as hell, he's sent me a letter...

(Reaches into his pocket)

KIRA

Andrei, I think we had better go home. You'll be late at the G.P.U. office, tomorrow morning.

(MOROZOV grasps and drops his hand hurriedly. Silence. The three look at one another.)

MOROZOV

(Giggling nervously)

Well, well, well, how foolish of me! And here I've been fooling you, setting a trap for you, Comrade Taganov, to catch you as a speculator, and report you to the Food Trust! As...as my social duty, you know. I...I bet you thought I was a speculator myself, didn't you? Funny, isn't it?

ANDREI

Very.

MOROZOV

(Mops his forehead with a napkin)

Of course, I should've known that Kira Alexandrovna wouldn't be out with a...speculator. That's a good one on me. Well, I do overstep, sometimes, you know, in my social loyalty, over zealous for the cause, you know how it is.

ANDREI

I do.

MOROZOV

Well, it's been a pleasure. I gotta be going now and...

(Reaches for his handkerchief. The letter falls to the floor. MOROZOV reaches for it with such a ferocious jerk that ANDREI stops him, seizing his wrist.)

ANDREI

What's that, Comrade Morozov?

MOROZOV

(Kicks the letter and it rolls out of reach, under the next table. Mops his forehead.)

Oh, that? Nothing, Comrade. Nothing at all. Just some scrap of wastepaper.

ANDREI

(Watching him)

Oh, just a scrap of wastepaper? Well, we'll let it lie there, we'll let the janitor throw it in the waste basket.

MOROZOV

(Eagerly)

Yes, that's it. Very well put, Comrade. We'll let the janitor throw it in the waste basket. Would you like another drink, Comrade? The next one's on me.

ANDREI

No, thank you.

MOROZOV

I...I always like a little drink, at night, before I go home.

ANDREI

About time you were going home, isn't it, Comrade Morozov?

MOROZOV

Oh!...well, I guess...well, it's not so late yet, and...

KIRA

(Rising)

But it is late for us, Andrei, and...

ANDREI

Sit down, Kira.

(She obeys reluctantly.)

(To Morozov)

I thought you were in a hurry a little while ago.

MOROZOV

I…well, no, I can't say that I'm in any particular hurry, and then such pleasant company…

ANDREI

What's the matter, Comrade Morozov? Anything you don't want to leave around here?

MOROZOV

Who, me? I don't know what that could be, Comrade.

ANDREI

It isn't that little scrap of wastepaper, down there under the table, by any chance, is it?

MOROZOV

Oh, that? Why, Comrade Taganov, I've forgotten all about that. What would I want with it?

ANDREI

(Slowly)

I don't know.

MOROZOV

That's just it, Comrade Taganov, nothing. Nothing at all.

KIRA

(Upsets her glass deliberately, it falls with a crash.)

Oh, I'm so sorry!

(Bends for it)

Won't you help me please, Andrei?

(MOROZOV tries to reach for the note, swiftly.)

ANDREI

(To Kira)

That's all right. The waiter will get it.

(To Morozov)

What are you bending for, Comrade Morozov?

MOROZOV

(Straightening himself quickly)

To tie my shoelaces. The shoelace is unfastened.

ANDREI

Where?

MOROZOV

(Stretches his feet out, giggles)

Well, isn't that funny? It really isn't unfastened at all. See? And I thought it was. You know how it is, this Soviet jun...these shoelaces nowadays. Not solid at all. Not dependable.

ANDREI

No. They tear like twine.

MOROZOV

Yes. They tear just like...like you would say...that's it, like twine.

KIRA

(Nervous, hurriedly)

They make better shoes abroad. A friend of mine got a pair of slippers from Riga, real patent leather. Have you ever seen foreign slippers, Andrei?

ANDREI

No.

KIRA

They're so much nicer than these old ones of mine.

(Extending her foot)

Aren't they terrible, Andrei?

(MOROZOV bends swiftly.)

ANDREI

Anything wrong under the table, Comrade Morozov?

MOROZOV

(Straightening himself quickly)

No. Not a thing, Comrade...Now speaking of the efficiency of production, Comrade Taganov, take for instance, in the capitalistic countries...in the...in the...

(Chokes)

ANDREI

Yes, Comrade Morozov, in the capitalistic countries?

(MOROZOV leaps ferociously for the letter. ANDREI seizes his wrist with one hand and reaches for the letter with the other. He opens it slowly, reads. MOROZOV and KIRA stare at him silently, frozen.)

ANDREI

(Raises his head slowly, folds the letter and puts it in his pocket. Looks at Morozov, without raising his voice.)

Get out of here.

MOROZOV

(Trembling)

Comrade...Comrade...let me explain...

ANDREI

Get out of here.

MOROZOV

Comrade, I'll pay, I'll pay anything you wish, I...

(ANDREI closes his fist. MOROZOV screams with the defiance of utter despair.)

Listen, you can't do anything to me! You can't do anything about it! Syerov's got a powerful friend at the G.P.U. who will see to it that you keep your mouth shut and...

ANDREI

Get out!

MOROZOV

I'll call him! I'll call him right now!

(Grabs his hat and exits hurriedly)

(KIRA stares at Andrei without a word.)

ANDREI

(Calmly)

Let's go, Kira. I'll take you home.

KIRA

Andrei, you wanted to leave it all...to go abroad...didn't you?

ANDREI

Yes.

KIRA

Then why are you starting something...against someone...to help the masters you no longer want to serve?

ANDREI

I'm going to find out whether they're still worth serving.

KIRA

What difference would that make to you?

ANDREI

I'm giving myself a last chance. I have something to put before them. I know what they should do about it. I'm afraid I know also what they're going to do about it. I'm still a member of the Party. In a very short while, I'll know how long I'll remain a member of the Party.

KIRA

You're making a test? At the cost of several lives?

ANDREI

At the cost of several lives that should be ended.

KIRA

Andrei!

ANDREI

Kira, please don't say anything. I don't want to learn how much you know about this case. I'm afraid I know already that you're not quite ignorant about it. I'm expecting the highest integrity from the men I'm going to face. Don't make me face them with less than that on my part.

KIRA

(Rises)

(Tense, holding on to the table for support, in a last desperate effort)

Andrei, I'm begging you—you understand?—begging you with all there is in me—if I ever meant anything to you, this is the only time I want to claim it—I'm begging you to drop this case, Andrei, for one reason only: for me!

ANDREI

(Looks at her, speaks slowly, coldly)

Who is involved in this case?

KIRA

I don't know! I...

ANDREI

Leo Kovalensky is, isn't he?

KIRA

No!

ANDREI

Kira, what is that man to you?

KIRA

(Controls herself with an effort, shrugs, speaks lightly)

Just a friend...I don't care, do as you wish...Will you take me home now?

(ANDREI rises.)

CURTAIN

ACT 3

SCENE 1

A few days later. Morning. Office of the G.P.U. headquarters. A small, bare, austere room. Door Center back. Window in wall Left. A large desk and chair in front of window; four chairs at walls. No other furniture. One large picture of Lenin on the wall.

At curtain rise, the head of the Economic section of the G.P.U. is sitting behind the desk. He is a suave, sinister individual of indefinite age; he wears a military tunic, tight breeches, high boots, and a gun on his hip. ANDREI is standing before the desk, facing him.

OFFICIAL

Comrade Taganov, you are not employed by the Economic Section of the G.P.U., are you?

ANDREI

No.

OFFICIAL

If I'm not mistaken, you belong to the Secret Service department?

ANDREI

Yes.

OFFICIAL

Yet I understand that you've been conducting some investigation in a case which comes under the jurisdiction of the Economic Section.

ANDREI

I have.

OFFICIAL

Who gave you the authority to do it?

ANDREI

My Party card.

OFFICIAL

What made you begin the investigation?

ANDREI

A piece of incriminating evidence.

OFFICIAL

Against a Party member?

ANDREI

Yes.

OFFICIAL

Why didn't you turn it over to us?

ANDREI

I wanted to have a complete case to report.

OFFICIAL

Have you?

ANDREI

Yes.

OFFICIAL

You will report it to me?

ANDREI

No. To my Chief, the Head of the Secret Service.

OFFICIAL

(Smiles, looks at him)
I suggest that you drop the entire matter.

ANDREI

If this is an order, I'll remind you that you are not my Chief. If it is advice, I do not need it.

OFFICIAL

Comrade Taganov, as Comrade Lenin has said, a Communist must be adaptable to reality. Have you considered the consequences on what you plan to expose?

ANDREI

I have.

OFFICIAL

Do you find it advisable to make public a scandal involving a Party member—at this time?

ANDREI

That should have been the concern of the Party member involved.

OFFICIAL

Do you know my…interest in that person?

ANDREI

I do.

OFFICIAL

Does the knowledge make any difference in your plans?

ANDREI

None.

OFFICIAL

Have you ever thought that I could be of service to you?

ANDREI

No. I haven't.

OFFICIAL

Don't you believe that it is an idea worth considering?

ANDREI

No. I don't.

OFFICIAL

How long have you held your present position, Comrade Taganov?

ANDREI

Two years and three months.

OFFICIAL

At the same salary?

ANDREI

Yes.

OFFICIAL

Don't you think a promotion desirable?

ANDREI

No.

OFFICIAL

You do not believe in a spirit of mutual help and cooperation with your Party comrade?

ANDREI

Not above the spirit of the Party.

OFFICIAL

You are devoted to the Party?

ANDREI

Yes.

OFFICIAL

Above all things?

ANDREI

Yes.

OFFICIAL

How many times have you faced a Party Purging Committee?

ANDREI

Three times.

OFFICIAL

Do you know that there is another Purging coming?

ANDREI

Yes.

OFFICIAL

And you're going to make a report on that case you've investigated—to your Chief?

ANDREI

Yes.

OFFICIAL

When?

ANDREI

I have an appointment to see him in half an hour.

OFFICIAL

(Glances at his wristwatch)

Very well. Will you kindly report here again at five o'clock this afternoon?

ANDREI

Yes. Is that all?

OFFICIAL

That's all, Comrade Taganov.

(ANDREI turns to exit.)

(*BLACKOUT*)
(*To indicate passage of several hours*)

Same office—late afternoon.

The OFFICIAL is sitting behind his desk. The CHIEF OF THE SECRET SERVICE, a thin, blond bearded, unctuous gentleman, is seated beside him. PAVEL SYEROV and MOROZOV occupy chairs facing the desk.

OFFICIAL

(Speaking into telephone)

Have Comrade Taganov come in.

(Hangs up)

MOROZOV

(Mopping his forehead)

Oh my lord! Oh my Lord Almighty!

OFFICIAL

Keep quiet!

(ANDREI enters. He stops on the threshold, looks at the gathering, startled.)

CHIEF

Sit down, Comrade Taganov.

(Rises and closes the door. ANDREI sits down.)

Congratulations, Comrade Taganov.

(ANDREI bows.)

You have done a valuable piece of work and rendered a great service to the Party. You've put into our hands just the case we needed and I, as your Chief, feel proud to thank you for it.

OFFICIAL

Allow me to add my compliments, Comrade Taganov. With the present difficult economic situation, the government has to show the masses who is responsible for their suffering. The treacherous counterrevolutionary activities of speculators, who deprive our toilers of their food rations, will be brought into the full light of proletarian justice.

CHIEF

We shall make an example of this case. Every newspaper, every club, every public pulpit[12] will be mobilized to the task. The trial of Citizen Kovalensky will be broadcast into every hamlet of the U.S.S.R.

ANDREI

(Rising)

Whose trial, Comrade?

CHIEF

The trial of Citizen Kovalensky. Oh, yes, of course, by the way, Comrade Taganov, that letter of Comrade Syerov's, which you attached to your report on the case—was that the only copy of it in existence?

ANDREI

Yes, Comrade.

CHIEF

Who has read it beside yourself?

ANDREI

No one.

CHIEF

(Slowly)

Comrade Taganov, you will forget that you ever read that letter.

(ANDREI stares at him silently.)

This is an order from the committee which acted upon your report. Do you realize the precarious equilibrium of our public opinion?

ANDREI

Yes, Comrade.

---

[12] Among the revisions Ayn Rand made to *We the Living* for the 1959 edition, she changed every instance of "pulpit" to "lectern."

CHIEF

In that case, I do not have to explain why a Party member's name must be kept from any connection with a case of counterrevolutionary speculation. Am I understood?

ANDREI

Thoroughly, Comrade.

OFFICIAL

(To Syerov)

Hereafter, Comrade Syerov, you will confine your literary efforts to matters pertaining to your job on the railroad.

SYEROV

Oh, sure, pal. Don't worry.

OFFICIAL

I'm not the one to worry in this case, I'll remind you.

SYEROV

Oh, hell, I've worried till I'm seasick. What do you want? One has only so many hairs to turn gray.

OFFICIAL

But only one head under the hair.

SYEROV

W...what do you mean? You have the letter, haven't you?

OFFICIAL

Not any more.

SYEROV

Where is it?!

OFFICIAL

In the furnace.

SYEROV

Thanks, pal.

OFFICIAL

You have good reason to be grateful. But remember, your aristocratic playmate, Citizen Kovalensky, will have to go on trial and...

SYEROV

Hell, do you think that will make me cry? I'll be only too glad to see that arrogant bum get his white neck twisted!

CHIEF

As to you, Comrade Morozov, your health requires a long rest and a trip to a warmer climate. I would suggest that you resign from the Food Trust. It would not be advisable to create a great deal of unnecessary comment about our Food Trust.

MOROZOV

(Mopping his forehead)

Oh, sure, Comrade, sure, I'll resign.

CHIEF

In acknowledgment of your resignation, we shall give you an assignment to a place in a House of Rest. A pleasant sanatorium in the Crimea. Restful and quiet. It will help your health a great deal. I would suggest that you take full advantage of the privilege, for—let us say—six months. I would not advise you to hurry back, Comrade Morozov.

MOROZOV

No, I won't hurry.

OFFICIAL

And if I were you, I wouldn't try to pull any wires for Kovalensky, even though he's going to the firing squad.

MOROZOV

Who, me, pull any wires? For him? Why should I, Comrade? Why should I? I had nothing to do with him. He owned that Food store, he alone. You can look up the registration. He alone. Sole owner.

CHIEF

Of course, Citizen Kovalensky was the real culprit and dominant spirit of the conspiracy. He will be arrested tonight. Does that meet with your approval, Comrade Taganov?

ANDREI

My position does not allow me to approve, Comrade. Only to take orders.

CHIEF

Very well said, Comrade Taganov. Of course, Citizen Kovalensky is an aristocrat by birth and the son of a father executed for counterrevolution. He is a living symbol of the class which is the bitterest enemy of the Soviet. Our working masses shall know who strikes deadly blows at the very heart of our economic life.

ANDREI

Yes, Comrade. A public trial with headlines in the papers and a radio microphone in the courtroom?

CHIEF

Precisely, Comrade Taganov.

ANDREI

And what if Citizen Kovalensky talks too much, and too near the microphone? What if he mentions names?

CHIEF

Oh, nothing to fear, Comrade Taganov. Those gentlemen are easy to handle. He'll be promised life to say only what he's told to say. He'll be expecting a pardon even when he hears his death sentence. One can make promises, you know. One doesn't always have to keep them.

ANDREI

And when he faces the firing squad—there will be no microphone on hand?

CHIEF

Precisely.

ANDREI

And, of course, it won't be necessary to mention that he was jobless and starving at the time he entered the employ of those unnamed persons?

CHIEF

What's that, Comrade Taganov?

ANDREI

A helpful suggestion, Comrade. It will also be important to explain how a penniless aristocrat managed to lay his hands on the very heart of our economic life.

OFFICIAL

Comrade Taganov, you have a remarkable gift for platform oratory. Too remarkable a gift. It is not always an asset to an agent of the G.P.U. You should be careful lest it be appreciated and you find yourself sent to a nice post—in the Turkestan, for instance—where you will have full opportunity to display it. Like Comrade Trotsky, for instance.

ANDREI

I have served in the Red Army under Comrade Trotsky.

CHIEF

At seven o'clock tonight, Comrade Taganov, you will report for duty to search Citizen Kovalensky's apartment for additional evidence in connection with this case. And you will arrest Citizen Kovalensky.

ANDREI

Yes, Comrade.
          (Turns to go)

CHIEF

Oh, incidentally, Comrade Taganov, no one else is to know about this case. If you observe the proper discretion, you will find yourself rewarded—*and* we won't bring Citizen Kira Argounova into the case.

ANDREI

          (Stops short)
I don't understand you, Comrade.

CHIEF

Oh, yes, I think you do.

ANDREI

Citizen Argounova has nothing to do with this.
          (SYEROV chuckles loudly.)

CHIEF

Comrade Taganov, do you happen to know where Citizen Argounova is living?

ANDREI

Certainly. With her parents.

CHIEF

Tell me, have you ever investigated Citizen Argounova—for your own sake?

ANDREI

I know all I have to know about her. You don't have to bring her into this. She is absolutely blameless politically.

CHIEF

Oh, *politically?* And in other respects?

ANDREI

If you're speaking as my superior, I refuse to listen to anything about Citizen Argounova, except her political standing.

CHIEF

Very well. I don't have to say anything. I was speaking merely as a friend. You should be careful, Comrade Taganov. You don't have many friends left—in the Party.

ANDREI

Is that all, Comrade?

CHIEF

That's all, Comrade Taganov.
  (ANDREI turns to go.)

CURTAIN

SCENE 2

Same evening. Leo's home. The room is neater, obviously more prosperous than when we saw it last. A new cupboard has replaced the kitchen table. The stove is gone. There are fresh flowers in vases. A fire is flaming brightly in the fireplace.

At curtain rise LEO is sitting in an armchair by the fire, in his shirtsleeves, weary, listless, an open book on the arm of his chair. ANTONINA PAVLOVNA sits facing him, her hat and coat on. Offstage OLGA IVANOVNA is playing the funeral march "You Fell As a Victim."

LEO

And then?

ANTONINA PAVLOVNA

He wouldn't say. Koko has been acting very strangely. I think he was at the G.P.U. today, but he wouldn't tell me anything.

LEO

Don't worry. They'll hush up the whole business of that fool letter. Syerov's friend is too powerful at the G.P.U. for any trouble. We're perfectly safe, all of us.

ANTONINA PAVLOVNA

I'm not so sure. There's something in the air. I thought I'd warn you.

LEO

Well, why worry? If we're caught—that'll be the end, so much the quicker.

ANTONINA PAVLOVNA

But Leo...

LEO

We've been expecting it all along, haven't we? Well, maybe it has come. And I can't really say I'm sorry.

ANTONINA PAVLOVNA

What's the matter, Leo?

LEO

I'm so tired...

ANTONINA PAVLOVNA

At your age, Leo! With your whole life before you and...

LEO

Life? What kind of life? In this damn century of ours?

ANTONINA PAVLOVNA

What's wrong with this century? One must be modern and broadminded. Of course, there's no place now for people with an arrogantly egotistical ideology such as...as Kira Alexandrovna, for instance. On the other hand, even the humblest citizen, if he is attuned to his collective, has a chance to rise and improve himself. Oh, don't misunderstand me, I'm not a Communist, but I'm trying to be fair.

LEO

By all means. We must always be fair. If we see two hundred million humans ground to a bloody pulp, we must always consider the possible good points of the picture.

ANTONINA PAVLOVNA

You've never talked like that before!

LEO

Even I have to be sober some time. That's the curse of it. You can never drown it all, for good, out of sight, to see nothing, nothing, to crawl lower than any of my brother men! The lower the better. If I could do something viler than what I'm doing—I'd be still happier.

Antonina Pavlovna

Leo darling, I don't understand you at all!

Leo

Don't try to. You know, I admire you tremendously. You're the perfect woman of our age. You've never had to squirm in agony because you still had something in you that choked every time you tried to swallow the life around us. But if you're cursed with it, it can be killed.

(Ferociously)

If I could slap my own face, if I could reach such utter contempt for myself that I'd feel lower, lower than anyone around me...

(His hands fall limply.)

...then I could rest. Rest.

Antonina Pavlovna

(Aghast)

You need a drink, Leo.

Leo

I certainly do.

(Walks to cabinet, gets bottle and two glasses, pours. Hands one glass to Antonina Pavlovna.)

Here. Forgive me. Forget what I said.

(Empties his glass in one swallow)

Antonina Pavlovna

(Raising her glass coquettishly)

To you, Leo darling!

(Drinks. Jerks her head at door Right, impatiently.)

Does that tenant of yours play all day long?

Leo

Usually.

Antonina Pavlovna

I wish to God she wouldn't play that funeral march!

(Walks to door Right. Knocks. The music stops. OLGA IVANOVNA opens the door.)

How do you do, Olga Ivanovna? Please excuse me, but would you mind stopping that funeral march? Really, it makes me nervous.

OLGA IVANOVNA

(With a dazed kind of stubbornness)

I'm sorry. I can't. I have to practice it for the club. So many Communists are dying these days, and they always play the revolutionary dirge for them.

ANTONINA PAVLOVNA

But couldn't you play some beautiful classic, like you used to?

OLGA IVANOVNA

No!

ANTONINA PAVLOVNA

Chopin or Bach or...

OLGA IVANOVNA

(Hysterically)

No! I won't! I'll never play them again! Never! What's the use? You think they're beautiful? That's why I'll never play them again! Not in this world! I won't! Never!

(Breaks down into hysterical sobs and rushes out, slamming her door. We hear her sobbing softly, offstage.)

ANTONINA PAVLOVNA

(Mopping her forehead)

Phew!...Really, Leo, you're living in an insane asylum...You know, I think Koko is getting ready to leave town.

LEO

What for? We have nothing to fear.

ANTONINA PAVLOVNA

And I don't think he'll take me along.

LEO

That's too bad.

ANTONINA PAVLOVNA

Oh, I don't know. It may have its...advantages. Would you like me to be free, Leo?

LEO

Really, Tonia, that's no concern of mine.

ANTONINA PAVLOVNA

Where's Kira Alexandrovna today?

LEO

Visiting her parents. She should be back by now.

ANTONINA PAVLOVNA

You love her very much, don't you, Leo?

LEO

That, my dear, is no concern of yours.

ANTONINA PAVLOVNA

Of course, of course...Only I can't help feeling, sometimes, that she doesn't know how to appreciate you.

LEO

Stop talking like a fool.

ANTONINA PAVLOVNA

I can't help feeling that you need the guiding hand of a more mature woman, a woman of the world who understands you and...

LEO

Will you please go home, Tonia, before I tell you that you make me sick?

ANTONINA PAVLOVNA

(Rising with dignity)

Really, Leo, I don't know what's happened to you. But I'll forgive you. I understand. The nervous strain and all...

(She is at the window. She throws a casual glance out and gasps, stunned, terror stricken.)

LEO

(Indifferently)

What's the matter?

ANTONINA PAVLOVNA

(Panicky, hysterical)

I've got to go! I've got to go at once! Leo, if they question you, remember, I had nothing to do with the store! I knew nothing about it! I didn't know where the money came from!

LEO

What are you getting panicky over? Go home. Forget about it.

ANTONINA PAVLOVNA

Leo, remember! Please remember!

> (She rushes out, madly.)

> (LEO shrugs, picks up his book, fingers the pages indifferently. A door-bell rings sharply. He pays no attention. Then LAVROVA's scream is heard offstage, a horrified scream. LEO raises his head, looks at the door. Steps are heard approaching. The door is thrown open. ANDREI enters, followed by TWO SOLDIERS with bayonets. ANDREI is wearing a black leather jacket with a holster on his hip. At a motion of his hand, a THIRD SOLDIER remains stationed beyond the door, closing it.)

> (LEO rises slowly, calmly, looking at them.)

LEO

Well, Comrade Taganov, didn't you know that some day we would meet like this?

ANDREI

> (Hands him a slip of paper; speaks as if he had never met him before)

Search warrant, Citizen Kovalensky.

LEO

(Bowing graciously)

Go ahead. You're quite welcome.

> (ANDREI motions to the soldiers sharply. One of them throws a book-case open and goes swiftly through the shelves, flinging the books to the floor; the other one opens the cupboard and looks through it, throwing out pans, dishes and sacks of food; ANDREI walks to a desk, opens the drawers, goes through them swiftly, mechanically, gathering all letters and papers, slipping them into his briefcase. LEO stands alone in the middle of the room; the others pay no attention to him. He leans against a table, half sitting, his legs sliding forward. He watches the search indifferently. Then:)

LEO

I'm sorry I can't oblige you by letting you find secret plans to blow up the Kremlin, Comrade Taganov.

ANDREI

Citizen Kovalensky, you are speaking to a representative of the G.P.U.

LEO

You didn't think I had forgotten that, did you?

(ANDREI continues his work silently. A soldier tears the covers off the bed, sticks his bayonet into the pillow; white flakes of down flutter out. LEO takes his cigarette case from his pocket, opens it, and extends it to Andrei.)

ANDREI

No, thank you.

(LEO lights a cigarette, the quiver of the match in his steady fingers, the first sign to betray his nervousness. A SOLDIER drops a vase with a loud crash.)

OLGA IVANOVNA

(Throwing her door open)

Lev Sergueievitch, what's the mat...

(She stops short with a choked gasp, seeing the searchers, and makes a swift sign of the cross. She rushes trembling, toward Andrei.)

Comrade! Comrade, I'm not guilty! I didn't know anything about this. I...

ANDREI

Keep quiet. This has nothing to do with you. Go back to your room.

(OLGA IVANOVNA crosses herself, hysterically, and rushes back into her room, slamming the door. The search continues.)

LEO

The survival of the fittest. However, the fittest are not always those to survive. Usually, it's the other way around. What are your philosophical convictions, Comrade Taganov? We've never had a chance to discuss that. And this is as good a time as any.

ANDREI

I would suggest that you keep silent.

LEO

And when a representative of the G.P.U. suggests, it's a command, isn't it? I realize that one should know how to respect the dignity and the grandeur of the authority under all circumstances, no matter how trying to the self respect of those in power.

(A SOLDIER raises his head menacingly and makes a step toward Leo. A glance from ANDREI stops him.)

(ANDREI opens the door of a wardrobe, disclosing Kira's dresses hanging in a row. With a sudden jerk, he reaches for one of them.)

LEO

What's the matter, Comrade Taganov?

> (ANDREI is holding Kira's red dress. He looks at it for a long moment, holding it spread out awkwardly in his two hands. Then he looks slowly at the open wardrobe.)

ANDREI

Whose are these?

LEO

> (With deliberate, mocking, insulting contempt)

My mistress's.

> (ANDREI straightens the dress slowly and hangs it back in the ward-robe, cautiously, a little awkwardly, as if it were of breakable glass. LEO chuckles.)

A disappointment, isn't it, Comrade Taganov?

> (ANDREI doesn't answer. He takes the dresses out slowly, one by one, and runs his fingers through the pockets and linings.)

> (Voices rise suddenly behind the door Left.)

GUARD'S VOICE

> (Offstage)

I say you can't, Citizen! You can't go in now!

> (There is the sound of a struggle behind the door, the sound of a body being thrown aside violently.)

KIRA'S VOICE

> (Offstage)

> (A savage, ferocious scream)

Let me in there! Let me in!

> (ANDREI walks to the door slowly and throws it open. KIRA stands on the threshold. She stares, frozen, horror stricken, when she recognizes him. He looks at her silently.)

ANDREI

> (Slowly, evenly)

Citizen Argounova, do you live here?

KIRA

> (Her eyes on his)

Yes.

(He lets her enter. She leans, helpless, against the wall, her hat in her hand.)

(The SOLDIER closes the door. ANDREI turns away from her, very slowly, with an immense effort. He walks back to the wardrobe. He orders the soldiers.)

ANDREI

Search that cabinet—and the boxes in the corner.

LEO

(To Kira)

I'm sorry, dearest. I hoped it would be over before you came back.

(She does not seem to have heard. She is staring at Andrei. ANDREI continues the search.)

ANDREI

(To the soldiers)

Look through all the pillows. And lift that rug.

(The SOLDIERS obey. The room is fast becoming a shambles.)

(Closing a last drawer, calmly, evenly)

That will be all.

(Turning to Leo)

Citizen Kovalensky, you're under arrest.

LEO

I'm sure this is the most pleasant duty you've ever performed, Comrade Taganov.

(He picks up his coat, walks to a mirror, adjusts his hair, his tie with deliberate precision. ANDREI stands waiting. LEO stops before Kira on his way out.)

Aren't you going to say goodbye, Kira?

(Takes her in his arms and kisses her)

I have only one favor to ask, Kira. I hope you'll forget me.

(She does not answer. A SOLDIER holds the door open. ANDREI walks out, followed by LEO and the SECOND SOLDIER who closes the door behind them.)

(KIRA stands, sagging, at the wall. The hat slips from her hand.)

CURTAIN

SCENE 3

Same evening. Andrei's room. The room is dark, lighted only by the glow of the fire in the fireplace.

ANDREI is sitting on a box by the fire, motionless, his hands hanging limply.

There is a sharp knock at the door.

ANDREI

(Without raising his head)

Come in.

(KIRA enters. She stands in the archway, Right, looking at him, her face menacing, loose, brutal. He rises without a word, looks at her.)

KIRA

(Savagely)

Well? What are you going to do about it?

ANDREI

(Slowly)

If I were you, I'd get out of here.

KIRA

And if I don't go?

ANDREI

Get out of here.

(She tears her hat and coat off, throws them aside in the darkness.)

Get out, you...

KIRA

Whore? Certainly. I just wanted to be sure you realized that that's what I am.

ANDREI

What do you want? I have nothing to say to you.

KIRA

But I have. And you'll listen. So you've caught me, haven't you, Comrade Taganov? And you're going to have your revenge? Go ahead! Have your revenge. And this is mine. I'm not pleading for him. I have nothing to fear any more. But, at least, I can speak. I have so much to say to you, to all of you, and I've kept silent for so long that it's going to tear me to pieces! I have nothing to lose. But you have.

ANDREI

Don't you think it's useless? Why say anything? If you have any excuses to offer...

KIRA

(Laughs)

You fool! I'm proud of what I've done! Hear me? I don't regret it! So you think I loved you, but you think I was merely unfaithful to you, on the side, as most women are? Well, then, listen: all you were to me, you and your great love, all they meant was only a pack of crisp, white, square ten ruble bills with a sickle and hammer printed in the corner! Do you know where those bills went? To a tubercular sanatorium in the Crimea. Do you know what they paid for? For the life of someone I loved before I ever saw you,[13] and now you're holding him in one of your cells and you're going to shoot him. Why not? It's fair enough. Shoot him. Take his life. You've paid for it.

ANDREI

(Stares at her, with fear, real fear for the first time, in his eyes)

Kira...I...I didn't know.

KIRA

You loved me? I was the highest of women to you? Well, look at me! I'm only a whore and you're the one who made the first payment! You think I loved you? I thought of Leo when you held me in your arms! Every kiss you got, every word, every hour was given to him, for him. I've never loved him as I loved him in your bed!...Go ahead! Kill him! Nothing you can do to him will compare with what I've done to you. You know that, don't you?

ANDREI

(Helplessly, as if speaking to himself, as if she were not present)

I didn't know.

KIRA

No, you didn't know. But it was very simple. He wanted to live. He had no right to that, had he? Your State said so. We tried to beg. We begged humbly. Do you know what they said? There was one big official and he told me that a hundred thousand workers had died in the civil war and why couldn't one aristocrat die in the face of the Union of Socialist Soviet Republics? And what is the Union of Socialist Soviet Republics in the face of one man? But that is a question not for you to answer. I'm really grateful[14] to that official. He gave me permission to

---

[13] In the novel, Kira does love Leo before she first sees Andrei; but in this version of the play, she meets Andrei shortly before meeting Leo.

[14] The typescript has "gratified."

do what I've done. I don't hate him. You should hate him. What I'm doing to you—he did it first!

ANDREI

Kira...I...I see now...I...

KIRA

You see now! But you didn't see when you started, you, and your official, and a million others, like you, like him, you didn't know the kind of salvation you were bringing mankind? Well, one of you has been paid. I paid it. In you and to you. For all the sorrow your comrades brought to a living world! How do you like it, Comrade Taganov of the All-Union Communist Party? If you taught us that our life is nothing before the state—well, then, are you really suffering? You loved a woman and she threw your love in your face? But the proletarian mines in the Don Basin have produced a hundred tons of coal last month! You had two altars and you saw suddenly that a harlot stood on one of them and Citizen Morozov on the other? But the proletarian State has exported ten thousand bushels of wheat last month! You've had every beam knocked from under your life? But the proletarian Republic is building a new electric plant on the Volga! It's still there, your Collective. Go and join it. Did anything really happen to you? It's nothing but a personal problem of a private life, the kind that only the dead old world could worry about, isn't it? Don't you have something greater—greater is the word your comrades use—left to live for? Or do you, Comrade Taganov?

ANDREI

Kira...please...don't...

KIRA

Now look at me! I was born and I knew I was alive and I knew what I wanted! Why do you think I'm alive? Because I have a stomach and eat and digest the food? Or because I know what I want, and that something which knows how to want—isn't that life itself? And who—in this endless, damned universe—who can tell me why I should live for anything but for that which I want? Who can answer that in human sounds that speak for human reason? But you've tried! You came to bring a new life to men. You tore that life you knew nothing about out of their very guts—and you told them what it had to be. You took their every hour, every nerve, every thought in the farthest corners of their souls—and you told them what it had to be. You came and you forbade life to the living. You've driven us all into an iron cellar and you've closed all the doors, and you've locked us air-tight, air-tight till the blood vessels of our spirits burst! Then you stare and wonder what it's doing to us. Well, then, look! Look at me!

> (He stands motionless, without a word. She laughs, approaches him, screams into his face.)

Why don't you speak? Have you nothing to say? Are you wondering why you've never known what I really was? Well, here's what's left of me after you took him—and do you know what it meant? Do you know what it meant when you reached for my highest reverence...

(She stops short. She gasps, a choked little sound, as if he had slapped her. She slams the back of her hand against her open mouth. She stands, silent, her eyes staring at something she understands suddenly, clearly, fully, for the first time.)

(He smiles slowly, very gently. He stretches out his hands, palms up, shrugging sadly an explanation she does not need. She moans:)

Oh, Andrei!...

ANDREI

(Calmly)

Kira, had I been in your place, I would have done the same—for the person I loved—for you.

KIRA

Oh, Andrei, Andrei, what have I done to you?

ANDREI

You've done me a great favor by coming here and telling me what you've told. Because, you see, you've given me back something I thought I'd lost. You're still what I thought you were. More than I thought you were. Only...it's not anything you've done to me...it's what you had to suffer, and I...I gave you that suffering, and all those moments were to you...to you...

(His voice breaks.)

KIRA

Andrei, I...[15]

ANDREI

(Controls himself with an effort. His voice is firm.)

Listen, child, we won't talk any more. I want you to keep silent for a while, quite silent, even silent inside, you understand? Don't think. Try not to think. You have to rest. I want you to sit down and just sit still for a few minutes.

(He leads her to a chair by the fire.)

KIRA

But...Andrei...you...

---

[15] In ARP 075-08x (see p. 349, under Version I), Rand made handwritten revisions to the rest of the exchange between Andrei and Kira, and cut Andrei's confrontation with Syerov (which follows it).

ANDREI

Forget that. Forget everything. Everything will be all right.

>(She does not resist, all her strength's gone. He sees her trembling. He takes his leather jacket and wraps it around her.)

This will keep you warm. It's cold here. The fire hasn't been on long enough. Now sit still.

>(She does not move. He stands in the darkness looking at her. Says slowly, thoughtfully.)

That letter...I could have taken photostats of it.

KIRA

What?

ANDREI

But I didn't...Still...

KIRA

What are you saying?

ANDREI

Never mind.

>(He whirls about sharply, walks resolutely to the telephone, lifts the receiver.)

Twenty-seven—forty-one, please...I want to speak to Comrade Syerov.

KIRA

>(Jerking her head up)

What are you doing?!

ANDREI

Never mind. Keep still.

>(Into receiver)

Allo, Syerov?...Andrei Taganov speaking. I want you to come to my house at once...yes, now...Don't let anyone see you...Never mind, you'll find out...I'm not going to argue. *I'd hurry if I were you.*

>(Hangs up)

KIRA

Andrei, what...

ANDREI

I don't want him to see you here. Can you go home now? I want you to go to bed. Rest and don't think of anything.

KIRA

But what are you...

ANDREI

Don't question me now. I'll tell you afterwards.
(Picks up her coat, helps her to put it on)
Will you be all right until you get home?

KIRA

Yes, but...

ANDREI

I want you to rest for a few days. Don't go anywhere. There's nothing you can do. Don't worry about...him. Leave that to me.

KIRA

(At the door)
Andrei...I...I understand...I...

ANDREI

(Slowly, gently)
Kira, don't you think it's better if we don't say anything—and just leave it to...to our silence, knowing that we both understand, and that we still have that much in common?

KIRA

(In a whisper)
Yes, Andrei...
(He takes her hand and presses her palm to his lips and holds it for a long time. Then she goes. He closes the door softly behind her.)
(He walks back into the room, stands still, lost in thought, then draws himself up with an effort. Turns on a light. There is a knock at the door.)

ANDREI

Come in.

SYEROV

(Entering belligerently)
Well, what the hell? What do you want?

ANDREI

Sit down.

SYEROV

What was the big idea calling me at this hour and ordering me to come, like a dictator or something?

ANDREI

You came, didn't you? You knew you had to.

SYEROV

I don't know what kind of bluff you're pulling. I thought you had learned a lesson in the last few days.

ANDREI

I have.

SYEROV

(Unbuttoning his coat)
What else do you want?

ANDREI

You better keep your coat on. You're going out—to the G.P.U.—and you haven't much time to lose.

SYEROV

Am I? Glad you let me in on the little secret. Otherwise I might have said that I had no such intention. And maybe I'll still say it. Where am I going, according to Comrade Mussolini Taganov?

ANDREI

To release Leo Kovalensky.

SYEROV

(Falling down on a chair, heavily)
What are you up to, Taganov? Gone insane, have you?

ANDREI

You better keep still and listen. I'll tell you what you have to do.

SYEROV

You'll tell me what I have to do?

ANDREI

And after that, I'll tell you why you will do it. You'll go from here to see your friend, and you know what friend I mean. The one at the G.P.U.

SYEROV

At this hour?

ANDREI

Get him out of bed, if you have to. What you'll tell him and how you'll tell it is none of my business. All I have to know is that Leo Kovalensky is released within forty-eight hours.

SYEROV

Now will you let me in on the little magic wand that will make me do it?

ANDREI

It's a little paper wand, Syerov. Two of them.

SYEROV

Written by whom?

ANDREI

You.

SYEROV

Huh?!

ANDREI

Photographed from one written by you, to be exact.

SYEROV

(Rising slowly, in a choked voice)

You God damned rat!

(ANDREI watches him silently. SYEROV screams.)

I'll go to see my friend all right! And you'll see Leo Kovalensky all right—and it won't take you forty-eight hours either! I'll see to it that you get the cell next to his. And then we'll find out what documents you . . .

ANDREI

There are two photostats, as I said. Only I don't happen to have either one of them.

SYEROV

What . . . what did you . . .

ANDREI

They're in the possession of two friends I can trust. Their instructions are that if anything happens to me before Leo Kovalensky is out—the photostats go to Moscow. Also—if anything happens to him after he is out.

SYEROV

You God damned...

ANDREI

You don't want those photostats to reach Moscow. Your friend won't be able to save your neck, then, nor his own, perhaps.

SYEROV

(Hoarsely)

You're lying. You've never taken any photostats.

ANDREI

Maybe. Want to take a chance on that?

SYEROV

(Falling down on a chair)

Sit down.

(ANDREI sits on the edge of a table, watching him.)

Listen, Andrei, let's talk sense. All right, you're holding the whip. Still, do you know what you're asking?

ANDREI

No more than you can do.

SYEROV

But, good lord in heaven, Andrei! It's such a big case and they're getting ready to...

ANDREI

Stop them.

SYEROV

But how can I?

ANDREI

Your friend can. Nobody knows who enters or leaves the G.P.U. Nobody will know if he keeps it quiet.

SYEROV

But how can I ask him? What am I going to tell him?

ANDREI

That's none of my business.

SYEROV

Andrei, one of us has gone insane. I can't figure it out. Why do you want Kovalensky released?

ANDREI

That's none of your business.

SYEROV

And if you've appointed yourself his guardian angel, then why the hell did you start the whole damn case? You started it, you know.

ANDREI

You said that I had learned a lesson.

SYEROV

Listen, let's talk as friend to friend. I take back all those things I said to you. I apologize. All right, you have your own game to play. I had mine and I made a misstep, but then we're both no innocent angels, as I can see, so we can understand each other and talk decently.

ANDREI

About what?

SYEROV

I have an offer to make to you, Andrei. A good one. That friend of mine, he can do a lot if I slip a couple of words to him, as you know, I guess. I guess you know I have enough on him for a firing squad, too. You're learning the same game, I see, and doing it brilliantly, I must hand it to you. All right, we understand each other. Now I can talk plain. Guess you know your spot in the Party isn't so good any more. After all that criticism you've been spouting about, making yourself enemies—really, you know, it won't be so easy on you at the next Party Purging.

ANDREI

I know.

SYEROV

In fact, you're pretty sure to get the axe, you know.

ANDREI

I do.

SYEROV

Well, then, what do you say if we make a bargain? You drop this case and I'll see to it that you keep your Party card, and not only that, but you can have any job you choose at the G.P.U. And name your own salary. No questions asked and no ill-feeling. What do you say?

ANDREI

What makes you think that I want to remain in the Party?

SYEROV

Andrei!

ANDREI

You don't have to worry about me. I may be thrown out of the Party or run over by a truck. That won't make any difference to you. Understand? But don't touch Leo Kovalensky. Watch him as you would watch your own child, no matter what happens to me. I'm not his guarding angel. You are.
(SYEROV rises unsteadily and draws himself up for a last effort.)

SYEROV

Listen, Andrei, I have something to tell you. I thought you knew it, but I guess you don't. Only pull yourself together and listen, and don't kill me on the first word. I know there's a name you don't want mentioned, but I'll mention it. It's Kira Argounova.

ANDREI

Well?

SYEROV

Listen, we're not mincing words, are we? Hell, not now we aren't. Well, then, listen: you love her and you've been sleeping with her for over a year. And...Wait! Let me finish...Well, she's been Leo Kovalensky's mistress all that time...Wait! You don't have to take my word for it. Just check up on it and see for yourself.

ANDREI

Why check up on it? I know it.

SYEROV

Oh!
(He stands, rocking slowly from heels to toes, looking at Andrei. Then he laughs, loudly, suddenly.)

Well, I should have known.

ANDREI

You better go now. We haven't much time to lose.

SYEROV

(Laughing)

I should have known why the saint of the Party would go in for blackmail. You fool! You poor, virtuous, brainless fool! So that's the kind of grandstand you're playing! Haven't you any sense left? Any pride?

ANDREI

Listen, we've talked enough. You seem to know a lot about me. Well, you should know that I don't change my mind.

SYEROV

(Buttoning his coat, grinning)

All right, Sir Galahad, or whatever it's called, Sir Galahad of the blackmail sword. You win—this time. It's no use threatening you with any retaliation. Fellows like you get theirs without any help from fellows like me.

(Stops in archway on his way out)

In a year—this little mess will be forgotten. I'll be running the railroads of the U.S.S.R. You'll be kicked out of the Party.

ANDREI

Yes. If I'm still here.

SYEROV

Huh?

ANDREI

You're a good member of the Party. Will you tell me something?

SYEROV

What?

ANDREI

What are we doing? Do we want to feed humanity in order to let it live? Or do we want to strangle its life in order to feed it?

(SYEROV shrugs and exits, slamming the door in the hall behind him.)

CURTAIN

SCENE 4

Two days later. Leo's home. Evening. Snowflakes flutter lazily behind the windows. The room still shows the after effects of the search; order is only half restored.

At curtain rise KIRA is sitting on the floor, sorting out a pile of clothing, lazily, indifferently, stopping frequently to stare blankly around her. OLGA IVANOVNA is playing the funeral march offstage.

KIRA jumps up suddenly, knocks furiously on door Right.

KIRA

(Screaming)

Stop it! Stop it, will you? I can't stand it!
        (The music stops, OLGA IVANOVNA comes out.)

OLGA IVANOVNA

(Sympathetically)

I'm so sorry, Kira Alexandrovna. I understand. I won't practice any more today.

KIRA

Thank you.
        (Falling wearily on a chair)
Forgive me for losing my temper.

OLGA IVANOVNA

Oh, I understand...But you know, the trouble with you is that you refuse the consolation of the faith. Listen, there's an old man, God's holy wanderer. I've been to see him. He says we are all being punished for our sins. Only through suffering and long bearing patience shall we become worthy of the Kingdom of Heaven...Only please don't mention that I told you, or they'll fire me from the Club.

KIRA

(Indifferently)

I won't tell anyone.

OLGA IVANOVNA

If there's anything I can...

        (LAVROVA enters, Left, kicking the door open with her foot, carrying a bowl of hot soup in both hands. OLGA IVANOVNA draws herself up with icy dignity the moment she sees Lavrova, and exits Right.)

LAVROVA

(Putting bowl down on table)

Here. I brought you some soup.

KIRA

Thank you, Citizen Lavrova, but I don't need it.

LAVROVA

Go on, eat it. You've eaten practically nothing for two days.

KIRA

I'm not hungry.

LAVROVA

Go on. Even a bourgeois has to eat.

(Doorbell rings. KIRA jumps up.)

Sit still. I'll answer it.

(Exits)

(KIRA listens eagerly, hearing steps approaching. GALINA PETROVNA rushes in, greatly agitated.)

KIRA

(With obvious disappointment, her voice flat, indifferent)

Oh...Good evening, mother.

GALINA PETROVNA

Kira, is it true, is it true what I've just heard?

KIRA

What?! Have you heard something about Leo?!

GALINA PETROVNA

No. Have you?

KIRA

Not a word. For two days.

GALINA PETROVNA

But I've heard about the passports. Is it true that they've refused your application for foreign passports?

KIRA

(Indifferently)

Oh, that?...Yes...Yes, they've refused. I got the notice yesterday.

GALINA PETROVNA

(Sitting down, unbuttoning her coat)

Of course, I fully expected it and I'd almost say thank God, if...if I were sure that you aren't going to...Listen, if you have any insane ideas of...of...Now, I want you to know that I won't allow it. I came here at once, when I heard, to tell you this. You know what it means if you attempt...if you even dare to think of leaving the country illegally!

KIRA

I've never mentioned that.

GALINA PETROVNA

No, you haven't. But I know you. I know how far your foolish recklessness will go. You still want to go abroad, don't you?

KIRA

Yes.

GALINA PETROVNA

And what would you do there? Have you thought of that?

KIRA

No.

GALINA PETROVNA

You have no money. You have no profession. How are you going to live?

KIRA

I don't know.

GALINA PETROVNA

What will happen to you?

KIRA

I don't care.

GALINA PETROVNA

But why do you want to do it?

KIRA

(Dully)

I want to get out.

GALINA PETROVNA

But you'll be all alone. Lost in a wide world, with not a...

KIRA

I want to get out.

GALINA PETROVNA

...with not a single friend to help you, with no aim, no future, no...

KIRA

(Screaming)

I want to get out!

GALINA PETROVNA

What are you after? What's wrong with this country? Of course, this is a transi-tory period of State Construction—but I received three pounds of real bread yesterday! And I've been elected *secretary* of the Teacher's Council. I've adapted myself. You'll outgrow your foolish notions. As I said at the Marxist Club, this is the land for young people. This is the country of opportunity, of honest toil, of freedom and justice, of...

KIRA

(Shaking, in a low choked voice)

Mother, if you don't stop, I'll get out of here.

GALINA PETROVNA

(Jumping up)

What?!

KIRA

We have nothing to say to each other. We never had. Let me...

GALINA PETROVNA

(Screaming)

Well, I'll have you know that you're still my daughter! I have something to say! I won't have you acting like a Communist, defying your mother, daring to...

> (The door is thrown open as LEO enters. KIRA gasps, is about to rush to him, stops short. His face is white; there is a strange, ominous look about him that stops her.)

GALINA PETROVNA

Leo! My lord in heaven!

KIRA

(Staring at him incredulously)
Leo...Leo...you're not...free, are you?

LEO

Yes. Free. Released. Kicked out.

KIRA

How...how could it happen?

LEO

I thought you knew something about that.

GALINA PETROVNA

Leo, my dear boy, I'm so happy!

LEO

Galina Petrovna, could you excuse me, please? I have to speak to Kira—alone.

GALINA PETROVNA

(Sensing trouble)
Certainly, I understand, I was going anyway. If you can speak to her—it's more than I can do!
(Buttons her coat, at door)
Good night.
(Exits)
(KIRA rushes to Leo, throws her arms around him. He flings her aside viciously.)

KIRA

Leo...what's the matter?

LEO

Don't you know?
(She shakes her head, frightened.)
Of course, I should thank you for giving me the pleasure of being released by your lover.

KIRA

My...
(Her voice breaks.)

LEO

You little bitch!

KIRA

Leo...

LEO

Shut up! You rotten little...I wouldn't mind if you were like the rest of us! But you, with your saintly airs, with your heroic speeches, trying to hold me up while you were...you were rolling under the first Communist bum that took the trouble to push you!

KIRA

(Standing straight, motionless, her face white)
Leo, who...

LEO

Shut up!...No! I'll give you a chance to talk. I'll give you a chance to answer just one word. Were you Taganov's mistress? Were you? Yes or no?

KIRA

Yes.

LEO

All the time I was away?

KIRA

Yes.

LEO

And all the time since I came back?

KIRA

Yes. What else did they tell you, Leo?

LEO

What else did you want them to tell me?

KIRA

Who told you?

LEO

Who didn't? Our dear friend Pavel Syerov and all the others. They all knew it at the G.P.U. They laughed and congratulated me—on my good judgment in selecting my protectors! Did you really expect me to thank you for it?

KIRA

Did...did Andrei tell you anything?

LEO

I didn't see him.

KIRA

That...that was a hard blow to you, Leo, when they told you, wasn't it?

LEO

That was the best piece of news I've heard since the revolution. Because, you see, that sets me free.

KIRA

Free...from what?

LEO

From a little fool to whom I had to lie about a great, unending love! A little fool I was afraid to face, afraid to hurt!...I won't even ask whether you had ever loved me. I'd rather think you hadn't. That will make it easier for the future.

KIRA

The...future, Leo?

LEO

Well, what did you plan it to be?

KIRA

I...

LEO

Oh, I know! Run away and get shot on the border. Or get a respectable Soviet job and rot over a Primus, and keep holy something in your fool imagination, your spirit, or soul or honor, something that never existed, that shouldn't exist, that is the worst of all curses, if it ever did exist! Well, I'm through with it. If it's murder—well—I don't see any blood. But I'm going to have champagne, and white bread, and limousines, and no thoughts of any kind, and long live the Dictatorship of the Proletariat!

KIRA

Leo...what...are you going to do?

LEO

I'm going away.

KIRA

Where?

LEO

Sit down.
          (He falls wearily down on a chair. She sits facing him.)
Citizen Morozov has left town.

KIRA

How do you know?

LEO

I stopped at Tonia's on my way here.

KIRA

Oh...Well?

LEO

Morozov has left Tonia—he wants no connections that could be investigated. But he's left her a nice little sum of money—oh, quite nice. She's going for a vacation in the Caucasus. She has asked me to go with her. I've accepted the job. Leo Kovalensky, the great gigolo of the U.S.S.R!

KIRA

          (Jumping up, shaking with terror)
Leo!!

LEO

She's an old bitch. I know. I like it better that way. She has the money and she wants me. Just a business deal.

KIRA

Leo...*you*...like a...

LEO

Don't bother about the names. You can't think of any as good as the ones I've thought of myself. What of it? I like it. At last I'll be one with our times and I'll feel nothing any longer...nothing...ever.

(Looks at her suddenly, rising)

You're not going to be fool enough to faint, are you?

KIRA

(Controlling herself with an effort)

No, of course not…Sit down…I'm all right…

(He sits down. She sits on the edge of the table before him, her two hands clutching the table edge convulsively. She looks at him. She whispers, choked.)

Leo…if you had been killed in the G.P.U.…or if you had sold yourself to some magnificent woman, a foreigner, young and fresh…

LEO

I wouldn't sell myself to a magnificent woman, young and fresh. I couldn't. Not yet. In a year—I probably will.

(Rises, looks at her, laughs softly, indifferently)

Really, you know, don't you think it's not for you to express any depths of moral indignation? And since we both are what we are, would you mind telling me just why you kept me on while you had him? Was it my money and his position?

KIRA

(Rises slowly, stands erect, facing him)

Leo, when did you decide to go with her?

LEO

When I heard I was going to be released.

KIRA

Before they told you about Andrei and me?

LEO

Yes.

KIRA

While you still thought that I loved you?

LEO

Yes.

KIRA

And that made no difference to you?

LEO

No.

KIRA

If they hadn't told you, you'd still go with her?

LEO

Yes. Only then I had to face the problem of telling you. They spared me that. That's why I was glad to hear it. Now we can say goodbye without any unnecessary scenes.

KIRA

Leo...please listen carefully...it's very important...please do me a last favor and answer this one question honestly, to the best of your knowledge: if you were to learn suddenly—it doesn't matter how—but if you were to learn that I love you, that I've always loved you, that I've been loyal to you all these years—would you still go with her?

LEO

Yes.

KIRA

And...if you *had to* stay with me? If you learned something that...that bound you to stay—would you try it once more?

LEO

If I were bound to—well, who knows? If I had to struggle here much longer—I might find my own firing squad, you know. Just one gun. That's also a solution.

KIRA

I see.

LEO

And why do you ask that? What is there to bind me?

KIRA

(Looking straight at him, her head high, with the greatest calm)
Nothing, Leo.

LEO

(Shrugging)
Really, you know, I still think you're wonderful. I was afraid of hysterics and a lot of noise. It's ended as it should have ended.

KIRA

Yes, Leo.

LEO

(Walks to a wardrobe, gets an old suitcase)

I'm leaving in three days. Until then, I'll move out of here.

KIRA

If you wish.

(He begins to pack hurriedly, nervously. She watches him silently. He turns to her suddenly.)

LEO

Aren't you going to say goodbye? Have you nothing to say?

KIRA

Only this, Leo: it was I against two hundred million people. I lost.

(He shrugs and continues his work silently. She stands at the window, her back to him.)

(Turning to him suddenly)

Leo, will you kiss me—once? And for one last moment, will you forget what we are? Kiss me for what we could have been.

(He looks at her, approaches, takes her in his arms, kisses her, a long kiss. Then she steps aside.)

LEO

(Softly)

Kira, I'll be back in Petrograd. I'll be back when years have passed, and years make such a difference, don't they? Then it won't hurt us so much. It will be strange to look back, won't it? We'll meet again, Kira. I'll be back.

KIRA

(Quietly)

I won't be here, Leo.

LEO

Where are you going?

KIRA

(With the intensity of a maniac)

Abroad.

CURTAIN

SCENE 5

A week later. Frontier post on the Russian-Latvian border. A small, crude log cabin, with bare rafters and unpainted log walls. One large window in wall Center and a narrow door by its side, Right. A crude table, a few benches, a narrow iron cot, bayonets and ammunition, a cast iron stove with a fire flickering in it. Pictures of Lenin and Stalin on the walls, a frayed sickle and hammer of gilded papier mache over the door. A radio on a table in a corner. Night. An endless snow plain stretches under a black sky beyond the window.

At curtain rise, TWO SOLDIERS in heavy winter coats are sitting at the stove, warming their frozen hands, listening to the radio over which the strains of "You Fell As a Victim," played by a military band, are coming solemnly. They sit silently, then one of them sings softly to himself in time to the music.

FIRST SOLDIER

(A husky, lazy fellow)

You fell in the sacred and glorious strife
For justice and emancipation,
And brutally tortured, the flower of your life
Was crushed by the foes of the nation.

SECOND SOLDER

(A lean, nervous youth, points at the radio)

That's from Leningrad...All the way from Leningrad, think of it!

FIRST SOLDIER

Uh huh...

(Pause)

SECOND SOLDIER

(Pointing at radio)

Whom are they burying today?

FIRST SOLDIER

Don't know. Never heard of him before.

(Pause)

SECOND SOLDIER

God, I wish I was back in Leningrad, now!

FIRST SOLDIER

Uh huh…

SECOND SOLDIER

(Rising abruptly)

What the hell do they have to play the funeral march for? Gives me the creeps.

(Turns radio off. Silence.)

FIRST SOLDIER

(Rubbing his hands)

I guess I froze my hands for good, yesterday…four hours in the snow.

SECOND SOLDIER

(At window, staring hopelessly into the night)

Snow…snow…snow…nothing but snow for miles and miles…I figure you could walk three days and you wouldn't see nothing but this damn white swamp around you. I think sometimes I'll go blind if I got to look at it much longer…God, I'd give anything for a heap of horse dung to make it look alive!

FIRST SOLDIER

(Helping himself to some sunflower seeds)

Get yourself a snort of vodka.

SECOND SOLDIER

It'll get me, some day, I tell you…Sometimes I ain't sure I'm alive no more. I get a funny feeling in my belly like that snow was on top of me, stuffed down my throat, and I can't yell, and there ain't a living soul, nowhere around to hear me!

FIRST SOLDIER

I wish there wasn't a living soul around. Then we wouldn't have to sit here. But there is. Seven of them counterrevolutionaries last week, trying to cross the border.

SECOND SOLDIER

Yeah, seven corpses in Moscow by this time.

FIRST SOLDIER

Uh huh.

SECOND SOLDIER

That's just it. Sitting here, hunting dead men. Dead beforehand, you know, 'cause the minute we get 'em, they're as good as shot already. You know what happens to all of them when we send 'em back.

FIRST SOLDIER

Serves 'em right, for trying to sneak out.

SECOND SOLDIER

But they keep coming, the damn fools, they keep trying. Like ghosts, crawling in the snow, all in white, the fools, think we won't notice 'em. All wrapped up in rabbit fur or flour sacks, or bed sheets. They don't seem alive, either, They're dead, but still moving.

FIRST SOLDIER

Shut up! You're going daffy, all right.
      (Dead silence)

SECOND SOLDIER

      (Panicky)
D'you hear it?

FIRST SOLDIER

What? I don't hear nothing.

SECOND SOLDIER

That's it: nothing. Nothing nowhere! Maybe we're dead already. Maybe we're dead and don't know it.
      (Turns the radio on)
Let's hear something. Something to shut it up!
      (The funeral march is coming to an end over the radio. Then the ANNOUNCER's VOICE is heard.)

ANNOUNCER'S VOICE

      (Over the radio)
And now, Comrades, you will hear Comrade Serguei Zubikov of the Leningrad Committee of the All-Union Communist Party, speaking at the memorial mass meeting at the Palace of Labor. Comrade Zubikov!

ZUBIKOV

      (Over the radio)
Comrades! Another name has been added to the glorious list of victims fallen on the field of honor of the revolution. That name may not be known to many, but it symbolizes the common ranks, the unsung heroes of our great Communist Party. In the person of Andrei Taganov we pay a last tribute to the unknown

warriors of the Army of the Proletariat. Comrade Taganov is dead. He committed suicide under the strain of a nervous collapse caused by overwork. His health was broken by the terrific, ceaseless task which his Party membership imposed upon him. And if, in these days of struggle and privation, some of us may weaken in spirit, let us look up to the great All-Union Communist Party that leads us, that spares not its strength, its energy, its lives! Let us...

SECOND SOLDIER

Who was he anyway?

FIRST SOLDIER

Never heard of him.

SECOND SOLDIER

What do them Party men have to commit suicide about?

FIRST SOLDIER

That's because they work so hard, and...

(Radio continues.)

(A shot is heard in the distance.)

SECOND SOLDIER

(Jumping up)

What was that?!

FIRST SOLDIER

Sit down!...Just Grishka out there, shooting a rabbit most likely.

SECOND SOLDIER

(Turns radio off)

Listen!

(No sound comes from outside.)

FIRST SOLDIER

What're you getting so jumpy about?

SECOND SOLDIER

God, I wish it was morning.

FIRST SOLDIER

You look out or someone'll report you for bourgeois ideology. You don't seem to get it through your head that it's an honorable job we have, guarding the borders of the U.S.S.R., the shock battalion, so to speak, of the only proletarian republic on earth the...the...what else was it?...You oughtta listen to the political instructor down at the Marxist Club, he knows, he can explain it all to you clear as day...Oh yes, he said we were the servants of humanity, the guardians of the freedom of all mankind, the...

(The door flies open. The THIRD SOLDIER, a tall, husky, loud voiced man, enters, a bayonet over his shoulder, carrying Kira in his arms. She is dressed all in white: a short jacket of white fur, unbuttoned over Galina

Petrovna's white lace wedding gown, with a long, torn train, white felt boots, white mittens, a white scarf wound tightly around her head, hiding her hair. She is unconscious. A narrow trickle of blood runs down her white gown, from under the left breast.

The TWO SOLDIERS jump up, startled. The SECOND SOLDIER gasps and, surreptitiously, makes the sign of the cross.)

FIRST SOLDIER

Where'd you get that, Grishka?

SECOND SOLDIER

Is she...is she dead?

THIRD SOLDIER

(Carrying Kira to the cot and putting her down)
Don't think so.

SECOND SOLDIER

(Staring at her, horrified)
A child...just a child...

FIRST SOLDIER

You never can tell what you'll catch, these days.
(SECOND SOLDIER removes Kira's jacket.)

THIRD SOLDIER

You better leave her alone. Pretty bad wound. We can't fix it here. Have to wait till morning. When the day shift comes, we'll take her to the hospital base.

SECOND SOLDIER

(Throwing the jacket aside)
What did you have to shoot her for?

THIRD SOLDIER

Tried to get away, the damn counterrevolutionary!

FIRST SOLDIER

(Looking at Kira, shaking his head)
She must have walked all night...

SECOND SOLDIER

Pretty young...

(Pause. KIRA stirs feebly, whispers, her eyes closed, her words unintelligible at first, then growing stronger and stronger.)

KIRA

Leo...Leo...It's such a beautiful morning...Wait for me...I'll be ready in a minute and we can walk, walk for hours, in the sun, we're so young and the world is so beautiful...I'll put on a white dress...it has to be white, so they won't see me...I love you, Leo. I've never told you, Leo...Leo...Leo...but I'll tell you there, abroad...and we'll live again...so much is still possible to us...if I can walk, if I can only walk, walk, walk...

(Jerks herself up to a sitting position, stares wildly around her, consciousness returning slowly. Tries to rise and falls back, her hand at her side. Looks at the hand: the mitten is stained with red. Looks at the soldiers.)

Who are you? Russian or Latvian?

THIRD SOLDIER

Well, what do you think?

(He points at sickle and hammer above the door.)

KIRA

Oh.

(Her head drops.)

THIRD SOLDIER

What's your name? Where do you come from?

(She does not answer.)

You better tell us now. They'll make you talk at headquarters.

SECOND SOLDIER

Leave her alone.

(Pours a glass of water from a pitcher and brings it to Kira; holds it to her lips with one hand and holds her head up with the other.)

Here. Have some water.

(She drinks. Raises herself slowly on one elbow. Tears her mittens and scarf off; her disheveled hair tumbles down over her shoulders.)

You better lie still. You're hurt.

KIRA

I'm all right.

FIRST SOLDIER

Where did you get the crazy get-up?

KIRA

That's all I had.

THIRD SOLDIER

Didn't help much, did it?—even with all that white.

KIRA

What are you going to do with me?

FIRST SOLDIER

What do you think? Think we'll take you to Paris, maybe? Back to Moscow you go, Citizen, and you'll have some pretty questions to answer—if you last that long.

THIRD SOLDIER

Say, there's a big meeting in Moscow tonight, they said on the radio.

FIRST SOLDIER

No, in Leningrad. We was listening to it.

THIRD SOLDIER

I wanted to hear it.

(Turns the radio on)

SECOND SOLDIER

(To Kira)
You better try to sleep, Citizen.

SPEAKER'S VOICE

(Over the radio)
...proletarian cause. The individual may fall, but the collective lives forever. Red banners flying, we are marching on into our radiant future!

(Applause over the radio)

ANNOUNCER'S VOICE

(Over the radio)
The next speaker, Comrades, will be Comrade Pavel Syerov, a brilliant young Party member, closest friend of Andrei Taganov.

(KIRA jerks her head up, listens attentively.)
Comrade Pavel Syerov!

Syerov's Voice

(Over the radio)

Comrades! We have lost a great man. Perhaps, I may be permitted to say that I feel the loss more keenly than many of you, for I was his best friend. Andrei Taganov is dead.

He committed suicide as a sacrifice to the revolution. What is the lesson all of us can learn from his example? The lesson of a Party comrade dying for the collective. The lesson of a Party that rules but to sacrifice itself to those it rules. Look at the world around you, Comrades!

(KIRA gasps.)

Third Soldier

What's the matter? Did you know him by any chance?

Kira

(Her head dropping, her voice choked.)
No ... No, I've never heard of him before ...

Look at the selfish rulers of the Capitalistic countries who crush their weaker brothers and stuff their own bellies! Then look at those who rule the U.S.S.R., who consecrate their lives to the unselfish service of the Collective! If you do, you'll understand me, when I say that the All-Union Communist Party is the only honest, selfless, idealistic body of men in the politics of the world today!

(Applause over the radio. KIRA's head drops with a deep breath, into her arms.)

Our only aim is the honest toil which profits not one but all. Andrei Taganov is dead, but his work, *our* work goes on. Andrei Taganov is dead, but *we* remain. Ours is the life and the glory and the victory. To us belongs the future!

(Applause over the radio. KIRA jumps up.)

Kira

(Screaming, hysterical)

Turn it off! Turn it off! I can't stand it!

Third Soldier

Say, who do you think you are to ...

Second Soldier

(Turns the radio down, to Third Soldier)

There! You can listen to it. Don't you see she is hurt?

(The radio continues as a low jumble of sound; the THIRD SOLDIER alone is listening, bending close to the radio.)

(SECOND SOLDIER turns to Kira.)

You better lie down, Citizen.

Kira

(Sitting down on the bed, with sudden, insane resolution)

Comrades, let me go!

FIRST SOLDIER

What?!

KIRA

Let me go! What difference would it make to you? I...

FIRST SOLDIER

Crazy, are you! With that slug in you and...

KIRA

I'm all right. I can walk. I have to get out. I...

FIRST SOLDIER

You'll croak if you take three steps.

KIRA

Well, then, what difference would it make to you? Let me go.

SECOND SOLDIER

We can't, Citizen. The State don't allow it.

KIRA

Of what use am I to you and to your State? You don't want me to live or to work or to eat. Why don't you let me out? You have enough people left without me. There...behind us...a whole country...a whole nation...it's all yours...What do you want me for?...You have millions and millions to rule. I have only my life...my one life...why don't you let me go?

FIRST SOLDIER

Shut up, you damn counterrevolutionary!

KIRA

You don't believe in God, do you? I don't either. I don't believe there's another life waiting for us anywhere. Here, now, a few short years, that's all we have, all we can be sure of. But so much is possible in these few years! What right have you to take it away from me? What right has anyone?

THIRD SOLDIER

Shut up! Let me listen to the meeting.

(Turns radio on louder. The funeral march comes over the air. KIRA makes a step forward, falls.)

SECOND SOLDIER

(Rushing to her)

Lie down, Citizen!

KIRA

(Pushing him aside, rises to her knees, on the floor, holding on to the bed.)

Let me go!...I'm still alive...You've taken most of it already. Once, when I was very young, I wanted to be an engineer, to work and build. You've taken that. I had a friend and you made me betray him. You've taken that. I loved some-one, someone who could have lived had he been born there, across the border. You've taken that. I have nothing left. Nothing but that I know I'm still alive and I can't give up...Let me go! Please let me go!...I can't give up!

(Rises slowly, swaying)

SECOND SOLDIER

Lie down, Citizen, you'll kill yourself!

KIRA

I can't go back. There, behind us, there's something that gets men, that kills something in them, have you seen it? Have you ever seen plants grown without sun, without air? It kills something. It got mother. It got Leo. It got Andrei. It won't get me!

(Staggers forward)

FIRST SOLDIER

Where are you going?

KIRA

(Staring around wildly, deliriously)

Do you see what's around us? Do you see them closing in on us? Do you see them staring, pointing, laughing at me? All the weak, the hopeless, the use-less ones of this world! All the blind eyes, the shaking hands, the still-born souls! All the botched, icy-blooded ones who huddle their skins and their sweat together to keep warm enough to stay alive! You think you've won? You think you've broken me? But I'm laughing at you! I'm alive! Come on! Who'll fight me first? Why do you shrink? There are so many of you and I'm alone! Or is that what's frightening you? Alone! The only title, the only crown of glory one can wear today! Stand back, you poor, unborn ghosts! You can't stop me!

(Staggers to door)

I can walk. I'll walk as long as I'm alive. I'll fight you all as long as I'm alive!

(Throws door open)

In the name of every living thing of every living world!

(Falls. The SOLDIERS look at one another; the first soldier shrugs. The radio thunders "You Fell As a Victim.")

CURTAIN

The Unconquered

by

Ayn Rand

(1939/40)

SYNOPSIS OF SCENES

ACT 1

Scene 1: Winter of 1924.
Leo's Home in Petrograd.

Scene 2: Spring of 1924.
Technological Institute.

Scene 3: Fall of 1924.
Railroad Office.

ACT 2

Scene 1: Spring of 1925.
Railroad Office.

Scene 2: Winter of 1925.
Railroad Office.

Scene 3: A few days later.
Andrei's Home.

Scene 4: A few days later.
Office of the G.P.U.

Scene 5: Same evening.
Leo's Home.

ACT 3

Scene 1: Same evening.
Party Club.

Scene 2: A week later.
Leo's Home.

CHARACTERS[1]

SOLDIER
LEO KOVALENSKY
NEIGHBORS
UPRAVDOM
KIRA ARGOUNOVA
PURGE COMMITTEE ATTENDANT
A STUDENT
PAVEL SYEROV
COMRADE SONIA
OLDER EXAMINER
ANDREI TAGANOV
MALASHKIN
COMRADE BITIUK
GIRL CLERK
BOY CLERK
COMRADE VORONOV
A YOUNG MAN
STEPAN TIMOSHENKO
KARP MOROZOV
ANTONINA PAVLOVNA
G.P.U. CHIEF
ASSISTANT G.P.U. CHIEF
SOLDIERS
PARTY CLUB ATTENDANT
YOUNG COMMUNISTS

---

[1] A number of minor revisions to this list were necessary: I changed the heading from CAST to CHARACTERS; changed NEIGHBOR to NEIGHBORS and moved it from the end of the list to where it belongs; added PURGE COMMITTEE ATTENDANT, as this character has a speaking part, and named him such (it is simply ATTENDANT in the text) to contrast him with PARTY CLUB ATTENDANT; and, I added A YOUNG MAN and SOLDIERS, which were inadvertently excluded.

ACT 1

SCENE 1

TIME: Winter of 1924. Afternoon.

SCENE: Leo's home. The room, a bedroom, still retains the aspect of
           stern, gracious luxury it once possessed, though it is beginning
           to show signs of wear. It is done in gray, silver, and black; two
           large, tall windows in wall Center; entrance door Left; door to
           bathroom Right. A black onyx fireplace downstage Right. The
           room has undergone a thorough search; drawers gape open,
           chairs are upturned, clothing, papers, splinters of broken glass
           are strewn all over the floor, the bed, the table.

AT RISE: The stage is empty. There is a sound of a knife grating loudly
           on door Left. The door is thrown open with a bang; it opens
           inward, showing a broken seal of red wax.

           A SOLDIER enters, holding door for LEO KOVALENSKY,
           who follows. LEO is tall, slender, young, unusually attractive,
           uncontrollably arrogant; he is wearing an old coat that had obvi-
           ously been expensive long ago.

Soldier

Well, here you are, Citizen.
            (Points at the seal on the door)
People who see this little seal clamped on their doors don't often come back to
see it broken. Better don't let it happen again.

Leo

            (With an insolent, exaggerated politeness)
May I address the same request to you?

Soldier

Huh?

Leo

Or to those who put that seal there.

Soldier

Being smart, eh? Don't you know how near you came to returning here in a
coffin?

Leo

I assure you I have never been more aware of it in my life.

Soldier

            (Tries to scratch the seal off the door, but the seal sticks)

Oh, hell, why bother? I'll leave it here—just as a little reminder.

> (The FIRST NEIGHBOR appears in doorway.)[2]

LEO

It is really quite unnecessary. We Soviet citizens have a great many reminders around us. It would be better to devise some means of letting us *forget*.

SOLDIER

You'd better watch what you're saying, or...

LEO

And now that this is *my* home again, would the Red Army mind getting out?

SOLDIER

(Shrugging)

Some people never learn nothing. They shouldn't have let you out at all.

LEO

I quite agree with you. Good day, Citizen.

SECOND NEIGHBOR

Yes, it's him all right.

FIRST NEIGHBOR[3]

Oh! He looks kind of sick.

> (SOLDIER exits, closing the door.)
>
> (LEO stands looking at the wrecked room. Picks up a few papers strewn over a desk, looks at them, throws them down indifferently, shrugs. Becomes aware of the hushed noise beyond the door Left, walks to it resolutely, throws door open; an assortment of NEIGHBORS are gathered on the threshold, having obviously been eavesdropping. They stare at him with curiosity.)

LEO

(Calmly)

No, Citizens, I have not been liquidated. My ears and nose are not cut off. I have no scars or burns to show you. Is that what you wanted to see?

NEIGHBOR GIRL[4]

We just...we...that is...

---

[2] The typescript has the terse "First Neighbor in door." He is the first of a number of curious neighbors who gather at the door, four of whom have speaking parts: two men, a woman, and a girl.

[3] The typescript has "Man Neighbor"; I take him to be the "First Neighbor."

[4] The typescript has "Girl."

NEIGHBOR WOMAN

Oh, Citizen Kovalensky, we're so glad to see you back!

LEO

(Charmingly)

Let us give you some helpful advice. Never set foot in my room again. Never recognize me when we meet. It will be much safer for you—and a little more tolerable for me.

(An imperious VOICE is heard beyond the door, approaching.)

UPRAVDOM'S VOICE

(Offstage)

Get out of here, Citizens! What are you staring at? Get out! All of you!

(The UPRAVDOM enters Left. He is a husky, middle-aged man, a peasant type, with high boots, a dirty shirt, a cap on the back of his head.)

UPRAVDOM

(Removing his cap, bowing awkwardly)

Citizen Kovalensky! God bless you, I'm sure glad to see you back.

LEO

I wouldn't say that too loudly, if I were you. They'll demote you from house manager back to janitor again, if they hear it.

UPRAVDOM

I don't care, Citizen, sir, let 'em! The world's all upside down.

(Catches himself abruptly, looks around cautiously)

Oh, I...I didn't mean no complaint, only...only...Well, if there's anything I can do for you, Citizen, if you need anything...

LEO

No, thank you...Has anyone asked for me today?

UPRAVDOM

No.

LEO

No one?

UPRAVDOM

No. Not that I know of.

(Hesitating)

There's...there's just a little question in regards to the rent on your room here...I don't know if I should charge you rent for the two months you've been in jail.

LEO

Most definitely. No one should enjoy such a privilege free.

(Coughs)

And I hope you had a fire here. There was none over there.

UPRAVDOM

I'd hate to see you get in trouble again and...It's twenty years I've worked in this house, when your father owned the place and...

(Catches himself abruptly. Then, involuntarily.)

God, I didn't think you'd ever return alive!

LEO

(Calmly)

I didn't either.

UPRAVDOM

And...and Admiral Kovalensky? He...is he back too?

LEO

(Abruptly)

No.

UPRAVDOM

Will he be...I mean when is he going to be released?

LEO

(In a hard, flat voice)

My father was executed two weeks ago.

UPRAVDOM

(Gasps)

Oh!...I...

(Then, dryly, frightened)

Well, I'll be going...I'm a busy man...I...

(Doorbell rings offstage.)

I'll open the door.

(Exits, obviously glad of an excuse to get out)

(LEO lights a cigarette, glancing at the door once in a while with an eagerness he wants to hide. The door opens. KIRA ARGOUNOVA enters. She is slender, eighteen, with wild, disheveled hair, with a hard young defiant precision in her voice, in her every movement. She wears an old black coat and hat. LEO stands motionless, only his hand with the cigarette descends slowly as he looks at Kira; she stops at the door, as if paralyzed, staring at him.)

KIRA

Leo...

LEO

(He stands looking at her. He smiles, shrugs lightly, deliberately, to hide his emotions.)

You haven't changed. You look nice. Your hair needs combing.

KIRA

Leo...

LEO

Take your coat off. Is it still raining?

KIRA

(Unbuttoning her coat mechanically, unable to tear her eyes away from him)

No...yes...yes, I think it is.

LEO

You shouldn't have come here.

(Approaching her)

But I knew you would.

KIRA

I just heard that you...you were...

LEO

(Seizing her in his arms violently, kissing her)

Oh Kira!

KIRA

Leo! You're safe! You're free!

LEO

Kira! Kira!

KIRA

You're free!

LEO

Oh, don't talk about it. I want to think that I've never been away. I've always been here, with you, holding you, looking at you...

(Breaking a little)

Kira...I didn't think I would again...

(Holding her silently. Laughs abruptly, releasing her.)

Really, the G.P.U. has a terrible influence on us. A moment longer and I'll say I love you.

KIRA

I've never heard it from you.

LEO

(Looking at her with all the adoration in the world)
You never will...Here, take your coat off.
(Removing her coat)
It's over. Done with. Don't tremble like that.

KIRA

(Laughing lightly and unconvincingly)
What have they done to your room?

LEO

It's the search. You should have seen it. It was most interesting. They found all my missing shirt studs, two handkerchiefs, and your hairpins. They were really suspicious of the hairpins...What have you been doing all this time?

KIRA

(Trying to sound just as matter-of-fact)
Working. Going to the Institute every day, learning all about steel and concrete and the law of gravity. Really, I worked very hard, I studied very thoroughly and...
(Breaking down suddenly, exultantly)
Leo! I didn't allow myself to be afraid. I knew you had to come back.
(Approaching him, sits down at his feet)
Only...only what did they do to you *there*?

LEO

Nothing. I had a nice cell all to myself and three meals a day, although the soup was rotten.

KIRA

Leo!

LEO

(His light tone changes slowly.)
Of course, I didn't sleep very much. They call you before the examiner every night and then...questions, questions, questions.
(Checks himself abruptly)

KIRA

What did they...

LEO

They asked me about father and his secret meetings. I didn't know anything. Father never wanted me to know. I only learned it there, from them.

KIRA

But you...

LEO

Oh, they kept me there until they got tired of me, then they let me go. The case is closed.

KIRA

Did you lose your job?

LEO

No. Not yet. They need me. They don't have many people to translate their damn foreign literature for them. Yes, tomorrow, Citizen Kovalensky will march back into the great State Publishing House, trying not to notice the cautious efforts of everyone trying not to notice him, not to utter a single counterrevolutionary "Good morning." Wonder how Citizen Kovalensky will make it. It will be curious to watch him in the evenings, alone.

KIRA

(Rises, looks about the room, asks quite matter-of-factly and with seemingly utter irrelevancy)
Have you got a large, flat table, Leo?

LEO

What?

KIRA

I'll need a large table for my blueprints.

LEO

For your what?

KIRA

(Lightly)
Oh, that's right, I haven't told you, have I?—that I'm coming to live here with you.

LEO

(Looks at her, then)
Do you know what you're saying?

KIRA

You've asked me to do it, haven't you?

LEO

Kira, don't you know that I'm an outcast now? That it may be dangerous to know me, even to speak to me?

KIRA

(Indifferently)

Yes.

LEO

That I have nothing to offer you?

KIRA

Yes.

LEO

That it's hard enough for you, with your family's past and...

KIRA

You want me to stay here, don't you?

LEO

(Softly)

Yes.

KIRA

That's all I have to know.

LEO

(Drawing her into his arms)

Darling, do you know that you're my worst enemy?

KIRA

Why?

LEO

Because I still have a reason for living.
(She buries her head on his shoulder, her arms around him.)
What will your parents say when you tell them?

KIRA

I've told them.

LEO

What did they say?

KIRA

Nothing much. Only that they never wanted to see me again.

LEO

But, Kira...

KIRA

I don't care.

LEO

Do they think...

KIRA

I don't care what they think. They've always fought against me. They've fought ever since I entered the Technological Institute. They can't understand it. A woman engineer! Mother says it's not a cultured profession for a young lady.

LEO

Well, it probably isn't.

KIRA

I think they hate me simply because I want a future—any future. They've given up. Father's crying for the factories they've taken away from him, mother's crying for the diamond necklace she's had to sell. They can't understand why I laugh about it. There's so much ahead of me!

LEO

Is there?

KIRA

To build, Leo. To build, to shape space, to raise girders in a net against the sky, to watch the sunrise from the top of a steel skeleton and to know that it's mine, every beam of it!

LEO

Of the building—or of the sun?

KIRA

Of the building. That's more important, because it's I who will have erected it.

LEO

To build for the Red State?

KIRA

No. To build just because *I* want to build…The Red State! Why do I have to know that it exists?

LEO

Sometimes I wish you'd lose that crazy, childish enthusiasm of yours.

KIRA

Why?

LEO

It will only make life harder for you.

KIRA

Why? It's beautiful to be alive. Haven't you ever felt it? It's like a strange treasure, waiting for you somewhere, something promised to you, and you can't even name or explain it, it's like a hymn and you don't know the music, but you feel it beating, like steps, your own steps into your own future!

LEO

…and into the G.P.U.

KIRA

Forget that, Leo. They'll leave us alone if we don't fight them. Why fight them? There are so many greater things in life. Someday, I'm going to build a skyscraper, the tallest one on earth. And a bridge, a white aluminum bridge…

LEO

And how long do you think they'll let you study? You can't build a bridge of aluminum, Comrade engineer…

KIRA

Leo!

LEO

You've heard of the purge, haven't you? It won't stop with political suspects. It will go through the courts, the army—the schools and the day nurseries. You'll be thrown out, don't worry.

KIRA

No. They won't touch us again. They'll forget us. Don't think about them, Leo, think about us. Think what it will be like—the two of us together.

> (Checks the happiness in her voice, looks at the room, tries to sound businesslike)

First of all, I'll have to clean this place. And gather all this broken glass. And sweep the floor. And...

> (She stops. She stands in the middle of the room, and spreads her arms wide, and laughs. She laughs defiantly, rapturously, triumphantly.)

Leo!...Leo! So much is still possible.

CURTAIN

SCENE 2

TIME: A few months later. Spring of 1924.

SCENE: Office of the Technological Institute.
             Late afternoon.

> A small, bare room. Two doors in wall Right; window—Center. Long table, set diagonally Left, with five chairs behind it. No other furniture, but a great profusion of gaudy posters on the wall, with red predominating; smoke-stacks, tractors, huge workers, appeals for donations to the Red Air fleet. On wall Left, behind the table, two pictures: of Lenin and Karl Marx. A prominent poster by window Center, with the word: "PURGING" standing out in huge letters. High above it—in a large cotton streamer, red with white sickle and hammer and white letters proclaiming: "PROLETARIANS OF THE WORLD, UNITE!"

AT RISE: An ATTENDANT with a list in his hand stands at upstage door Right. Five PEOPLE sit behind the table which is loaded with papers, documents, and file folders. PAVEL SYEROV, president,[5] sits in the Center; he is a youth in his middle twenties, but looks older, pale with an unhealthy, washed-out blond grayness, immaculately dressed, his manner alternating between servility and arrogance. To his Left sits COMRADE SONIA; she is a stocky, husky girl with short, stubby hair, a masculine leather jacket, and flat shoes. The three other EXAMINERS at the table are older men and quite obviously figureheads, awed and dominated by Syerov. Behind the table, in upstage Left corner, stands ANDREI TAGANOV. He is tall, slender, in his middle twenties, with the hard, uncompromising face of a medieval soldier. He wears a Communist black leather jacket and high military boots. He stands silently, rarely moving; he is an ominous presence, like a court of final appeal, like a judge and an executioner at once. When he speaks, even those at the table are uncomfortable.

> A STUDENT, a nervous, hysterical youth, is standing before the table. She is shaking with panic.

---

[5] I assume this means "presiding"; perhaps it is a typographical error.

STUDENT

(Screaming)

No, Comrades! No! You can't! You can't do this! Why? What have I done?

SYEROV

(Coldly)

It is not a personal matter, Comrade. You, as an individual, do not concern us. You are expelled from the Technological Institute of Leningrad as a representative of the social class of exploiters which must be liquidated.

STUDENT

But what have I ever done to you?

COMRADE SONIA[6]

You're not the only one. Thousands are being purged today from all the schools of the country. All the children of former capitalists.

SYEROV

(Pointing to a paper that lies before him)

Your questionnaire states that your father owned a laundry before the revolution.

STUDENT

But I can't help it! I can't help what parents I was born to!

SYEROV

(Sternly)

Comrade, science is a weapon of the class struggle. Proletarian schools are for the Proletariat. We shall not educate our class enemies. That's all. It's very simple.

STUDENT

But if I'm expelled, I'll lose my ration card! And there's my mother...if I lose my card, what'll become of us?

OLDER EXAMINER[7]

(Timidly, uneasily, to Syerov)

Comrade Syerov, perhaps an exception could be made to...

ANDREI

(Quietly, with implacable authority)

---

[6] The typescript is inconsistent, sometimes reading "Sonia," other times "Comrade Sonia." I always print the latter.

[7] The typescript is inconsistent, sometimes reading "Old Examiner," more often "Older Examiner." I always print the latter.

The Comrade is expelled. Next case.

> (They ALL look at Andrei. The STUDENT chokes the plea she was about to utter. SYEROV points silently to the door downstage. The STUDENT exits, crushed. The ATTENDANT throws the other door open, calling from the list.)

Attendant

Ivan Malashkin!

> (MALASHKIN enters hesitantly. He is a small, cringing boy with an obsequious smile. He stops uncertainly at the door, removing his hat.)

Syerov

Come here, Comrade Malashkin.

Malashkin

Yes, Comrade Syerov, yes indeed, Comrade Syerov.

> (Approaching the table and stands, crumpling his hat nervously in both hands)

Syerov

> (Looking at a questionnaire with a puzzled frown)

Comrade Malashkin, your questionnaire is *most* unusual. Now, who were your parents?

Malashkin

> (Earnestly)

A peasant woman and two workers.

> Syerov

What?!

Malashkin

> (Miserably)

Well, not exactly two *workers*. One of them was a worker, a butler, but the other...the other one was the Prince Voronsky.

Syerov

Which one of them was your father?

Malashkin

> (Desperately)

I don't know!

Syerov

What? But your mother...

Malashkin

My mother doesn't know, either!

SYEROV

Oh...hm, yes, I see...Well, this is a problem...
(To the others at the table)
Now what are we going to do, Comrades?

COMRADE SONIA

(After a moment's thought, brightly)
Why, it's simple. If his father was the butler, then it had obviously been a love match and this comrade's birth was a hundred percent proletarian, but if it was the prince—then his poor mother had been *forced*, in which case she was a victim of the social system, in which case her son must not be penalized.

OLDER EXAMINER

Very well reasoned out, Comrade Sonia.

COMRADE SONIA

I make it a point to see the woman's angle in all matters.

MALASHKIN

(Eagerly)
Then I can remain in school?

SYEROV

Yes, I believe we can allow Comrade Malashkin to remain.
(The OTHERS at the table nod their assent.)

MALASHKIN

(Beaming)
Oh, thank you, Comrades, thank...

ANDREI

To remain—pending further investigation.

MALASHKIN

(Somewhat deflated, to Andrei)
Oh!...But he said...

OLDER EXAMINER

Comrade Malashkin, one doesn't argue with a representative of the G.P.U.

MALASHKIN

(Terrified)
The G.P.U.?
(Exits hastily)

COMRADE SONIA

(Looking at her wrist watch)

Time to strike off for lunch? I'm hungry.

SYEROV

Just one more case.

(To Attendant)

Next!

ATTENDANT

(Throws door open, calls)

Kira Argounova!

(KIRA enters and approaches the table. She stands straight, her face set, betraying no emotion.)

SYEROV

(Looking at a questionnaire)

Comrade Argounova, your father owned a factory before the revolution?

KIRA

Yes.

SYEROV

I see. And your mother? Did she work before the revolution?

KIRA

No.

SYEROV

I see. What was your grandfather's occupation?

KIRA

He was the owner of the same factory.

SYEROV

And your great-grandfather's occupation?

KIRA

I don't know.

SYEROV

Regrettable. Shows a lack of interest in your social heredity...Are you a member of the Communist Party?

KIRA

No.

SYEROV

Are you a member of our Trade Union?

KIRA

No.

SYEROV

Are you a member of our Marxist Club?

KIRA

No.

SYEROV

Well, what *are* you, then?

KIRA

I'm Kira Argounova.

SYEROV

A perfectly meaningless answer—socially.

COMRADE SONIA

(Looking through a report)

I have here a most unfavorable report on Comrade Argounova's behavior. She has done nothing but attend her classes. She has shown no social spirit whatever. She has refused to join our Club of Marxism, our Club of Leninism, and our Club of Historical Materialism.

SYEROV

(To Kira)

Just why did you come here at all?

KIRA

To study engineering.

SYEROV

For what reason?

KIRA

To learn a work I like only because *I* like it.

Syerov

That is not a valid reason. Your personal emotions are of no importance in the world of today.

Older Examiner

(Hastily picking up another report and passing it to Comrade Sonia[8])

Comrades, I have here a report on Comrade Argounova's scholastic record. In view of the unusual ability she has demonstrated in her studies, couldn't we overlook the...

Comrade Sonia

(Pushing the report aside)

Scholastic ability has nothing to do with a student's right to an education.

Syerov

Furthermore, Comrade Argounova, the report on your choice of personal acquaintances is most distressing. You are known to be on friendly terms with several people of aristocratic descent.

Kira

(With the first flash of anger)

That is my private business.

Syerov

Comrade Argounova, nothing is private in the Soviet Union.

Comrade Sonia

Why just yesterday I personally saw Comrade Argounova in a restaurant with Leo Kovalensky, son of a counterrevolutionary.

Kira

What right have you to inquire into that?

Syerov

Our right, Comrade Argounova, is anything which we choose to make our right... How well do you know Citizen Kovalensky? What can you tell us about him?

Kira

Nothing.

Syerov

What do you know about his political views?

---

[8] The typescript has "Hastily picking up a report," but the next stage direction seems to require something more here.

KIRA

Nothing.

SYEROV

(Leaning forward, confidentially)

Comrade Argounova, you know that you're about to be expelled, don't you?

KIRA

Yes.

SYEROV

But, on the other hand, the State appreciates those who put their social duty above any petty personal loyalty. *And*—exceptions are known to have been made for those willing to furnish some information which...

(He waits. She doesn't move.)

Well? What will you say?

KIRA

Nothing.

SYEROV

(Slamming the table angrily)

Comrade Argounova, when we demand...

ANDREI

Comrade Argounova is expelled.

(KIRA stands still, rigid, emotionless.)

SYEROV

Now she must answer about...

ANDREI

That will be all.

COMRADE SONIA

Fine. Now we can have some lunch.

(The OTHERS rise. KIRA turns to go.)

ANDREI

(To Kira)

Wait. I want to speak to you.

(She stops. The ATTENDANT and two of the EXAMINERS exit. The OLDER EXAMINER approaches Andrei.)

OLDER EXAMINER

Comrade Taganov, why don't you let her go? She's expelled, so why be so harsh now and...

ANDREI

You are not wanted here—till after lunch.

(The OLDER EXAMINER exits.)

COMRADE SONIA

(Taking Syerov's arm imperiously, with a smile which she believes to be coquettish)

Come on, Pavel. Let's go together. Seems as if I never get a chance to see you alone. We'll have time for a little walk after lunch. It's spring, you know. The sunshine, you know, and the flowers, and I've got a brand new pair of shoes— and double soles!

SYEROV

(Shaking his head with helpless reproach)

Honest, Sonia, that's not the way to go about it, that's not the way at all.

COMRADE SONIA

Oh, come on!

(She grabs Syerov's arm and they exit, SYEROV following her reluctantly.)

(KIRA and ANDREI stand studying each other silently. She is the first to speak.)

KIRA

(Brusquely)

Well? What do you want?

ANDREI

(Quietly)

I'm curious about you.

KIRA

What else do you want to ask me, Comrade G.P.U.?

ANDREI

You know, once, years ago, before the revolution, I was sentenced to three years in jail—for belonging to a secret Party. The judges offered me a chance to be spared—if I told them where to find another man, a comrade of mine...I went to jail...I know what you felt just now.

KIRA

Now you must know also what the Czar's judges felt when they sentenced you.

ANDREI

Yes. And I felt sorry for them—a few minutes ago...

(Adds in a hard voice)

I'm not grateful to you for the lesson. I don't understand it. When I faced those judges, years ago, I had a great mission to give me courage. You have no mission. You're just a selfish woman without any social value. Why did you do it?

KIRA

Perhaps, because I have a higher mission, and that is—contempt for all missions. I don't exist for the sake of any State. I live for myself. Not for any brother of mine, not for any cursed holy cause. My life is its own reason.

ANDREI

You're speaking to an agent of the G.P.U.

KIRA

That's what you resent?

ANDREI

That's what I admire.

(She looks at him, astonished.)

Do you think I enjoy seeing those people cringe before us? I loathe it. It frightens me. I don't want to think that...that this is what we're causing people to become.

KIRA

Yet you're doing it.

ANDREI

We have to. A few must suffer—to save a greater suffering for many in the future. There's a new sun rising, such as the world has never seen. We're in the path of its first rays. Every pain, every cry of ours will be carried by these rays down the centuries. Every little figure will grow into an enormous shadow that will wipe out decades of future sorrow for every minute of ours...Nothing can hurt me—when I think of that. But I must learn also to see others suffer—and that's harder. Thank you for meeting it as you did.

KIRA

(Slowly)

You're a most unusual agent of the G.P.U.

ANDREI

You know, whether you like it or not, you're a living symbol of my cause—and of our future.

KIRA

I?

ANDREI

I'm fighting against you—in order to make all men what you are. To give them all a chance to be what you are. To be free and honest—and very brave. But also—I want to kill your kind of selfishness in all of them.

KIRA

If you kill that—are you sure you'll like what's left?

ANDREI

I'm sure I don't like you as a complete human being either. But I do—as a symbol. That's all that matters. An actual person is of so little importance.

KIRA

I've learned that today.

ANDREI

You know, it was a test for me, in a way. I wanted to save you. I wanted to save you against all rules—for no other reason than that I wanted it. And that's a reason upon which I have never acted. I have always believed that when men learn to forget even the conception of a personal desire—then our earth will be worth living upon. And so I didn't defend you before the purging committee. I've sacrificed you—because it was hard for me to sacrifice you...I don't suppose you can understand that.

KIRA

I understand...Well...I guess I won't be a builder after all. I guess I won't build any aluminum bridges...

(Tries to laugh)

It's all right, because everybody always told me that one can't build a bridge of aluminum anyway.

ANDREI

What are you going to do now?

KIRA

I...I don't know.

ANDREI

You'll need a job. It will be hard for you to get one—with your family past.

KIRA

A...job?

ANDREI

You've lost your student's ration-card, you know.

KIRA

Oh...I hadn't thought of that.
          (Dully)
...Yes, I suppose I'll need a job.

ANDREI

What would you rather...

KIRA

Anything. Does it matter...now?

ANDREI

I can get you a job in a railroad office. Pavel Syerov works there. I'm afraid you won't like it, but the work won't be too hard.

KIRA

Thank you.

ANDREI

Where do you live? I'll bring you a letter to...

KIRA

No, don't come to my house! He wouldn't allow me to invite a Communist!

ANDREI

          (Frowning)
Who?

KIRA

          (Looks at him, catching herself, realizing that she's said too much. Then answers.)
My...father. You see, I live with my parents—and you know what they are. Ex-factory owners. They'd be afraid of you.

ANDREI

Yes, of course.
          (Writes a few words on a piece of paper)
Here's my address. Come tomorrow morning and I'll leave a letter there for you.

KIRA

          (Looks at him with a faint, amused smile)
For whom are you doing this? For an actual person—or for a symbol?

ANDREI

(With the same smile)

For a little fool—who'd make such a great fighter on our side. And who might join us, perhaps, some day.

KIRA

Oh...So that's what you're after? Well, it will mean a long struggle between us.

ANDREI

Yes.

KIRA

I'll be glad to fight against you. One must always be proud of one's enemy.

CURTAIN

SCENE 3

TIME: A few months later. Fall of 1924.
         Late afternoon.

SCENE: Railroad Office. A large, grimy, unkempt room in which every-
         thing is old, battered, dusty—except a vast crop of red posters
         and slogans on the walls, new and glaring, like a bright mildew
         growing over ruins. Entrance door Left. Smaller, private door
         set diagonally in upstage Right corner, bearing a sign: "Comrade
         Voronov." One narrow window in wall Center, admitting scant
         light, opening upon a webbing of steel beams.

AT RISE: The office work is in full swing. The staff consists of COMRADE
         BITIUK, the office manager, a tall, thin, military-looking
         woman, seated at a large desk in Center of room; PAVEL
         SYEROV, at a smaller desk to her Right; KIRA and the two
         other young CLERKS, a boy and a girl. The GIRL is punching
         a typewriter—with great determination and two fingers, stop-
         ping frequently after a few taps to gaze about and at the ceiling,
         blithely, and counting a tall pile of pamphlets in red paper cov-
         ers. COMRADE BITIUK is gushing loudly into a telephone.[9]

COMRADE BITIUK

...yes, Comrade, it's all arranged. The comrade peasants of the Siberian delegation arrive tomorrow. At one o'clock sharp they will go to the Museum of
the Revolution. At three o'clock sharp they will visit our Marxist Club. At five
o'clock they will attend a lecture on Historical Materialism. At seven o'clock

---

[9] Comrade Bitiuk is here doing the same sort of work that she did in the House of the Peasant (in the novel and in the other version of the play in this volume).

they go to the opera—to hear "Aida"...Yes, Comrade, we have arranged every-thing on a strict schedule, to the minute...What?...No, I can't tell you about their train—it may be late—just an hour or two...Yes, that's right. Goodbye, Comrade.

(Hangs up, whirls around in her chair, snapping a military command)

Comrade Argounova! Do you have the requisition for the special lecturer for the Siberian delegation?

KIRA

No, Comrade Bitiuk.

COMRADE BITIUK

Where is it?

KIRA

In Comrade Voronov's office. He hasn't signed in yet.

COMRADE BITIUK

Some people do not realize the tremendous importance of the cultural side of a railroad!

SYEROV

(Suavely, but with unmistakable menace)

What was that, Comrade Bitiuk?

COMRADE BITIUK

(Hastily)

Of course, I didn't mean to criticize our chief, Comrade Voronov. I meant you, Comrade Argounova. You do not show sufficient interest in your work. That's what happens when one has to employ bourgeois who have Communist friends...Of course I didn't mean to criticize Comrade Taganov.

SYEROV

(To Kira)

I hear Comrade Taganov's been taking you to the theater.

COMRADE BITIUK

And to the opera—and the ballet—and the museums.

KIRA

I haven't seen Comrade Taganov for weeks.

SYEROV

Really? What happened?

KIRA

I don't know.

SYEROV

Maybe he realized that being seen with you so often wasn't doing him much good in the Party.

>(VORONOV enters from door Right.)

>(There is a stir in the office at his entrance as if the staff were subtly[10] coming to attention.)

VORONOV

>(Handing some papers to SYEROV)

Comrade Syerov, will you be so kind and take this to the Freight Department?

SYEROV

>(Jumping up eagerly, servilely)

Yes, Comrade Voronov. So glad to be of assistance to you, Comrade Voronov.

>(SYEROV exits Left.)

>(VORONOV turns to go. Kira stops him.)

KIRA

Comrade Voronov, could I speak to you for a moment, please? It's very urgent.

VORONOV

I'm sorry, Comrade Argounova, but I've told you once, I haven't the time today.

>(Exits Right into his office)

>(She returns to her desk, obviously upset.)

COMRADE BITIUK

What is this, Comrade Argounova? Do you think our chief has time for every stray clerk in the place?

>(KIRA doesn't answer.)

What's the matter with you lately? When you came here five months ago you had spirit enough. Now you tramp around like a ghost.

KIRA

I have some trouble . . . at home, Comrade Bitiuk.

COMRADE BITIUK

Your personal troubles aren't important to us and . . .

>(Telephone rings. She picks up receiver.)

---

[10] This is almost certainly an error, and should read "suddenly."

Allo?...Yes, speaking...Oh, yes, the comrades workers of the Ukranian delegation are expected at a lecture on "The Red City and Village" as soon as they arrive...Yes, the lecturer is all ready, but you can have a choice of subjects: "The Red City and Village" or "The Work Bench and the Plow" or "Marxism in Streets and Fields" or "Leninism in Farm and Factory."

(With indignation)

What?...No, we have no lecturers on beauty culture!

(A YOUNG MAN storms in from the door Left, and rushes to Comrade Bitiuk.)

YOUNG MAN

(Furiously)

Who the hell ordered the freight train from Kharkov to be held up?!

COMRADE BITIUK

(With ominous dignity)

I did.

YOUNG MAN

Why, for God's sake? Don't you know what's on that train?

COMRADE BITIUK

Merely some wheat.

YOUNG MAN

Merely some wheat!

COMRADE BITIUK

(Into phone)

You'll take "Leninism in Farm and Factory"?...Fine...Goodbye, Comrade...

(Hangs up)

YOUNG MAN

The co-operatives of the twelfth district haven't had any bread for three weeks! What the devil possessed you...

COMRADE BITIUK

Kindly control your vocabulary, Comrade. That train had to wait in order to let the train from Armenia pass.

YOUNG MAN

Well?

COMRADE BITIUK

The train from Armenia carries marble for the Soviet Pavilion at the International Exposition in Dresden.

YOUNG MAN

But what the devil...

COMRADE BITIUK

Don't you know how important foreign public opinion is to us?

YOUNG MAN

But God damn it all! Those poor devils in the twelfth district have to eat occasionally!

COMRADE BITIUK

That will be all, Comrade. We're busy.

(He hesitates.)

Do you want to be reported for sabotage?

(The YOUNG MAN whirls about and exits.)

KIRA

(Looks at her, makes up her mind. Resolutely.)

Comrade Bitiuk, could I please have an advance on my salary for three months?

COMRADE BITIUK

(Gasps)

What? Have you lost your mind?

KIRA

It's...for a friend of mine. He's ill. He...he has tuberculosis.

COMRADE BITIUK

Oh, how dreadful!

KIRA

The doctor said that another winter in Petrograd would be as certain as a firing squad for him. I have to send him south. To the Crimea. Please let me have the advance. It will be just enough to start him off.

COMRADE BITIUK

There are State Hospitals to take care of that.

KIRA

He's applied to State Hospitals. He's been refused. Just let me have the money. I'll send him to a private sanatorium.

COMRADE BITIUK

What's his name?

KIRA

(After a moment's hesitation)

Leo Kovalensky

COMRADE BITIUK

Not a relative of Admiral Kovalensky, by any chance?

KIRA

His son.

COMRADE BITIUK

Indeed! And you have the impertinence to ask help for *him*?

KIRA

But don't you see? It's your fault! It's their fault! He became ill in jail, months ago, in the G.P.U.

COMRADE BITIUK

(Horrified)

In the G.P.U.?

(All her sympathy gone)

Comrade Argounova, go back to your work and don't ever let me hear another word about it!

KIRA

But Leo's not guilty of anything! He's never...

COMRADE BITIUK

An advance of *three months*! What do you think this is, a capitalistic country! How can you be sure that you'll be working here another month, let alone three? There's to be a reduction of staff here next week, you know.

KIRA

I...

(A sharp bell rings loudly somewhere in the building. The entire office is jerked into a frantic activity of slamming desks and reaching for coats, all eager to get out first.)

COMRADE BITIUK

(Stopping at the door on her way out)

Comrades, I shall remind you that you have just barely time for dinner. At six o'clock you are to report at the Palace of Labor for the street demonstrations in honor of the visiting delegations of British Trade Unions. Your attendance is voluntary, of course. If any of you are absent, the name will be reported to me. Good night, Comrades.

> (Exits)

> (The OTHERS follow her in a rush, all except KIRA who remains behind, looking at Voronov's door. The door opens, COMRADE VORONOV comes out, dressed for the street. She stops him.)

KIRA

Comrade Voronov, please . . .

VORONOV

> (Impatiently)

Well, what is it? What is it?

KIRA

Comrade Voronov, I have a friend who—he's going to die. He has consumption. You know what that means here, in Petrograd. I have to send him South. To a sanatorium in the Crimea.

VORONOV

My dear, what has that to do with me?

KIRA

We've tried every hospital in town. We've spent nights waiting in line. They won't even register him. But you . . . in your position . . . you could arrange it for him.

VORONOV

Is he a State employee?

KIRA

No. He lost his job at the State Publishing House. He can't find work. He's unemployed.

VORONOV

> (Sternly)

Comrade Argounova, there is no unemployment in Soviet Russia.

KIRA

> (Hastily)

Oh no, of course not.

VORONOV

Is he a member of a Trade Union?

KIRA

No.

VORONOV

(Dryly)

You don't seem to grasp our present-day reality, Comrade Argounova.

KIRA

Comrade Voronov, don't you see? I love him. And he will die. And they will let him die because they didn't write his name on a piece of paper and call it membership in a Trade Union. I know they are important, these things, the Unions and the papers and all. And if one has to sacrifice and suffer for them, I don't mind. Perhaps, I haven't always understood you and all those things, but I can be obedient and learn. Only…only when it comes to life itself, then we have to be serious, don't we? We can't let those things take life!

VORONOV

Comrade Argounova, your feelings or mine are of no consequence in the matter.

KIRA

(She speaks slowly, softly, but her voice rises until she is screaming on the last words.)

Comrade Voronov, there are things that must not be touched. You understand, don't you? Well, he is that to me, and you can't take him away from me, because you can't let me stand here and look at you and talk and breathe and move, and then tell me you'll take him—we're not insane, both of us, are we, Comrade Voronov?

VORONOV

There's nothing I can do.

KIRA

But he's going to die!

VORONOV

But he's not a Trade Union Member!

(Enter ANDREI and TIMOSHENKO)

ANDREI

Good evening, Comrade Voronov.

VORONOV

Comrade Taganov! Haven't seen you here for such a long time!

KIRA

(Stepping forward, eagerly)

Andrei…

ANDREI

(Nods to her curtly and turns to Voronov, dismissing her completely)
Where's Pavel Syerov?

VORONOV

He's down at the freight office across the hall, Comrade Taganov.

ANDREI

(To Timoshenko)
See if you can find him.
        (TIMOSHENKO nods silently and exits.)

VORONOV

If there's anything I can do for you, Comrade Taganov...

ANDREI

No. Good night, Comrade.

VORONOV

(Bowing)
Good night.
        (Exits)
        (ANDREI walks to Syerov's desk, stands, looking at papers, his back to
        Kira.)

KIRA

Andrei, I want to speak to you.

ANDREI

(Without turning)
Sorry, Kira. Not now.

KIRA

Andrei, do you know that it's been two months since I saw you last?

ANDREI

Yes.

KIRA

I've telephoned you five times. I've written to you. You didn't answer.

ANDREI

No.

KIRA

Andrei, if there's been some misunderstanding between us...

ANDREI

(Turning to her)

Has there been a misunderstanding between us?

KIRA

I thought...if you wanted to explain...

ANDREI

I have nothing to explain.

KIRA

Andrei, what have I done?

ANDREI

Nothing.

(Turns away again, as the door opens and SYEROV enters, followed by TIMOSHENKO.)

SYEROV

Andrei, my pal, so glad to see you! What did you want to...

ANDREI

(To Kira)

Isn't it time for you to go home, Kira?

KIRA

I must speak to you, Andrei.

ANDREI

(Points to Voronov's office)

You wait in there.

(KIRA looks at the three men, astonished, gathers a few papers from her desk, then exits into Voronov's office.)

SYEROV

(With a note of apprehension)

What is this, Andrei?

ANDREI

We're going to have a little talk, Syerov.

SYEROV

(Looking at Timochenko)

Private?

TIMOSHENKO

(Leaning insolently against a desk)

Very private.

SYEROV

(Looking from one to the other)

What's the matter?

ANDREI

Merely a warning, Syerov. About certain activities of yours on this railroad. And the next time it won't be in private.

SYEROV

What do you mean? What have I done? I'm the best worker they've got here. Next year, when I graduate from the Institute, I'll have a better job. I'll have old Voronov's job. He doesn't know it, but I will.

ANDREI

Not if I can prevent it.

SYEROV

Why? What have you got against me?

ANDREI

You've been making too many friends around here, Syerov—strange kind of friends for a Party member.

SYEROV

Who?

ANDREI

There are many people around a railroad terminal. Speculators, for instance. People who smuggle things from abroad. Aren't there?

SYEROV

(Dangerously)

You have no proof of what you're driving at.

ANDREI

(Pointing to Syerov's wristwatch)

That watch wasn't made in Russia, was it?

SYEROV

(Nervous, flustered)

Well...I...

ANDREI

The Party is fighting speculators to the death, but things have a way of slipping by at *railroad stations*...haven't they?

SYEROV

Andrei...I...you see...

ANDREI

Yes. I see. And I don't want to see any more of it.

SYEROV

Andrei, who the hell reported on me?

TIMOSHENKO

(Quietly)

I did.

SYEROV

(Whirling toward him angrily)

Oh, so that's it? Who gave you the authority to spy on me?

ANDREI

I did.

SYEROV

(Whirls to Andrei, but has to control himself and to speak ingratiatingly)

Andrei, my pal, what's the matter? We're such old friends, did you have to hire stray sailors to watch me?

TIMOSHENKO

(Pleasantly)

Just *one* sailor, Comrade Syerov. One single sailor of the Baltic Fleet. And not hired, either. More in the nature of a labor of love.

SYEROV

Of what?

TIMOSHENKO

Of love, Comrade—for the kind of man you ain't.

(Very pleasantly)

You see, I don't like your snoot.

SYEROV

Who the hell are you to...

TIMOSHENKO

Stepan Timoshenko. Stepan Timoshenko—of the Red Baltfleet.

SYEROV

Aw hell, what's a watch anyway? You can't go through life wearing nothing but a halo. Do you want to live in a rat hole forever? Don't you want to rise in the world?

ANDREI

That's not what I fought for in the revolution.

SYEROV

You fought? Didn't I? Didn't we fight in the trenches together in the civil war, shoulder to shoulder?

ANDREI

Yes. We did. We made the revolution, you and I. And sometimes I wonder which of us won.

SYEROV

What are you talking about?

ANDREI

About men whom something has killed since the civil war, killed without bullets, without blood. We owe them a thought and a glance back once in a while, Syerov...The men who lived in rat holes and defied the world—in the days of the Czar. The men who owned nothing but their lives and stood ready to sacrifice that willingly.

SYEROV

(Uneasily)
Andrei, why...why talk about it?

ANDREI

Do you remember that you were one of them?

SYEROV

I only...

ANDREI

Syerov, do you know how many members of the Communist Party there are in this country? One million in a country of a hundred and seventy millions...We are not a Party, Syerov. We're a sacred order. We should carry our Party cards as a banner, not as a burglar's pass-key!

SYEROV

Andrei, it's because...because I've never had anything. I know it was rotten to buy from a speculator. I guess I was weak. I'll...I'll never do it again.

ANDREI

All right. That's all.

SYEROV

Thanks. So long.

 (Exit TIMOSHENKO and SYEROV)

ANDREI

 (Walks to Voronov's office, calls)

Kira!

KIRA

 (Enters)

Andrei...

ANDREI

Well? What did you want?

KIRA

Andrei, you know that I need your help, don't you?

ANDREI

How could I?

KIRA

I thought the G.P.U. knew everything...about everyone.

ANDREI

The G.P.U.? I've never made use of that to spy on my friends, Kira. Not on your private life. Why, I don't even know where you live.

KIRA

Andrei, will you help me?

ANDREI

What is it?

KIRA

Do you remember Leo Kovalensky?

ANDREI

Yes. I met him once. I don't like him.

KIRA

He's ill. Dangerously ill. He has to be sent south.

ANDREI

Well?

KIRA

You can do it. You have the power to do it. You can arrange a place for him in a State sanatorium.

ANDREI

(Looks at her, asks in a strange, new, hard voice)

Is he a good friend of yours, Kira?

KIRA

He...

(Watches him, finishes cautiously)

...he's one of my friends.

ANDREI

He's not the type of person you should associate with. And you should know better than to ask my help for a notorious counterrevolutionary.

KIRA

But he's ill.

ANDREI

He shouldn't be helped.

KIRA

He's a human being. Doesn't that mean anything to you?

ANDREI

All human beings mean so much to me, Kira, that not a single one counts. Not even myself.

KIRA

But he's going to die!

ANDREI

(Looking straight at her, implacably)

One hundred thousand workers died in the civil war. Why—in the face of the Union of Socialist Soviet Republics—can't one aristocrat die?

KIRA

(She steps away from him, her eyes wide with terror. She makes an effort to control herself. She whispers.)

Andrei...I have no one else to help me[11]...I thought you were my friend...

---

[11] The typescript has "help"; I follow Version V A ("help me").

ANDREI

(Approaching her)

Your friend...?

(He seizes her in his arms. He kisses her. She tears herself away violently, falls back.)

KIRA

Andrei!

ANDREI

Now do you know why I couldn't see you?...I don't know when it started. I knew only that it must end—because I couldn't stand it. To see you and laugh with you and discuss the future of humanity—and to think only of when your hand would touch mine. To lie, to hide it, to...

KIRA

Andrei...I didn't know...

ANDREI

I didn't want you to know. I've tried to stay away from you. To break it. You don't know what it's done to me. I was beginning to hate my work, my position, my high salary, which others envy.[12]

(Her eyes open wide to a sudden thought. She looks at him.)

...the men I deal with, my job, everything. I hate myself...You shouldn't have spoken to me. I'm not your friend. I don't care if I hurt you. I don't love you. I want you. I've never wanted anything in my life. I've taught myself to have no desires. It's some kind of revenge perhaps. Every wish I ever could have had is now in one. I want you. I'd give everything I have, everything I could ever have—Kira—for something you can't give me!

KIRA

(She whispers.)

What did you say, Andrei?

ANDREI

(Looks at her. His voice is suddenly very soft and low.)

Or is it something you...can...Kira?

KIRA

I love you, Andrei.

(She is in his arms. He kisses her. Her head falls back. She screams, a cry of sheer despair.)

...No one must know!...No one must know!

CURTAIN

---

[12] The typescript has "my high salary which others envy."

ACT 2

SCENE 1

TIME: Six months later. Spring of 1925.
Late afternoon.

SCENE: Railroad Office.

AT RISE: COMRADE BITIUK sits at her desk. KIRA and the two CLERKS are standing before her. KIRA is wearing a red dress. Syerov's desk is now occupied by COMRADE VORONOV who doesn't look quite as imposing as before. COMRADE BITIUK is addressing her staff.

Comrade Bitiuk

…And I must impress upon you, Comrades, that this is "Railroad Efficiency Week." I want you all to do your best.

> (SYEROV enters from what had been Voronov's office. He has some papers in his hand.)

Syerov

> (Imperiously)

Voronov!

> (VORONOV jumps to his feet. SYEROV walks to him and throws the papers down on his desk.)

Why aren't you taking your instructions with the others?

Voronov

Yes, Comrade Syerov, of course, Comrade Syerov.

> (Hurries to take his place with the group)
>
> (SYEROV exits Right.)

Comrade Bitiuk

Now the following are the events on which we must concentrate and make certain that they are carried out in perfect order. First, there's the dedication of the Station Library Lenin's Nook. After that—the porters' and ticket collectors' mass meeting to open the "Fight Vodka and Fascism Week"—Comrade Argounova, see that the red bunting is delivered on time. Then there's the firemen and engineers' rally to help the children of the strikers of New Zealand. And above all, don't forget the City Tournament of Marxist Clubs. If our club wins the award for the best thesis—we'll get the Order of Lenin and two pounds of liverwurst each!

The Others

Yes, Comrade Bitiuk…Of course…Yes, Comrade Bitiuk…

COMRADE BITIUK

Now let me see you go to it. You know our slogan: "To reach and to over-reach!"

(The GROUP breaks up to return to their work.)

VORONOV

(Hesitantly)

Comrade Bitiuk, I... I was just preparing a report on a little matter that requires some attention. It's that question of fuel delivery.

COMRADE BITIUK

Well? What about it?

VORONOV

I really think we should suggest some action to the proper department. I have here a report on that train from Kiev, which was six days late. It seems they ran out of fuel, so the engineer stopped the train in the middle of a forest and made the passengers go out to chop some wood.

COMRADE BITIUK

Yes, of course. We'll attend to it—as soon as "Railroad Efficiency Week" is over.

VORONOV

But last week you said we would...

COMRADE BITIUK

Now, Comrade Voronov, the most important thing is the proper revolutionary ideology. As I think you've realized.

VORONOV

(With resignation)

Yes, Comrade Bitiuk.

(Returns to his desk)

COMRADE BITIUK

(Turning to Kira)

Comrade Argounova, will you get out the inventory for the State Library Lenin's Nook as soon as possible?

KIRA

(Very cheerfully)

Yes, Comrade Bitiuk.

COMRADE BITIUK

You actually seem to sound happy. Quite a pleasant change.

KIRA

May I use the telephone, Comrade Bitiuk?

COMRADE BITIUK

What, *again*?

KIRA

Yes, please.

COMRADE BITIUK

Well, go ahead. But be quick about it.

KIRA

> (Picks up phone receiver)

Give me the Station Commandant's office please...Comrade, can you tell me please what time the train from the Crimea will arrive?...Oh!...Yes, connect me with him, please...

COMRADE BITIUK

What's all the impatience? Whom are you expecting?

KIRA

He's coming back on that train.

> (Into telephone)

Allo, Comrade?...Can you tell me what time the train from the Crimea will arrive?...Oh! Well, switch me to him then...

COMRADE BITIUK

Who's coming back?

KIRA

My...a friend of mine.

> (Into telephone)

Allo, Comrade?...Can you tell me what time the train from the Crimea will arrive?

> (Eagerly)

It *has* arrived?

> (Is about to hang up, stops as the voice over the wire continues)

What?

> (Crestfallen)

Oh, it hasn't?...It *will* arrive in a few minutes?...You aren't sure? Well, can't you find out?...Can't you connect me with someone who knows?...

> (Shrugs with resignation and hangs up)

COMRADE BITIUK

What did they say?

KIRA

That the train may be here any minute now—or any day.

COMRADE BITIUK

But it will get here, won't it?

KIRA

Yes. Today or tomorrow.

COMRADE BITIUK

Well, what are you complaining about? That's a pretty close margin. Who's on that train? Your friend who has tuberculosis?

KIRA

Who *had* tuberculosis. Not any more. He's cured, Comrade Bitiuk. He's spent all winter in the Crimea. He's actually cured. We... *he* stopped it in time.

COMRADE BITIUK

That's lovely. You see? You had nothing to worry about. And I remember what scenes you created here. As I always say, everything works out for the best, it doesn't matter how.

KIRA

(Her face dark, her voice dull for a moment)

No. It doesn't matter how.

(Then cheerfully again)

Oh, no, it doesn't matter!

COMRADE BITIUK

And just why are you so happy about this man returning? Comrade Taganov won't like that.

KIRA

(Stopping short)

What?

COMRADE BITIUK

Oh, don't look so innocent. I have my own little suspicions. You've been pretty friendly with Comrade Taganov all this past winter, haven't you?

KIRA

(Looking straight at her)

Yes. Friendly. What else?

COMRADE BITIUK

(Retreating)

Oh, well, I didn't mean to insinuate that...Comrade Taganov's always been the great scholar[13] of the Party who never even looked at women.

(SYEROV enters Right. EVERYONE gets very busy.)

SYEROV

(Walks to Voronov's desk, throws some papers down)

From the Station Commandant's office. Immediate attention.

VORONOV

Yes, Comrade Syerov.

SYEROV

(Handing a paper to Comrade Bitiuk)

Here's the order for that freight car. I've signed it personally. See that it's put through without delay.

COMRADE BITIUK

Yes, Comrade Syerov.

SYEROV

(To boy clerk)

Go down to the yard and ask where the hell's the report they promised me? Don't come back without it—or else they'll find their rears in the gutter—and you too, for good measure!

BOY CLERK

Yes, Comrade Syerov.
(Exits like a streak)

COMRADE BITIUK

(Raising her head from the paper Syerov has given her)

Oh, Comrade Syerov, I'm so sorry about that butter!

SYEROV

(Brusquely)

It's not our fault. It couldn't be helped.

COMRADE BITIUK

But a whole carload of it! Of *real* butter! And all of it rancid. Such a pity!

---

[13] "Saint" is more appropriate. In the novel (pt. 1, ch. 7), Sonia says to Kira about Andrei, "And if you have any intentions in a bedroom direction, Comrade Argounova—well, not a chance. He's the kind of saint that sleeps with red flags." See also *We the Living*, the play, p. 29.

SYEROV

Accidents will happen.

COMRADE BITIUK

But couldn't we do something? Our State co-operatives haven't had any butter for months. So many people are waiting for it.

SYEROV

(Shortly)
The expert of the Food Trust has condemned it. There's nothing to be done. You wouldn't want our toilers to be poisoned with rotten stuff, would you?

COMRADE BITIUK

Oh dear, no! Only...
(Resolutely)
Look, Comrade Syerov, could I...could I have a pound of it? Just one pound. I don't mind if it does smell, I don't mind a bit, I've been saving for two months now to get some butter. If it's going to be dumped anyway, couldn't I just...

SYEROV

Certainly not. And really, I don't see why there has to be so much talk on the subject. The less said about it—the better. We don't want any criticism of our freight department.

COMRADE BITIUK

Oh, I wasn't criticizing anybody, Comrade Syerov. I *never* criticize anybody. But could I...could I just see that butter before they...

SYEROV

What's the matter, Comrade Bitiuk? Are you distrusting your superiors?

COMRADE BITIUK

(Frightened)
Oh, God forbid, Comrade Syerov!

SYEROV

Then shut up about it!

COMRADE BITIUK

(Meekly)
Yes, Comrade Syerov.
(A band and chorus singing the Internationale are heard offstage.)

SYEROV

(Glancing at his wrist watch)
Has anyone asked for me?

COMRADE BITIUK

No, Comrade Syerov.

SYEROV

(At window)

There goes the demonstration for the delegates of the Rumanian Trade Unions. I want my office to be represented.

COMRADE BITIUK

Yes, of course, Comrade Syerov.

SYEROV

You'd better start at once. The delegation will arrive in a few minutes—on the train from the Crimea.

KIRA

(Jumping up)

The train from the Crimea?!

SYEROV

(Looks at her, astonished)

Well! What's the matter?

KIRA

The...the train from the Crimea? It's here?

SYEROV

It's just getting in. What's the matter with you?

(KIRA rushes to the door. COMRADE BITIUK stops her.)

COMRADE BITIUK

Comrade Argounova, you will please control yourself. Your personal affairs can wait. You will take part in the demonstration with the others.

KIRA

But I'll miss him—if I stand there with the crowd! He's my...friend. I haven't seen him for six months.

COMRADE BITIUK

I don't care if it's your grandmother and if you hadn't seen her for six years. Social duty comes first. The toilers of the Rumanian Trade Unions must have a proper reception.

SYEROV

Get out of here. All of you.

COMRADE BITIUK

Yes, Comrade Syerov.
> (Distributes red flags to Kira, Voronov, and the Clerks)

Come on, Comrades.
> (They file out with the flags.)

> (SYEROV stands looking out of the window. COMRADE SONIA enters Right. SYEROV starts with surprise, stops short, his mouth falling open as a sudden recollection strikes him. He utters involuntarily, in a choked moan.)

SYEROV

Oh, my Lord!

COMRADE SONIA

> (Stopping coquettishly)

Merely surprised, Pavel?

SYEROV

Why, no, I'm...I'm delighted, Sonia my dear! I just...I didn't expect you and...

COMRADE SONIA

> (Coyly)

Pavel! You should have expected me *today*.

SYEROV

Yes, of course...that is...should I?...I mean...
> (Then resolutely)

Listen, Sonia darling, I have an appointment, I can't talk now, you really mustn't be seen here.

COMRADE SONIA

You mean because of last night? I don't mind. I'm not old-fashioned.

SYEROV

Last...night?

COMRADE SONIA

It was lovely, wasn't it, Pavel?

SYEROV

Oh...oh yes, very lovely. A very lovely party. The vodka was excellent.
> (Looking at her anxiously)

Say, Sonia, I'm sorry if I did drink a bit too much and...

COMRADE SONIA

You were wonderful, Pavel. Of course, I've always known that you liked me.

SYEROV

Oh sure, certainly, I've always liked you, Sonia, only...only I never would permit myself to...that is, I *hope* I wouldn't...I mean I...

COMRADE SONIA

(Smiling)

Why, Pavel! I could almost think that you don't remember!

SYEROV

(Shattered)

Oh, Christ!

(KARP MOROZOV enters Right. He is a heavy, middle-aged man, well-dressed, awkward and peasant-like in his manner, shrewd, sly and naïve at once. He smiles brightly, approaching Syerov with outstretched hand.)

MOROZOV

Good afternoon, Pavel, soul of mine! How well you're looking!

SYEROV

Sonia darling, this is an urgent business matter, I must...

COMRADE SONIA

Of course...

(Looks at Morozov)

Of course...See you later, Pavel.

(Exits Right)

SYEROV

(Lowering his voice a little)

I don't think it's a good idea, Morozov—your coming here. Too many people around to see you.

MOROZOV

Why, pal, that's why it's good. Open and aboveboard. Official business. No one can suspect nothing.

SYEROV

I don't like it. We've got to work it differently. Through Antonina only. Understand? I don't want to see you. When's Antonina coming back?

MOROZOV

She's here. Just arrived. And she's got news for us.

SYEROV

Well, talk fast.

MOROZOV

But first, how about that carload of butter, pal?

SYEROV

(Lowering his voice)
It's done. You'll have it tonight. The usual place...Wait a few days before you dispose of it. Don't take any chances.

MOROZOV

We won't have to take any chances at all from now on. We can open that food store. I've got the man. Just the kind we've been looking for.

SYEROV

Who?

MOROZOV

Antonina's found him. They've just got back together on the same train. They're waiting outside. A broken-down aristocrat. Young. Poor. Desperate. Ready for anything.

SYEROV

You speak to him first. If he's all right—send him in to me.

MOROZOV

Antonina's checked up on him.

SYEROV

And remember this: when we open that store, I want my share in advance on each load. I'm not to be kept waiting. And I don't want to see him or you here again. Antonina will deliver the money to me. No one else.

MOROZOV

Sure, pal, anything you say.
(MOROZOV opens the door Right, calls out)
Come in, Tonia.
(ANTONINA PAVLOVNA[14] enters, followed by LEO. LEO looks tanned, healthier than before. ANTONINA PAVLOVNA is a stout woman in her forties, flashily, expensively dressed, with obviously dyed red hair and too much make-up.)

---

[14] The typescript is inconsistent, sometimes reading "Antonina," other times "Antonina Pavlovna." I always print the latter.

Morozov, cont.

(To LEO, as he enters)

Come right in, Lev Sergueievich, soul of mine.

Antonina Pavlovna

(Rushing to Syerov)

Pavel my dear! So glad to see you again!

(SYEROV nods curtly.)

Morozov

Citizen Syerov—this is Citizen Kovalensky.

(The two MEN bow, looking at each other coldly.)

Antonina Pavlovna

It was my idea, Pavel. The moment I saw Leo, I knew he was just the man we've been looking for. And Koko can't refuse me anything.

Syerov

(To Leo, in the grand manner of a big executive)

I'll let Citizen Morozov explain the matter to you. Then I may speak to you later.

(Exits into his office)

Morozov

Sorry to've grabbed you like that, practically off the train steps, as one might say, but it's urgent business, Lev Sergueievich. Gotta be settled quickly.

Leo

Well?

Morozov

Well, Lev Sergueievich, it's like this: the man we want must be young, independent and...and with a social past, as they say, an aristocrat or...well, someone who wouldn't be liable to have too many Soviet ideals in his head.

Leo

You can count on me for *that.*

Morozov

And he mustn't be too well off...so that he'd be...or...rather eager to make money and...wouldn't mind taking a little chance if necessary.

(LEO sits on the edge of a desk.)[15]

---

[15] I have added this stage direction, to match the next one, which has Leo stand.

LEO

I haven't a brass coin to my name. I haven't a prospect in the world. I don't give a damn about any chances. Is that what you want?

MOROZOV

Splendid, Lev Sergueievich, splendid... Oh, that is, I'm sorry... Well... Well, it's like this: we're planning a big business, and first of all we got to have a private food store—for protection. Now a private trader is no easy title to bear these days. The government allows them to exist, for the time being, but it doesn't like them—Lord, no, it doesn't like them. I couldn't take it upon myself, and my partner—he's a Communist, so he can't even think of it.

LEO

Well?

MOROZOV

Well, your part of it will be to get the store. We'll...
(KIRA comes in, Right. She stops short, with a choked gasp, as she sees Leo. He rises slowly, stands looking at her.)

LEO

(Quietly)
Allo, Kira.

KIRA

Leo...
(She runs to him, forgetting everything. She doesn't kiss him. She buries her face against him, unable to speak. He says softly)

LEO

Kira... my little fool... Stop it, Kira...

KIRA

Leo, I... I've been looking for you all over the station... I...

LEO

(Controls himself, puts her aside gently, turns to the others, his voice a warning and a reminder to her)
Kira, this is Antonina Pavlovna Platoshkina—Kira Alexandrovna Argounova.
(ANTONINA PAVLOVNA bows coolly, studying Kira shrewdly.)
And Karp Karpovich Morozov.

MOROZOV

Honored to meet you, Kira Alexandrovna, soul of mine.

LEO

(To Kira)

Tonia and I were together in the Sanatorium and...

ANTONINA PAVLOVNA

(Coming to them)

I was taking a rest cure for my nerves—and what sensitive person isn't a nervous wreck these days? But I'm so glad to be back. I'm sure the Sanatorium lost all its charm now that Leo's gone.

(To Kira)

He was the most fascinating man there—and everybody admired him so much—oh, purely platonically, my dear—if you're worried.

KIRA

I'm not.

ANTONINA PAVLOVNA

Leo has told me that we can trust you to keep secrets. Leo and I used to sit in the sun together and talk about our friends. I told him all about Koko. Poor Koko! You mustn't let him astonish you. He's really very artistic. He's really a gentleman at heart. He even reads poetry. Ah, you two will get along beautifully in business.

MOROZOV

(To Leo)

Well, you'll have to get the store for us, Lev Sergueievitch. We'll pay for it, but you gotta get the license in your name. You'll be the sole, official, registered owner. Our partner has plenty of pull on this railroad. All he's got to do is see that the food shipments for the State Co-operatives are damaged a wee bit and pronounced worthless. That's all.

LEO

And then?

MOROZOV

The rest is simple. The shipment goes quietly to the basement of your little shop. Nothing suspicious in that—is there?—just supplies for the store. We break up the load and we ship it to our own customers, private traders all over the city, reasonable and discreet.

KIRA

Leo! Are you insane?!

LEO

Kira, keep quiet, please.

KIRA

If that's a new way of committing suicide, there are much simpler ones!

ANTONINA PAVLOVNA

Really, Kira Alexandrovna, you're unnecessarily tragic about it.

MOROZOV

Now, now, Kira Alexandrovna, soul of mine, there's nothing to be afraid of. If anything should go wrong, Syerov has . . .

KIRA

Who?

MOROZOV

Our partner.

KIRA

Oh.

MOROZOV

He has a powerful friend in the G.P.U. One of the chiefs. I'd be scared to mention his name.

LEO

Oh, I suppose we'll be safe from that quarter, if we have enough money.

MOROZOV

Money? Why, Lev Sergueievich, soul of mine, we'll make so much money that you'll be rolling ten-ruble bills to make cigarettes. We split it three ways, you understand, me, yourself, and Syerov. And we gotta take care of his friends here. But then, you must remember that on the face of it you're the sole owner. It's your store, in your name.

LEO

Don't worry. I'm not afraid.

ANTONINA PAVLOVNA

(To Morozov)

I told you.

KIRA

Leo! Don't you see what they're doing? They're investing money. You're investing your life!

LEO

I'm glad to find some use for it.

KIRA

Don't you know that it's the firing squad for anyone caught in a criminal speculation?

MOROZOV

Kira Alexandrovna, why use such strong names for a simple business deal which is perfectly permissible and *almost* legal?

LEO

Listen. Kira, I know that this is as rotten a deal as could be made. And I know I'm taking a chance on my life. And I still want to do it. You understand?

KIRA

Even if I begged you not to?

LEO

Nothing you can say will change things. I didn't get cured in order to start starving to death all over again and let it take longer this time. Do you think I'll spend the rest of my life crawling, begging for a job they'll never give me? Do you think I'll let your uncle in Budapest send us money as he did all winter? So they shoot speculators? What is there left to me? I have no career. I have no future. I'm not risking much when I risk my life.

MOROZOV

(With admiration)

Lev Sergueievich, soul of mine, how you can talk!

ANTONINA PAVLOVNA

Indeed, Leo, I'm surprised! If you let yourself be influenced and do not seem to be grateful...

LEO

Drop it. Why use the wrong words? You need me and I need you. That's all.

MOROZOV

(Placatingly)

Sure, sure, that's how it is. Then it's all settled? You'll take the job?

LEO

Yes.

MOROZOV

Splendid.

(To Antonina)

It's all right, Tonia, soul of mine, you come along now.
    (To Leo)
We don't want to be seen here all together, you understand, so we'll be going, and you just step in to see Pavel Syerov, he'll settle all the details with you.
    (Points to Syerov's office)
God bless us all.

    (ANTONINA PAVLOVNA exits without looking at them. MOROZOV bows low to Leo and Kira and exits Right.)

KIRA

Leo...Leo, you won't do this...you *can't* do this...now, when I thought I had saved you...

LEO

Yes. Now. Because you saved me.
    (Moves away from her)
Did you think I'd accept and forget? Write at once to your uncle. Thank him and tell him not to send us money any longer.

KIRA

Leo...are you doing this...because of...that money?

LEO

Yes. Because I want to repay it. To repay it quickly. To him—and to you.

KIRA

Oh, Leo, it doesn't matter! We don't have to think of that! We...

LEO

I've thought of nothing else all winter long. Do you think I'm going to live off you for the rest of my days? Do you think I'm going to stand by and watch you slaving in a Soviet office? You poor little fool! You don't know what life can be. You've never seen it. But you're going to see it. And I'm going to see it before they finish me!

KIRA

Leo, if I told you that I'd bless this office, and every demonstration I'd have to attend, and every Club, and every red flag—if only you wouldn't do this—would you still...

LEO

If I knew for certain that it's the firing squad in six months—I'd still do it!
    (He turns abruptly and exits into Syerov's office.)
    (KIRA stands at her desk, helplessly, crushed.)
    (COMRADE BITIUK enters Right, followed by VORONOV and the two CLERKS. They are dragging their red flags, obviously exhausted.)

COMRADE BITIUK

Oh Lord, do my feet hurt!

(The GIRL CLERK mutters something to the boy.)

What was that, Comrade? A complaint?

GIRL CLERK

(Hastily)

Oh, no, Comrade Bitiuk! I was just saying how lucky we are that we only had to meet the delegation, not parade all the way to the Square with the others.

COMRADE BITIUK

Well, I...

(She turns and notices Kira.)

Well, Comrade Argounova! What have you got to say for yourself?

(KIRA raises her head, looks at her, says nothing.)

So you ran away? You left the demonstration? You ignored orders?

KIRA

Yes, Comrade Bitiuk.

COMRADE BITIUK

Well, I warned you. You can't say I didn't.

KIRA

No, Comrade Bitiuk.

COMRADE BITIUK

I shall report this to the editor of our Wall newspaper. You will see your name on the blacklist of Social Slackers in the next number—and you know what that means. You will...

(ANDREI enters Right.)

COMRADE BITIUK, CONT.

Oh!

(Looks at Kira)

Oh...

(Too brightly)

Why, good evening, Comrade Taganov.

ANDREI

Good evening.

(Bows to Kira, noncommittally, as if they were mere acquaintants)

Good evening, Comrade Argounova.

KIRA

(In the same manner as his)
Good evening, Comrade Taganov.

ANDREI

(To Comrade Bitiuk)
Is Comrade Syerov in?

COMRADE BITIUK

I'll see…He…

KIRA

(Hastily)
He's in a conference.

COMRADE BITIUK

Was he expecting you, Comrade Taganov?

ANDREI

No. No, he wasn't expecting me. Nothing urgent. Comrade Syerov is a very busy man.

COMRADE BITIUK

Oh yes, indeed, Comrade Syerov is the most active worker we've got.

ANDREI

By the way, when are we going to get that butter?

COMRADE BITIUK

(Uneasily)
Butter?

ANDREI

That carload from Novgorod. Why hasn't it been delivered?

COMRADE BITIUK

Oh, Comrade Taganov, it has arrived, but it can't be distributed. It's rancid.

ANDREI

Rancid? All of it?

COMRADE BITIUK

Yes. The whole load. Such a pity! But it's not our fault, Comrade Taganov. Such things happen everywhere. Why, last week, at the Baltisky Terminal, they had a load of eighty dozen pairs of shoes delivered, and when they opened the boxes—all the shoes were for the left foot!

ANDREI

What is going to be done with that butter?

COMRADE BITIUK

Why, Comrade Syerov takes care of that, with the experts of the Food Trust.

ANDREI

Do you keep records of it?

COMRADE BITIUK

Certainly. They're in perfect order. Countersigned by an official of the Food Trust.

ANDREI

Who countersigns for the Food Trust?

COMRADE BITIUK

Comrade Karp Morozov himself.

ANDREI

I see.

COMRADE BITIUK

Anything wrong, Comrade Taganov?

ANDREI

No. Nothing at all.

> (The closing bell rings loudly offstage. The STAFF leaps into frantic hurry, eager to get out. COMRADE BITIUK rises.)

COMRADE BITIUK

Comrades, don't forget, at six o'clock you are to report at the Smolny Institute for the street demonstration of protest against labor conditions in France. Your attendance is voluntary. See you all tonight.

> (COMRADE BITIUK exits and the three other EMPLOYEES follow her hastily. KIRA is about to go also. ANDREI stops her.)

ANDREI

Kira...wait...

KIRA

> (Glances anxiously at Syerov's office)

We can't talk here, Andrei. Not now.

ANDREI

Why not?

KIRA

I'll come to your house later.

ANDREI

I have something to give you. I was paid today.
>   (Reaches into his pocket, produces some bills, hands them to her)

KIRA

>   (A little too violently)

No, Andrei. Not any more. I don't need it. And I won't need money again.

ANDREI

But your parents...

KIRA

You've given me enough for them. All winter long. They can manage now.
Father's found a job.

ANDREI

I'm sorry. I was selfish enough to be glad that I was doing something for you.

KIRA

You've done too much for me.
>   (SYEROV and LEO enter Right. KIRA sees them, but ANDREI has his
>   back turned to the office and doesn't see them at once. SYEROV comes
>   out, slapping Leo's shoulder with obvious approval, but stops short, seeing
>   Andrei, and turns to Leo loudly, obviously bluffing.)

SYEROV

I've got more shipping clerks than I can take care of. I don't know why people
keep bothering me. There are no openings here, Citizen...
>   (Then, as if noticing Andrei for the first time)

Oh, good evening, Andrei!

ANDREI

Good evening.

SYEROV

What are you doing here?
>   (Looks at Kira)

Oh, of course...
>   (To Kira)

Well, if anyone asks for me, send them to hell...Good night, Comrades.

(Exits Left)

(LEO picks up his hat and stands by door waiting.)

LEO

(To Kira)

Are you coming? I mean, could I have the pleasure of escorting you to your home, Comrade Argounova?

ANDREI

No.

LEO

What?

ANDREI

Comrade Argounova has work to finish. You can go.

LEO

Thank you. I believe you know where to find me, Comrade Argounova, whenever your official duties release you.

(Exits Left)

ANDREI

What did he mean by that?

KIRA

I don't know.

ANDREI

That's the man you wanted me to place in a State Sanatorium, isn't it?

KIRA

Yes.

ANDREI

He seems to have survived without my help. Do you see much of him?

KIRA

I haven't seen him for months...Why are you questioning me? He's not important to you, Andrei. Neither am I, for that matter. But we must be careful. You've promised me that no one would know—about you and me. You've promised that no one would know even...even after it's ended.

ANDREI

No one will know that it's ended, Kira. No one will see it end. Not you or I. Never.

KIRA

Never?
                (She approaches him, puts her hand over his; he does not move—and it is
                the sudden, tense immobility of his body that shows he has not become
                indifferent to her nearness. He is about to draw closer, controls himself
                with an effort and is the first one to withdraw his hand. She smiles.)
You see? That's what I mean to you. Just that. The touch of my hand on yours.
My body against yours. That's all we have been to each other, Andrei. And
that doesn't last. That shouldn't be wanted to last. It can end and leave you
unhurt...Say that you want me, Andrei.

ANDREI

I love you.

KIRA

No. Say that you like my dress, my hair, my mouth.

ANDREI

I love you.

KIRA

I don't like to hear you say it so pitilessly, as if it were a death sentence or a
prayer.

ANDREI

                (Quietly)
It is, Kira. A life sentence—and a prayer.

KIRA

Andrei, there is something I have wanted to tell you for a long time. I couldn't
say it before. Now I will. I must. Andrei, we can't go on like this.

ANDREI

                (Calmly)
I know it. Will you marry me, Kira?
                (She stares at him, silently, stunned.)
Why do we have to hide and live in this agony of counting days between our
meetings? And when you're gone, why have I no right to approach the house
where you live? Sometimes, I look at all the people in the street—and it frightens me, that feeling that you're lost somewhere among them, and I can't get to

you. Then I begin to hate people, all those masses of people that seem to have swallowed you...

KIRA

You beginning to hate people? *You*, Andrei?

ANDREI

Sometimes.

KIRA

(She looks at him, astonished.)

Andrei, let's break it—now and completely. Let's leave each other. Let's end it. Before it's too late.

ANDREI

It *is* too late, Kira. You see, I've spent a whole life in the service of others. And suddenly I've discovered what it is to feel things that have no reason but myself, and I've seen how sacred a reason that can be, and I've learned that a life is possible whose only justification is my own joy. And now everything else suddenly seems very different to me.

KIRA

Have I...have I done that to you?

ANDREI

Yes, it's what I've learned through you. I've never known anything but other men's future. You taught me my present.

KIRA

Andrei, what's happening to you?

ANDREI

I don't know. But it's so simple. I think of you, and I look at the people around me—and suddenly I think that they don't know what I feel and I don't want them to know, I don't want them to touch it. And then I'm suddenly aware of my own body—apart from all those others. You're not essential in that moment—*I* am, nothing counts but the strange feeling that my existence is important, more terribly important than I had ever guessed.

KIRA

Oh, Andrei!

ANDREI

I don't understand, as yet. But I'm beginning to learn. I don't know the answer—but I'm seeing the question for the first time. I love you, Kira. I need you. I need you with a greater need than love.

(She looks at him helplessly.)

Don't you see? You can't leave me now.

(She shakes her head slowly.)

Say that you won't leave me. Say you'll never leave me.

KIRA

I...

ANDREI

Say it.

KIRA

I won't leave you, Andrei.

(Desperately)

I don't want to hurt you. Oh, Andrei, I don't want to hurt you!

CURTAIN

SCENE 2

TIME: A few months later.
             Winter of 1925. Evening.

SCENE: Railroad office. It is dark beyond the window. The office staff is
             gone, the desks are closed for the night. A single lamp is burn-
             ing in the room.

AT RISE: The curtain rises to discover SYEROV and ANTONINA
             PAVLOVNA. She wears a heavy winter fur coat. She is sitting on
             the edge of a chair, watching Syerov anxiously, apologetically.

SYEROV

(Furiously)

...and I'll be damned if I let you get away with it! I won't wait another minute!
Not one minute!

ANTONINA PAVLOVNA

(Soothingly)

Now, now, Pavel, be reasonable...It's only...

SYEROV

I've told that hog Morozov! I've warned him that I'm not to be kept waiting!
But he's done it again! The second time this winter. He's spent my share! He's
ten days late on that last load! If he thinks I'm going to...

ANTONINA PAVLOVNA

You'll have that money, Pavel, so help me God, you'll have it, in a couple of days...

SYEROV

(Advancing furiously upon her)

In a couple of...

ANTONINA PAVLOVNA

I mean, *tomorrow*, Pavel! Tomorrow for sure!

SYEROV

That's what you said last week!

ANTONINA PAVLOVNA

Well, you know how it is, things are so uncertain, and with Koko so busy—poor Koko, he works so hard! I'd positively wilt of loneliness if our dear Leo wasn't gallant enough to take me out once in a while. And how Leo can spend money! It's simply thrilling to watch.

SYEROV

Yes! *My* money! I'm taking all the chances—so that the rest of you can go around strewing thousands into every gutter that Citizen Kovalensky fancies! But this is going to be the last of it! If I don't get my share—if I don't get it tomorrow morning...

ANTONINA PAVLOVNA

You'll have it, Pavel! I promise! For certain!

SYEROV

Just tell your Koko...tell that damned piece of tripe...What does he think I am? A ration card slave, like the rest of them? A stray mongrel eating outta slop pails all his life? I'll show him. I'm a great man. Some day, I'm going to make foreign capitalists look like mice. That's what: *mice*!

ANTONINA PAVLOVNA

(Edging toward exit door)

Yes, of course, Pavel, you will, that's right...May I go now, Pavel? It's getting late. It's...

SYEROV

Go on, get out. I don't want to be seen with you outside. I'll wait a few minutes.

ANTONINA PAVLOVNA

So silly of me, I'm getting to be so nervous lately, over nothing at all...only...I had the oddest experience tonight, on my way here...there was a man who...I'm sure he was following me all the way down...A sailor.

SYEROV

(Stopping short)

A *sailor*?

ANTONINA PAVLOVNA

Of the Baltic Fleet.

SYEROV

What did he do?

ANTONINA PAVLOVNA

Nothing. Just walked. And of course, I can't be sure he was following me, it just seemed strange...I don't know...

SYEROV

(Shrugging)

Forget it.

ANTONINA PAVLOVNA

Oh, I suppose it's all right. Men usually follow me for a perfectly *innocent* reason. Only I don't like sailors.

(She exits.)

(SYEROV paces nervously, chews sunflower seeds, stops as he hears voices.)

GUARD'S VOICE

But Comrade Syerov's gone! He's not here! He's...

COMRADE SONIA'S VOICE

Let me in or I'll report you!

(The door flies open as COMRADE SONIA enters.)

SYEROV

(Too cheerfully)

Sonia, my dear! It's you!

COMRADE SONIA

Why the guard, Pavel?

SYEROV

My dear, I'm so sorry. I was busy and I had given orders...but had I known it was you...

COMRADE SONIA

(Dismissing the subject briskly)

It's quite all right.

(Throws her briefcase on the table, unwinds a heavy scarf from around her neck, feeling quite at ease and at home.)

I had to see you about something important.

SYEROV

Yes, dear. What is it, dear?

COMRADE SONIA

(Quite matter-of-fact)

Pavel, we're going to have a baby.

SYEROV

(Stops dead. His mouth falls open.)

A...

COMRADE SONIA

(Firmly)

A baby.

SYEROV

Why didn't you tell me sooner?

COMRADE SONIA

I wasn't sure.

SYEROV

But hell! You'll have to...

COMRADE SONIA

It's too late for that now.

SYEROV

(Falls heavily on a chair before her and stares at her muffled calm)

Are you sure it's mine?

COMRADE SONIA

(Not raising her voice)

Pavel, you're insulting me.

SYEROV

(Jumps up, paces the room, falls down again and jumps up)

Well, what the hell are we to do about it?

COMRADE SONIA

We're going to be married, Pavel.

SYEROV

(Leans toward her menacingly, his fist slamming the table)
You've gone crazy.
(She looks at him silently, waiting.)
You're crazy, I tell you! I have no such intention.

COMRADE SONIA

But you'll have to do it.

SYEROV

I will, will I? You get out of here, you...

COMRADE SONIA

(Evenly)
Pavel, don't say anything you might regret.

SYEROV

Listen...what the...we're not living in a bourgeois country. Hell! There's no such thing as a betrayed virgin—and you were no virgin anyway and...Well, if you want to go to court, try and collect for its support—and the devil take you—but there's no law to make me marry you! Marry! Hell! You'd think we lived in England or something!

COMRADE SONIA

Pavel, don't misunderstand me. My attitude is not old-fashioned in the least. I am not concerned over morals or public disgrace or any such nonsense. It is merely a matter of our duty.

SYEROV

Our...what?

COMRADE SONIA

Our duty, Pavel. To a future citizen of our republic. Our child shall have the advantage of a Party mother—and father.

SYEROV

Hell, Sonia! That's not at all up to date. There are day nurseries and you know, collective training, one big family.

COMRADE SONIA

Our child shall have a perfect home. Our child...

SYEROV

Our child! God damn you! You've done it deliberately! You let it go on purpose! Just to trap me! Just like any old-fashioned slut!

COMRADE SONIA

Pavel, am I to understand that you intimate that I...

SYEROV

Oh, no, no, of course not. You know that I love you, Sonia...But I have a career to think about.

COMRADE SONIA

I could help you Pavel. Think of the prestige I'd give you in the Party. You've heard of my father, haven't you? A real revolutionist, a real victim of the Czar, who's spent four years in jail in Siberia. Could you marry into a better family? And besides, if certain activities of yours should attract attention.

SYEROV

What do you mean...?

COMRADE SONIA

Well, you seem to have a great deal of money lately—and in case anyone should notice it, it won't do any harm to be married into the right family.

SYEROV

Listen, Sonia, give me two days, will you—to think it over and get sort of used to the idea?

COMRADE SONIA

Certainly. Think it over. My time's up anyway. Have to run. Have three meetings at eight o'clock—and promised to attend them all...So long, Pavel.

(He lifts one hand weakly, without looking at her. She exits.)

SYEROV

(Grabs telephone)

Call Morozov again! Keep ringing!

(Starts writing a letter)

CURTAIN

SCENE 3

TIME:　　A few days later. Evening.

SCENE:　 Andrei's home. A fire is burning in the fireplace.

AT RISE: KIRA is sitting on the floor by the fire. ANDREI is standing
by the window. The music of a gay foreign operetta tune comes
from beyond the window.

KIRA

Andrei, where does that come from?

ANDREI

Abroad...It's the radio in the Party Club next door.

KIRA

Abroad...Such a place does exist somewhere, doesn't it?...

ANDREI

I like that music. I don't know why.

KIRA

It's the kind of music I liked...long ago...when I was a child...Andrei, have
you ever felt as if something had been promised you in your childhood, and you
look at yourself and you think: "I didn't know, then, that this is what would
happen to me"—and it's strange, and funny, and a little sad?

ANDREI

No. I was never promised anything. There were so many things that I didn't
know then, it's hard to be learning them now.
> (Turns away from the window abruptly, as if remembering something.
> Picks up a box and throws it down to Kira.)

It's something—from abroad.

KIRA

Oh, Andrei, I've asked you not to buy presents for me.

ANDREI

I've had this here for two weeks. I was waiting for you.

KIRA

I'm sorry. I couldn't come sooner.
> (Opens the box and produces a beautiful white, fluffy, gay-looking fur
> coat. She holds it up incredulously.)

Andrei...where did you get this?

ANDREI

I bought it. At the G.P.U. headquarters.

KIRA

Oh, Andrei! Do they wear things like that abroad!

ANDREI

Evidently.

KIRA

How...oh, how silly and how lovely!

ANDREI

Put it on. I want to see it.
>   (She puts the coat on. He watches her happily, smiling.)

KIRA

Well?

ANDREI

You look funny. You don't look like yourself at all.

KIRA

Not like a woman engineer.
>   (Tries to change her mood)
Andrei, where did the G.P.U. get a coat like this?

ANDREI

It was confiscated—from someone who tried to escape across the border.

KIRA

Wearing *this*?

ANDREI

Most of them dress in white and crawl through the snow, past the sentries—they try to.

KIRA

Do they get out?

ANDREI

A few have done it. Not many.

KIRA

Where?

ANDREI

Down on the Latvian frontier. North of Ostrov. There are some deep ravines down there that give them a chance...

KIRA

How good a chance?

ANDREI

One in a thousand.
(Looks at her, sees her eagerness, asks brusquely)
You're not mad enough to be thinking of *that*?

KIRA

I...

ANDREI

(Angrily)
Don't ever think of it!

KIRA

(Starts taking off the coat. Looks at the coat as she is removing it and stops
short suddenly.)
Oh!

ANDREI

What's the matter?

KIRA

(Showing him the back of the coat)
Andrei...there's a hole...a...
(He seizes the coat roughly. Looks at it. She says in a dull voice.)
So they took it away from a woman who was trying to cross the border...A
bullet hole?

ANDREI

I didn't know...I'm sorry, Kira. I wanted to give you something lovely...some-
thing cheerful...

KIRA

(Picks up the coat, says dully)
I want to keep it. A coat that almost got abroad...
(There is a sharp knock at the door. ANDREI raises his head impatiently,
snaps brusquely.)

ANDREI

Who's there?

Timoshenko's Voice

(Offstage)

It's me, Andrei. Stepan Timoshenko.

Andrei

I can't see you now, Stepan. I...

Timoshenko

(Throwing the door open)

Gotta see you, Andrei. Urgent. Very urgent.

(Sees Kira)

Oh...sorry to butt in like this, Andrei.

Kira

Good evening, Stepan.

(Walks away from them)

Andrei

What is it?

Timoshenko

I have a present for you, Andrei—a present from the pocket of Comrade Morozov. Comrade Morozov is drunk. I am sober. You know, Andrei, it's funny. Once upon a time we made a revolution. We had fools who thought in their doomed hearts that we made it for all those downtrodden ones who suffer on this earth. But you and me, Andrei, we have a secret. We know that the revolution—it was made for men like Comrade Syerov, the winners among those who crawl. That, pal, is the great slogan of the men of the future: those who crawl.

Andrei

What are you talking about?

Timoshenko

There was a man once, Andrei. A man executed at the G.P.U. He said something...and I can't forget it...He said, it was our own fault: once men were ruled with a god's thunder; then they were ruled with a sword; now they're ruled with a breadcard. Once they were held by reverence. Then they were held by fear. Now they're held by their stomachs. Only you don't hold heroes by their stomachs.[16] It was our own fault...

Andrei

Stepan...

---

[16] On revisions to this passage, see Appendix 3, "A Note on George Abbott."

TIMOSHENKO

Want proof of it?

(Fishes in his pocket and produces a crumpled piece of paper)

Listen to this: "Dear Morozov, you bastard! If you don't come across with what's due to me before tomorrow morning, you'll eat breakfast in the G.P.U." Signed—*Pavel Syerov.*

ANDREI

(Seizing the note)

How did you get this?

TIMOSHENKO

I've been picking pockets for the good of humanity.

ANDREI

Thank you, Stepan.

TIMOSHENKO

I'm not too sure you'll thank me before you get through this. I'm not too sure the Party will thank you either.

ANDREI

Stepan, don't you think that I see it all too? But we can still fight.

TIMOSHENKO

(Stops at door, grins somberly)

Sure, go on fighting. But I can't help you. You should take me by the scruff of my neck and kick me out, and then go and bow very low and lick a very big boot. But you won't do it. And that's why I hate you, Andrei. And that's why I wish you were my son. Only I'll never have a son. My sons are strewn all over the cat houses of the U.S.S.R... Good night, Comrades.

(Waves to them and exits)

ANDREI

You'll have to go home now, Kira.

KIRA

(Trying to sound calm)

Andrei, who is involved? Syerov and... Morozov?

ANDREI

(Looks at her, then)

Yes.

KIRA

Of course, they're powerful enough for any secret deal they'd want to make, aren't they?

ANDREI

(Still looking at her)

Yes.

KIRA

I've never trusted Syerov.

ANDREI

Kira, is he still a friend of yours?

KIRA

Who? Syerov?

ANDREI

No. Leo Kovalensky.

KIRA

(Stares at him, frozen, then)

Why do you ask that?

ANDREI

You're not interested in politics, are you?

KIRA

No. Why?

ANDREI

You've never wanted to sacrifice your life uselessly in jail or exile? Have you?

KIRA

What are you driving at?

ANDREI

Keep away from Leo Kovalensky.

KIRA

(Very slowly)

What do you mean?

ANDREI

He owns a certain private food store, doesn't he?

KIRA

Are you being the G.P.U. agent with me, and...

ANDREI

No, I'm not questioning you. I have nothing to learn from you. I know he runs that store and that's all I need to know. But I want to be sure that you don't let your name be implicated in any way.

KIRA

Implicated—in what?

ANDREI

Kira, I'm not a G.P.U. agent—with you or to you.
    (Silence)

KIRA

Andrei, Leo Kovalensky was the least guilty of the three. He had no other chance. He had no choice. He...

ANDREI

Kira, I don't want to learn how much you know about this case. I'm afraid I know already that you're not quite ignorant about it. I'm expecting the highest integrity from the men I'm going to face. Don't make me face them with less than that on my part.

KIRA

Andrei, listen and don't question me. I'm begging you—with all there is in me. If I ever meant anything to you, this is the only time I want to claim it—I'm begging you to drop this case, Andrei, while it's still in your hands!

ANDREI

    (Looks at her, asks slowly, icily)
Kira, what is that man to you?

KIRA

Just a friend...

ANDREI

Don't think of him. Not now. I need you. I need you more than I ever did. I'm sick of seeing what I see around me. I'm giving myself a last chance. Now I have something to put before the leaders of my Party. I know what they should do about it. In a very short while, I'll know whether I'll want to remain a member of the Party.

KIRA

Why make the test? You don't want to know the answer. You may lose too much.

ANDREI

I'll still have you.

(She looks at him.)

No matter what happens, I still have you. No matter what human crimes I see around me, I still have you. And—in you—I still know what a human being can be.

KIRA

(In a whisper)

Andrei, are you sure you know me?

ANDREI

That's the only thing I am sure of. That's the only certainty left to me. My highest reverence—and my only one.

KIRA

Andrei!...Don't say that!

ANDREI

(Quietly, firmly)

My highest reverence—and my only one.

(Drawing her into his arms)

Don't be afraid...I'm not complaining...I'm happy...happy that I'm sure of nothing but you...nothing...but you...

CURTAIN

SCENE 4

TIME: A few days later. Morning.

SCENE: Office of the G.P.U. Headquarters. A small, bare, austere room. Door Center back. Window in wall Left. A large desk and two chairs in front of window; three chairs facing it. No other furniture. One single large picture of Lenin on the wall.

AT RISE: The CHIEF of the G.P.U., a thin, blonde-bearded, unctuous gentleman, is seated behind the desk; his ASSISTANT, a suave sinister individual of indefinite age, sits beside him; PAVEL SYEROV and MOROZOV occupy the chairs facing the desk.

CHIEF

(Speaking into telephone)

Have Comrade Taganov come in.

(Hangs up)

MOROZOV

(Mopping his forehead)

Oh my Lord! Oh my Lord in Heaven! Oh my lord. My lord in heaven.

CHIEF

Keep quiet!

SYEROV

(Approaches the Assistant in a low voice)

Honest, pal, I don't want to hear all this, I was counting on you . . .

CHIEF

Sit down.

    (SYEROV obeys reluctantly.)

    (ANDREI enters. He stops on the threshold, looks at the gathering, startled.)

Close the door, Comrade Taganov.

    (ANDREI obeys.)

Sit down.

    (ANDREI sits down, facing the desk.)

My congratulations, Comrade Taganov.

    (ANDREI looks at him silently.)

You have done a valuable piece of work and rendered a great service to the Party by exposing a flagrant case of criminal speculation. The committee which investigated your report authorized me, as your chief, to extend to you the gratitude of your comrades in the G.P.U.

    (ANDREI bows curtly.)

ASSISTANT

Allow me to add my compliments, Comrade Taganov.

    (ANDREI bows.)

CHIEF

You have put into our hands just the case we needed. With the present difficult economic situation, the government must show the masses who is responsible for their suffering. The treacherous activities of speculators who deprive our toilers of their food rations, will be brought into the full light of proletarian justice . . . We shall make an example of this case. Every newspaper, every Club, every public pulpit will be mobilized for the task. The trial of Citizen Kovalensky will be broadcast into every hamlet of the U.S.S.R.

ANDREI

(Rising)

Whose trial, Comrade?

CHIEF

The trial of Citizen Kovalensky...Oh, yes, of course, by the way, Comrade Taganov, that letter of Comrade Syerov's, which you attached to your report on the case—was that the only copy of it in existence?

ANDREI

Yes, Comrade.

CHIEF

(Slowly)

Comrade Taganov, you will forget that you have read that letter.

(ANDREI looks at him silently.)

Do you know what is going on in our villages at the present time, Comrade Taganov?

ANDREI

Yes, Comrade.

CHIEF

Are you aware of the mood in our factories?

ANDREI

Yes, Comrade.

CHIEF

Do you realize the precarious equilibrium of our public opinion?

ANDREI

Yes, Comrade.

CHIEF

In that case, I do not have to explain to you why a Party member's name must be kept from any connection with a case of counterrevolutionary speculation. Am I understood?

ANDREI

Thoroughly, Comrade.

CHIEF

As to Comrade Syerov...

ASSISTANT

(Hastily, with forced lightness)

Hereafter, Comrade Syerov will confine his literary efforts to matters pertaining to his job on the railroad.

(SYEROV throws a slow, mocking glance at Andrei.)

I assume full responsibility for Comrade Syerov. I have known him for a long time, and even though he did allow himself a—shall we say—a lapse of discipline? I have full confidence that he will erase it from his record in the future.

SYEROV

(Leaning back in his chair comfortably)
Oh, sure, pal, sure. Don't worry.

CHIEF

I suggest a lesser degree of levity in the matter, Comrade Syerov. If it weren't for the kindness of your friend here . . .

(Points to his Assistant)

SYEROV

Well, I've worried till I'm seasick. What do you want? One has only so many hairs to turn gray.

CHIEF

But only one head under the hair.

SYEROV

What do you mean?
(To Assistant)
You have the letter, haven't you?

ASSISTANT

Not any more.

SYEROV

Where is it?!

ASSISTANT

In the furnace.

SYEROV

(Relaxing)
Thanks, pal.

ASSISTANT

You have good reason to be grateful. However, your aristocratic playmate, Citizen Kovalensky, will have to go on trial and . . .

SYEROV

Hell, do you think that will make me cry? I'll be only too glad to see that arrogant bastard get his white neck twisted!

CHIEF

(Turning to Morozov)

As for you, Comrade Morozov, your health requires a long rest and a trip to a warmer climate. I would suggest that you resign from the Food Trust. It would not be advisable to create a great deal of unnecessary comment about our Food Trust.

MOROZOV

(Mopping his forehead)

Oh, sure, Comrade, sure, I'll resign.

CHIEF

In acknowledgment of your resignation, we shall give you an assignment to a pleasant sanatorium in the Crimea. I would suggest that you take full advantage of the privilege for—let us say—six months. I would not advise you to hurry back, Comrade Morozov.

MOROZOV

No, Comrade, I won't hurry.

ASSISTANT

And if I were you, I wouldn't try to pull any wires for Kovalensky, even though he's going to the firing squad.

MOROZOV

Who, me, pull any wires? For him? Why should I, Comrade? Why should I? I had nothing to do with him. He owned that Food Store, he alone. You can look up the registration. He alone, sole owner. Sole owner.

CHIEF

Of course, Citizen Kovalensky was the real culprit and the dominant spirit of the conspiracy. He will be arrested tonight. Does that meet with your approval, Comrade Taganov?

ANDREI

My position does not allow me to approve, Comrade. Only to take orders.

CHIEF

Very well said, Comrade Taganov. Citizen Kovalensky is an aristocrat by birth, a living symbol of the class which is the bitterest enemy of the Soviets. Our working masses shall know who strikes deadly blows at the very heart of our economic life.

ANDREI

Yes, Comrade. A public trial with headlines in the papers and a radio microphone in the courtroom?

CHIEF

Precisely, Comrade Taganov.

ANDREI

And what if Citizen Kovalensky talks too much and too near the microphone? What if he mentions names?

CHIEF

Oh, nothing to fear, Comrade Taganov. Those gentlemen are easy to handle. He'll be promised life to say only what he's told to say. He'll be expecting a pardon even when he hears his death sentence.

ANDREI

And when he faces the firing squad—there will be no microphone on hand?

CHIEF

What's that, Comrade Taganov?

ANDREI

And it won't be necessary to explain how a penniless aristocrat managed to lay his hands on the very heart of our economic life.

CHIEF

Comrade Taganov, you have a remarkable gift for platform oratory. Too remarkable a gift. It is not always an asset to an agent of the G.P.U. You should be careful lest it be appreciated and you find yourself sent to a nice post—in the Turkestan, for instance, where you will have full opportunity to display it. Like Comrade Trotsky, for instance.

ANDREI

I have served in the Red Army under Comrade Trotsky.

CHIEF

I wouldn't remember that too often, Comrade Taganov, if I were you.

ANDREI

I shan't, Comrade. I shall do my best to forget it.

CHIEF

At seven o'clock tonight, Comrade Taganov, you will report for duty to search Citizen Kovalensky's apartment for additional evidence in connection with this case. No one else is to be informed. You will observe the strictest secrecy. And you will arrest Citizen Kovalensky.

ANDREI

Yes, Comrade. Is that all?

CHIEF

That's all, Comrade Taganov.

> (ANDREI turns and exits, closing the door slowly behind him.)

CURTAIN

SCENE 5

TIME: Same evening.

SCENE: Leo's home.

AT RISE: LEO is alone and is getting dressed for the evening. He has black trousers and a formal shirt on: he stands before a mirror, adjusting his tie. The doorbell rings. He glances at his wrist watch. There is a knock at the door.

LEO

Come in.

> (ANTONINA PAVLOVNA enters: she wears a magnificent fur wrap over a fleshy[17] evening gown. She is visibly nervous and upset. LEO waves to her lightly.)

Allo, Tonia...Sorry. Not quite ready yet. Sit down, will you? I'll be with you in a minute.

> (She sits down without a word, watching him nervously, a little astonished. He proceeds with his tie, his back turned to her.)

What will it be tonight? The European Roof Garden? The Club Monaco? Or is there any new place?

ANTONINA PAVLOVNA

> (Doesn't answer for a moment, then)

Leo...

LEO

> (Without turning)

Yes?

ANTONINA PAVLOVNA

Leo, are you sure you want to go out tonight?

---

[17] This should perhaps read "flashy"; otherwise, understand "revealing."

LEO

(Lightly)

I'm quite sure I haven't the slightest desire to. Not tonight nor at any other time. But what else is there to do?

(Turning)

Why?

ANTONINA PAVLOVNA

Is this a pose, Leo—or aren't you human?

LEO

No—to both questions, my dear. What's the matter?

ANTONINA PAVLOVNA

What's the matter?! With the G.P.U. investigating us...

(She looks at him. He says nothing, but smiles with a faint shrug, a smile which is not gay. She continues.)

...investigating us at this very minute, and God knows what they're going to do or when they're going to do it, how can you...

(She stops.)

LEO

(Calmly)

Yes?

ANTONINA PAVLOVNA

You know, I think Koko was at the G.P.U. office today. He's acting very strangely. But he won't tell me anything.

LEO

That's fortunate. Do you really enjoy hearing Koko talk? I don't.

ANTONINA PAVLOVNA

(She is almost screaming.)

Leo! Don't you realize how serious this is?!

LEO

(Quietly)

I realize it too well, my dear.

ANTONINA PAVLOVNA

Then why did you ask me to go out with you tonight?

LEO

That is precisely why.

ANTONINA PAVLOVNA

What do you mean?

LEO

What alternative would you suggest? Shall I sit at home, waiting, and amuse myself by thinking of what last words I'll say before the firing squad?

ANTONINA PAVLOVNA

We could try to do something.

LEO

What?

ANTONINA PAVLOVNA

(Helplessly)

Well...

LEO

Well, why worry? If we're caught—it'll be the end, so much the quicker.

ANTONINA PAVLOVNA

But, Leo...

LEO

We've been expecting it some day, haven't we? Well, maybe it has come. And I can't really say I'm sorry.

ANTONINA PAVLOVNA

What's the matter, Leo?

LEO

I'm so tired...

ANTONINA PAVLOVNA

(Uncertainly)

But, Leo, I thought you were happy. I thought you were enjoying it, these past months, all the wonderful evenings we've had together and we were just beginning to be such good friends, you and I, and...

LEO

Oh, yes. It's been wonderful. Throwing money away, night after night, in contemptible dives, among people I loathed, on drinks that tasted rotten, with a companion like you. Knowing all the while that I was paying with my life for every ruble and every minute of it...Well, that was my only answer to them. You don't fight with beautiful gestures today. Let the gestures fit the adversary.

Antonina Pavlovna

That doesn't make sense.

Leo

What do you think is easier? To go before the firing squad, quivering with love for that life you're leaving behind? Or to be so sick of it, so sick that even the squad comes to you as the sublime relief?

Antonina Pavlovna

Leo, I don't know what's happening to you!

Leo

Nothing, my dear. Just the charm of your company.

Antonina Pavlovna

Well, I did think that I could cheer you up on occasion. You can't have a good time with Kira Alexandrovna, who...

Leo

Shut up!
 (Looks at her, chuckles bitterly, adds)
No, you're right. Go on, talk about her. It's lovely—talking about her to *you*.

Antonina Pavlovna

Well, I only...

Leo

You're right. I couldn't take her to those places. She's like a reminder. A reminder of my future.[18] I must live up to her. But not you. With you, I can be what one has to be if one is to survive these days. With you—I'm so safe.

Antonina Pavlovna

Leo darling, I don't understand you at all.

Leo

That's why I like to be with you...You know, I admire you tremendously.

Antonina Pavlovna

 (Smiling happily)
I've really waited a long time to hear you say that.

---

[18] In the typescript, this line continues (but is crossed out): "—the future I should have had. The future I'll never have."

L E O

You're the perfect woman of our age. You've never had to squirm in agony, try-ing to accept the life around us. But if I'm cursed with that, it can be killed.

(Fiercely)

If I could reach such utter contempt for myself that I'd feel lower, lower than anyone around me...

(His hands fall limply.)

...then I could rest. Rest.

A N T O N I N A P A V L O V N A

Really, Leo, this is the craziest way I've ever heard a man make love to me. Or are you making love to me?

L E O

Certainly. Consider that I'm making love to you.

(Doorbell rings.)

Open that door, Tonia, will you please? I think the neighbors went out. I'll be ready in a moment.

(ANTONINA PAVLOVNA exits. LEO picks up a comb, stands combing his hair before the mirror. There is the sound of a door opening offstage; then ANTONINA'S scream, a horrified scream.)

(LEO stops still. Then, very slowly, very quietly, he puts the comb down. Then he turns, without haste, to look at the door.)

(Steps are heard approaching. The door is flung open. ANDREI enters followed by TWO SOLDIERS with bayonets. ANDREI is wearing a black leather jacket with a holster on his hip. At a motion of his hand, a THIRD SOLDIER remains stationed beyond the door, closing it.)

(LEO stands calmly, looking at them.)

L E O

Well, Comrade Taganov, didn't you know that some day we would meet like this?

A N D R E I

(Handing him a slip of paper, his voice impersonal, official, expressionless)

Search warrant, Citizen Kovalensky.

L E O

(Bowing graciously)

Go ahead. You're quite welcome.

(ANDREI motions to the soldiers sharply, one to the bed, the other to the bathroom. ANDREI walks to a desk, opens the drawers, goes through them swiftly, gathering all letters and papers, slipping them into his briefcase. LEO stands alone in the middle of the room; the OTHERS pay no attention to him. He watches the search indifferently. Then...)

Shall I step out? Or do you intend going through me, too, like this? I wish you would. I'd be curious to know what you'd find inside of me.

ANDREI

You're to remain here.

(The search continues. SOLDIER at bed has gone through suitcase and thrown it to back of sofa. LEO takes a cigarette case from his pocket, opens it and extends it to ANDREI.)

No, thank you.

(LEO lights a cigarette, the quiver of the match in his unsteady fingers— the first sign to betray his nervousness.)

(ANDREI crosses to mantle. Opens briefcase and throws out papers and envelopes.)

LEO

The survival of the fittest. However, the fittest are not always those to survive. Usually, it's the other way around. What are your philosophical convictions, Comrade Taganov? We've never had a chance to discuss that. And this is as good a time as any.

ANDREI

I suggest that you keep silent.

LEO

And when a representative of the G.P.U. suggests, it's a command, isn't it? I realize that one should know how to respect the dignity and the grandeur of authority under all circumstances, no matter how trying to the self-respect of those in power.

(A SOLDIER raises his hand menacingly and makes a step toward Leo.)

ANDREI

Get back!

(SOLDIER from bathroom appears in doorway.)

(ANDREI opens the door of a wardrobe, disclosing Kira's dresses hanging in a row. With a sudden jerk, he reaches for one of them.)

LEO

What's the matter, Comrade Taganov?

(ANDREI is holding Kira's red dress. He looks at it for a long moment, holding it spread out awkwardly in his two hands. Then he looks at the open wardrobe.)

ANDREI

Whose is this?

LEO

(With deliberate, mocking, insulting contempt)

My mistress's.

> (ANDREI straightens the dress out slowly and hangs it back in the wardrobe, cautiously, a little awkwardly, as if it were of breakable glass. LEO chuckles.)

A disappointment, isn't it, Comrade Taganov?

> (ANDREI doesn't answer. He takes the dresses out one by one, and runs his fingers through the pockets and linings. Voices rise suddenly behind the door Left.)

SOLDIER'S VOICE[19]

(Offstage)

I say you can't, Citizen! You can't go in now!

> (There is the sound of a struggle behind the door, the sound of a body being thrown aside violently.)

KIRA'S VOICE

(Offstage. A savage scream.)

Let me in there! Let me in!

> (ANDREI nods to SOLDIER to open door. KIRA stands on the threshold. She stares, frozen, as she sees him. He looks at her silently. Then:)

ANDREI

(Slowly, evenly)

Citizen Argounova, do you live here?

KIRA

(Her eyes on his)

Yes.

> (The SOLDIER closes the door. ANDREI turns away from her, very slowly, with an immense effort. He orders the soldiers.)

ANDREI

Search that box in the fireplace.[20]

---

[19] The typescript has "Guard's Voice."

[20] This refers to the small stoves called "bourgeoise," which were inserted into the fireplaces in many middle-class homes (hence the name). These appear regularly in the novel, and one is described in act 1, scene 3, of the other play (see above p. 35).

LEO

(To Kira)

I'm sorry, dearest. I hoped it would be over before you came back.

(She does not seem to hear. She is staring at Andrei.)

ANDREI

(To the soldiers)

Search that.

(The SOLDIERS obey, searching sofa and tearing open a pillow. The room is fast becoming a shambles.)

That will be all.

(Turning to Leo)

Citizen Kovalensky, you're under arrest.

LEO

I'm sure this is the most pleasant duty you've ever performed, Comrade Taganov...Shall I change my clothes?

ANDREI

We haven't the time.

LEO

As you wish.

(ANDREI stands waiting. LEO gets his hat and overcoat. He stops before Kira on his way out.)

Aren't you going to say goodbye, Kira?

(Takes her in his arms, violently, possessively, and kisses her. ANDREI stands looking at them.)

I have only one favor to ask, Kira. I hope you'll forget me.

(She does not answer. A SOLDIER holds the door open. ANDREI walks out, followed by LEO and the SECOND SOLDIER, who closes the door behind them. KIRA stands, sagging, at the wall.)

CURTAIN

ACT 3

SCENE 1

TIME: Same evening.

SCENE: Party Club. The room is in semi-darkness, lighted only by a single lamp. The light is focused upon the speaker's pulpit and the scarlet banner behind it.

AT RISE: A sloppy ATTENDANT is preparing the room for a meeting. He lines the chairs around the table, polishes a few ash trays, shuffling about lazily, indifferently. KIRA enters. She stops at the door, looking about vaguely. Her face is set, hard; she does not seem to see anything around her; there is an air of such unnatural calm about her that the ATTENDANT looks at her, startled and a little uncomfortable, even before she notices him and approaches him slowly.[21]

ATTENDANT

Your Party card, Comrade?
        (Extends his hand for it)

KIRA

        (In a dead, implacable voice, unconscious of his request)
I want to see Comrade Taganov.

ATTENDANT

Strangers ain't allowed at Club meetings, Citizen. Comrade Taganov is...

KIRA

        (Stonily)
He is here. He is making a speech here tonight. Call him.

ATTENDANT

Oh, yes. Comrade Taganov's going to read a thesis tonight, on the...on the...
        (Picks up a bulletin from the table, glances at it)
...that's it: on the "Basic Philosophy of Communism."

KIRA

Tell him to come here.

---

[21] For both scenes in act 3, I have added TIME, SCENE, and AT RISE (which are missing in the typescript), and divided the text (otherwise without change) accordingly.

ATTENDANT

(Scratching his head)

Well, Citizen, it's against the rules, on the one hand, and on the other...

(ANDREI enters. He is wearing his black, leather jacket, as in the preceding scene. He stops short. KIRA turns to look at him. Without tearing his eyes from her, he motions the ATTENDANT to get out, with a quick jerk of his thumb over his shoulder. The ATTENDANT exits hastily, frightened. KIRA and ANDREI stand looking at each other silently. Her face is suddenly menacing, loose, brutal.)

ANDREI

(Slowly)

If I were you, I'd get out of here.

(She doesn't move.)

Get out of here.

(She tears her hat and coat off, throws them aside.)

What do you want? I have nothing to say to you.

KIRA

But I have! And you'll listen. So you've caught me—haven't you?—and you're going to have your revenge? Go ahead. Have your revenge. And this is mine. I'm not pleading for him. I have nothing to fear any more. But, at least, I can speak. I have so much to say to you, to all of you, and I've kept silent for so long! I have nothing to lose. You have.

ANDREI

Don't you think it's useless? Why say anything? If you have any excuses to offer...

KIRA

You fool! I'm proud of what I've done! Hear me? I'm proud! So you think I loved you? Well, then listen: all you were to me, all you meant was only a pack of white, crisp, square ten ruble bills with a sickle and hammer printed in the corner! Do you know where those bills went? To a tubercular sanatorium in the Crimea. Do you know what they paid for? For the life of someone I loved before I ever saw you, and now you've locked him in a cell and you're going to shoot him. Why not? Shoot him. Take his life. You've paid for it.

(She looks at him. He does not seem hurt or angry: he seems frightened.)

ANDREI

Kira...I...I didn't know...

KIRA

No, you didn't know. But it was very simple. He wanted to live. He had no right to that, had he? Your State said so. We tried to beg, we begged humbly. But then someone[22] told me that one hundred thousand workers died in the civil war and why couldn't one aristocrat die—in the face of the Union of Socialist Soviet Republics?...

(Laughs, approaching him)

Remember? Remember that? Do you know the answer now?

ANDREI

Kira...

KIRA

You didn't know, you and your comrades? You came and you forbade life to the living. But one of you has been paid. I paid it. How do you like it, Comrade Taganov of the All-Union Communist Party? If you taught us that our life is nothing before the State—well, then, are you really suffering? You loved a woman and she threw your love in your face? But the proletarian mines in the Don basin have produced a hundred tons of coal last month! You've lost your faith. But the proletarian Republic is building a new electric plant on the Volga! It's still there, your Collective. Go and join it. Did anything really happen to you? It's nothing but a personal problem of a private life, isn't it? Don't you have something greater—to live for? Or do you, Comrade Taganov?

(He does not answer. She laughs, approaching him, screams in his face.)

Why don't you speak? Have you nothing to say? Are you wondering why you've never really known me? Here's what's left of me after you took him—and do you know what it meant when you reached for my highest reverence...

(She stops short. She gasps, a choked little sound, as if he had slapped her.)

(She slams the back of her hand against her open mouth. She stands, silent, her eyes staring at something she understands suddenly, clearly, fully, for the first time.)

(He smiles, slowly, very gently. He stretches his hands out, palms up, shrugging sadly an explanation she does not need. She moans.)

Oh, Andrei...

ANDREI

Kira...I understand.

KIRA

Oh, Andrei, Andrei, what have I done to you?

ANDREI

It's not what you've done to me...It's what you had to suffer...and I...I gave you that suffering, and all those moments were to you...to you...

(His voice breaks.)

---

[22] Andrei (see p. 220 above); but it was someone else in the novel and the other version of the play.

KIRA

Andrei...

ANDREI

I want you to go home now. You must rest. Rest for a few days. Don't go any-where. There's nothing you can do. Don't worry about...him. Leave that to me.

KIRA

But you, Andrei...

ANDREI

(Slowly, gently)

Kira, don't you think it's better if we don't say anything—and just leave it to...to our silence, knowing that we both understand and that we still have that much in common?

KIRA

(In a whisper)

Yes.

(She slowly crosses to door and exits.)

(ANDREI turns slowly, walks away from the door, stops. He stands motionless, looking up at the words on the red banner over the pulpit. Then goes to the door and calls off.)

ANDREI

Tell Pavel Syerov to come here.

YOUNG COMMUNIST

Yes, Comrade.

(After a pause the door opens and SYEROV enters breezily. He stops short, taken aback, seeing Andrei; then recovers himself quickly, and throws at him in a forcedly light, mocking voice.)

SYEROV

Well, what is it?

ANDREI

(Stonily)

I want to speak to you.

SYEROV

(Rudely, but stopping, nevertheless)

I'll hear enough of you at the meeting.

ANDREI

I don't think you want the others to hear what I'm going to tell you.

SYEROV

Maybe I don't want to hear it either. Still going strong, eh? I thought you had learned a lesson in the last few days.

ANDREI

I have.

SYEROV

What else do you want?

ANDREI

You're not staying for the meeting tonight. You're going out and you haven't much time to lose.

SYEROV

Am I? Glad you let me in on the little secret. Where am I going?

ANDREI

To release Leo Kovalensky.

SYEROV

Gone insane, Taganov, have you?

ANDREI

You'd better keep still and listen. You'll go from here to see your friend, and you know what friend I mean. What you'll tell him and how you'll tell it is none of my business. All I have to know is that Leo Kovalensky is released within forty-eight hours.

SYEROV

Now will you let me in on the little magic wand that will make me do it?

ANDREI

It's a little paper wand, Syerov. Two of them.

SYEROV

Written by whom?

ANDREI

You.

SYEROV

Huh?!

ANDREI

Photographed from one written by you, to be exact.

SYEROV

You God damned rat!

(ANDREI watches him silently.)

(SYEROV screams.)

I'll go to see my friend all right! And you'll see Leo Kovalensky all right—and it won't take forty-eight hours either! You'll get a cell next to his. And then we'll find out what documents...

ANDREI

There are two photostats, as I said. Only I don't happen to have either one of them.

SYEROV

What...what did you...

ANDREI

They're in the possession of two friends I can trust. Their instructions are that if anything happens to me before Leo Kovalensky is released—the photostats go to Moscow. Also—if anything happens to him after he's out.

SYEROV

You God damned...

ANDREI

You don't want those photostats to reach Moscow. Your friend won't be able to save your neck, then, nor his own, perhaps.

SYEROV

(Hoarsely)

You're lying. You've never taken any photostats.

ANDREI

Maybe. Want to take a chance on that?

SYEROV

(After a pause)

Listen, Andrei, let's talk sense. All right, you're holding the whip. Still, do you know what you're asking?

ANDREI

No more than you can do.

SYEROV

But, good Lord in heaven, Andrei! It's such a big case and they're getting a first class propaganda campaign ready, and...

ANDREI

Stop them.

SYEROV

But how can I?

ANDREI

Your friend can. Nobody knows who enters or leaves the G.P.U. Nobody will know if he keeps it quiet.

SYEROV

But how can I ask him? What am I going to tell him?

ANDREI

That's none of my business.

SYEROV

Andrei, one of us has gone crazy. I can't figure it out. Why do you want Kovalensky released?

ANDREI

That's none of your business.

SYEROV

And if you've appointed yourself his guardian angel, then why the hell did you start the whole damn case? You started it, you know.

ANDREI

You said that I had learned a lesson.

SYEROV

All right. You win—this time. It's no use threatening you with any retaliation. Fellows like you get theirs without any help from fellows like me. In a year, this little mess will be forgotten. I'll be running the railroads of the U.S.S.R. You'll be kicked out of the Party.

ANDREI

Good luck, Comrade Syerov.

SYEROV

Good luck, Comrade Taganov.

> (Exits)[23]

> (COMRADE SONIA enters, followed by a group of COMMUNISTS.)

FIRST COMMUNIST

> (To Comrade Sonia)

My congratulations!

SECOND COMMUNIST

What's that?

FIRST COMMUNIST

Didn't you know? Comrade Sonia and Pavel Syerov were married yesterday.

COMRADE SONIA

> (In another group)

Who's the speaker tonight?

THIRD COMMUNIST

Andrei Taganov.

---

[23] There is a problem with the next set of lines, and I have revised them in the hopes of restoring sense (in part relying on Version V A). What follows are the sequence both in Version V A and in Version V B:

> *Version V A*:
> (SONIA and TWO YOUNG COMMUNISTS enter followed by other party club members.)

FIRST COMMUNIST: What's that?
SECOND COMMUNIST: Didn't you know? Comrade Sonia and Pavel Syerov were married yesterday.
FIRST COMMUNIST: (To Comrade Sonia) My congratulations!
THIRD COMMUNIST: (In another group) Who's the speaker tonight?
FOURTH COMMUNIST: Andrei Taganov.
THIRD COMMUNIST: Oh, *that one*? Still here? I'd like to see the list of the next Party purging!

> *Version V B*:
> (SONIA and TWO YOUNG COMMUNISTS enter followed by other party club members.)

FIRST COMMUNIST: What's that?
SECOND COMMUNIST: Didn't you know? Comrade Sonia and Pavel Syerov were married yesterday.
FIRST COMMUNIST: (To Comrade Sonia) My congratulations!
COMRADE SONIA: (In another group) Who's the speaker tonight?
FOURTH COMMUNIST: Andrei Taganov.
COMRADE SONIA: Oh, *that one*? ~~Still here? I'd like to see the list of the next Party purging!~~
[Next to these crossed out words, Rand added, in pencil: "That makes it nice!"]

COMRADE SONIA

Oh, *that one*? How nice. I'd like to see the list for the next Party purging!

(The OLDER EXAMINER sees the CHIEF enter and raps for the members to take their seats at the table. ANDREI joins them. The CHIEF nods a curt greeting and takes his place at the head of the table. He looks at the papers before him, then strikes his gavel.)

CHIEF

I declare this meeting of the All Union Communist Party Club of the Eleventh District of Leningrad open. First on the order of the day is a thesis on the "Basic Philosophy of Communism" by Comrade Andrei Taganov. Word is now given to Comrade Taganov.

(ANDREI rises and mounts the speaker's pulpit. Stands looking at the room; then speaks, his voice dull, mechanical, as if he were unconscious of his own words.)

ANDREI

Comrades...In these days of struggle, when the eyes of the world are upon us, we hear many people condemning our methods, while admiring profoundly our ideals. It is, therefore, imperative for us to keep clear in our minds the basic principles of our great cause, which shall justify all our actions...The rock upon which we build is our faith in the supremacy, the preeminence, the all-inclusive power of the Collective. The State, which is the symbol of men's brotherhood, recognizes no right but its own right, no will but its own will. The Collective is our single god and the State is its single prophet. To this great conception all else must be sacrificed...To this great conception...all else...even the most precious woman on earth...even the lovely...the single...the unrepeatable...

CHIEF

Comrade Taganov!

(Strikes gavel)

I'm calling you to order.

(A wave of whispers runs through the room.)

ANDREI

Yes, Comrade Chairman...To this great conception...What was I saying, Comrade Chairman?...Oh, yes. To this great conception all else must be sacrificed. Man does not exist save as a useful servant to all other men. The good of all is good for all. When this is reached, no man on earth shall go hungry. Such is our faith. Such is our great work...Our great work...We came and we forbade life to the living.

CHIEF

Comrade Taganov! I'm calling you to order!

ANDREI

Comrades! Brothers! Listen to me! Listen, you consecrated warriors of a new life, you who seek the great and the sacred! Nothing is great but Man. Nothing is sacred but his freedom. He is not the means to any end. He is the end and the reason of reasons. He has a right which no brother, not even all his brothers together, can take away from him—the right to the aim and the meaning of his own life. For there are things in men, in the best of us, which must not be touched by others. You cannot change it. You cannot change it because that's the way man is born, alone, complete, an end in himself. But we've tried. Now look at those whom we allow to triumph. Deny Man's ego—then look at those who will be able to survive. Whom are we sacrificing—and to whom? Do we want the crippled, crawling, lying monstrosities that we're producing? Are we not castrating life in order to perpetuate it?

CHIEF

Comrade Ta...

ANDREI

Brothers! We have to answer this! What are we doing? Do we want to feed humanity in order to let it live? Or do we want to strangle its life in order to feed it?

CHIEF

Comrade Taganov! I deprive you of speech!

ANDREI

I...I...I have nothing more to say.

(Staggers down the pulpit steps)

CURTAIN

SCENE 2

TIME: A week later.

SCENE: Leo's Home. Afternoon. Snowflakes flutter lazily beyond the windows.

AT RISE: LEO is standing at a window, looking out, motionless, a forgotten cigarette burning in his hands. The strains of "YOU FELL AS A VICTIM," the revolutionary funeral march, played by a military band, are coming from the street, approaching. THE NEIGHBOR rushes in; she is dressed for the street.

NEIGHBOR

Citizen Kovalensky, I left soup cooking on my Primus stove, will you watch it for me please?

LEO

Yes.

NEIGHBOR

Aren't you going to the funeral?

LEO

No.

NEIGHBOR

I'll be fired if I don't march in the procession. By the way, whom are they burying?

LEO

A Communist.

NEIGHBOR

But who was he anyway?

LEO

Don't you hear that music? Know the words? "You fell as a victim...of endless devotion to the people." Funny. They used to sing it secretly under the Czar. Now it's their official dirge.

NEIGHBOR

But what's his name? Who was he?

LEO

Just a victim of endless devotion.

NEIGHBOR

(Glancing at window)

Lord help me, I'll be late! Don't let my soup burn please, Citizen!

(Rushes out)

(LEO stands motionless. The cigarette burns out; he shudders, as it reaches his fingers; throws it away; takes another cigarette from a box on the table and looks vaguely, absent-mindedly for a match, even though the matches are right before him; drops the cigarette; stands staring ahead; notices the match box, picks it up and looks at it, wondering, for he has forgotten what he wanted; drops the matches, walks to window again. The music swells, then begins to die down slowly as the funeral procession passes.)

(KIRA enters. She is dressed for the street. LEO whirls about, looks at her fixedly, without a word. She removes her coat and hat silently, wearily, her movements slow, spent, indifferent.)

LEO

You didn't follow the procession to the end?

KIRA

No.

LEO

They're burying him in state, aren't they?

KIRA

Yes.

LEO

A nice little trick of propaganda. The papers are full of it.
(Picks up a newspaper, reads)
"Glory eternal to the victims of the revolution! Comrade Andrei Taganov, who committed suicide under the strain of overwork, in his service to the Party..."

KIRA

Leo, please...

LEO

Of course, you don't want to hear it. I understand.
(She looks at him.)
I wonder whether the revolution really killed him, or you did, or both.

KIRA

(Whirling toward him)
Leo!

LEO

Of course, this is not a good time to speak about it. Right on the day of your lover's funeral.

KIRA

My lover...

LEO

Shut up!...No, I'll give you a chance to talk. I'll give you the chance to answer just one word. Were you Taganov's mistress?

KIRA

(She looks at him, then:)

Yes.

LEO

All the time I was away?

KIRA

Yes.

LEO

And all the time since I came back?

KIRA

Yes.
   (Silence)

LEO

Would you mind telling me just why you kept me on while you had him? Was it my money and his position?

KIRA

   (Sits)
Who told you, Leo?

LEO

Our dear friend Pavel Syerov. He stopped me on the street this morning—to congratulate me.
   (She says nothing.)
Really, you know, it's funny. You and your Communist hero! I thought he had died making a great sacrifice, saving me for you. But he was just tired of you, he probably wanted to leave you on my hands. So much for the sublime in the human race.

KIRA

We don't have to speak of him, do we?

LEO

Still love him?

KIRA

That makes no difference to you—does it?

LEO

No. None. I won't even ask whether you had ever loved me. That, too, makes no difference. I'd rather think you hadn't. It will make the future...easier.

KIRA

The ... future, Leo?

LEO

Well, what did you plan it to be?

KIRA

I want ...

LEO

Oh, I know. Try to run away and get shot on the border. Or beg for a respectable Soviet job and rot while they're refusing it. You want me to begin all over again—as we did once—don't you? ... To begin again—to struggle, to beg, to wait, to hold on—and to suffer! Well, I'm through with it. I'm going to have champagne and white bread and limousines and no thoughts of any kind, and long live the Dictatorship of the Proletariat!

KIRA

Leo ... what ... are you going to do?

LEO

I'm going away.

KIRA

Where?

LEO

(She sits down facing him.)
Citizen Morozov has left town.

KIRA

Well?

LEO

He's left Tonia—he wants no connections that could be investigated. But he's left her a nice little sum of money—oh, quite nice. She's going for a vacation in the Caucasus. She has asked me to go with her. I've accepted the job. Leo Kovalensky, the great gigolo of the U.S.S.R.!

KIRA

Leo!

LEO

You're not going to be fool enough to faint, are you?

KIRA

Leo...*you*...like a...

LEO

Don't bother about the names. You can't think of any as good as the ones I've thought of myself...I'm happy when I think of those names. That's my solution. From now on, nothing that anyone could do to me will be worse than what I've done myself. That, too, is a kind of freedom...

KIRA

Leo! What have they done to you!

LEO

(In an even, indifferent voice)

Did it ever occur to you what fools we are? We torture ourselves seeking joy, beauty, honor, thinking that our holy quest will give us relief from the agony. We can't be hurt through the things we hate. Only through the things we love...But to give up and give in, to accept our century as it is, to hold nothing precious and nothing sacred, never to be hurt again nor astonished—*that*, my dear, is the only enviable achievement left to us...

(And suddenly, like an explosion, his voice is eager, desperate.)

Kira!

(She looks at him, a silent, startled question in her eyes.)

Kira, did you ever love me?

KIRA

I...

LEO

If you did, if you can remember it, if you can remember one single moment when I was precious to you, in the name of that, in the name of a last charity, the kind of charity one grants at a death bed—*don't try to stop me* now, Kira!...Don't... try...to stop me...

KIRA

Leo, when did you tell her that you'd go with her?

LEO

Three days ago.

KIRA

Before you knew anything about Andrei and me?

LEO

Yes.

KIRA

While you still thought that I loved you?

LEO

Yes.

KIRA

If they hadn't told you, you'd still go with her?

LEO

Yes.

KIRA

Leo... please listen carefully... it's very important... please answer this one question honestly, as honestly as you can: if you were to learn suddenly—it doesn't matter how—but if you were to learn that I love you, that I've always loved you—would you still go with her?

LEO

Yes.

KIRA

And... if you *had to* stay with me? If you learned something—from the past—that... that bound you to stay—would you try it once more?

LEO

If I were bound to—well, who knows? I might do what your other lover did. That's also a solution. Why do you ask that? What is there to bind me?

KIRA

(Looking straight at him, her head high, with the greatest calm of her life.)

Nothing, Leo.

LEO

(Looks at her silently. Then:)

Really, you know, I still think you're wonderful. I was afraid of hysterics. It's ended as it should have ended.

KIRA

Yes, Leo.

(He rises. She stands looking at him. Then she asks, very quietly.)

Leo, will you kiss me—once? You see, I'm not quite as strong as you hoped I'd be. And for one last moment, will you forget what we are? Kiss me for what we could have been.

> (He looks at her, approaches, takes her in his arms, kisses her, a long kiss. Then she steps aside.)

LEO

(Softly)

Kira, I'll be back in Petrograd. I'll be back when years have passed, and years make such a difference, don't they? Then it won't hurt us so much...We'll meet again, Kira. I'll be back.

KIRA

(Quietly)

I won't be here, Leo.

LEO

Where are you going?

KIRA

(With the intensity of a maniac)

Abroad.

LEO

How?

> (She walks to wardrobe, takes out the white fur coat.)

Kira! That's certain death!

KIRA

Probably. But I'll try to get out...to get out...only to get out...

LEO

Do you think they'll let you out?

KIRA

Of what use am I to them? They have a whole country, a whole nation. They have millions to rule. I have only my life...my one life...

LEO

Kira, why take the chance? Why struggle? What is there left?

KIRA

Nothing. Nothing but that I know I'm still alive—and can't give up.

LEO

Give up? What? It's been taken away from you.

KIRA

Has it?…Leo, listen to me. I'd like you to remember this—even though you can't understand it any longer. I wanted two things. To be a builder—and you. They took the building away from me. Now they've taken you. But there's something they can't take. That thing in me which knew how to want. That thing which chooses its desires—and is more important than its choice or its desire. You were my only love,[24] Leo—and that doesn't matter. It matters only that *I* loved you. *I*, Leo.

LEO

But you're going out to be killed.

KIRA

Perhaps. I don't know. It doesn't matter. It matters only that I keep—to the last minute—something they can't destroy, the thing they're destroying here. And that's what I hate them for. For the thing they've killed in you. I'll keep it, Leo—to the last minute—for you…for Andrei Taganov…and perhaps for many others whom I'll never know.

LEO

What thing?

KIRA

The spirit, Leo—not of the people, not of the masses—but the greatest and the only one that matters—the spirit of a single human being alone.

CURTAIN

---

[24] They typescript has "You were my only my love."

PART II

Additional Materials

Excerpts from Other Versions

I. Five Miscellaneous Scenes

1. Kira and Comrade Sonia at the Student Purging

From act 1, scene 2, of Version II D. Students are waiting to hear the results of the recent purging.

First Girl

Oh, why don't they hurry!

Second Girl

Comrade Sonia, do you know when the list will come out?

Comrade Sonia

(Slaps her affectionately on the shoulder)

What's the matter, dear? You're not afraid of such a little matter as this purging? You're a member in good standing of my Marxist Club, so you have nothing to fear. Comrade Sonia is your friend. Comrade Sonia is everybody's friend!

First Girl

Good God, Comrade Sonia! I didn't know it made a difference—belonging to your club, I mean. You said...you said, when you were enrolling members, that it was strictly voluntary, that we didn't have to join.

Comrade Sonia

(Coldly, ominously)

No. You didn't have to.

First Girl

You said it was *voluntary*!

Comrade Sonia

It was. And you didn't find it necessary to join, did you, dear? So we received a voluntary expression of your attitude toward your social duties. It was eloquent.

First Girl

But I didn't know! I...

(Breaking down suddenly)

Oh, I can't! I can't! I can't lose my place here!...I've got to graduate!...I've got to get a job!...Mother's starving...if I'm thrown out...what'll become of us?

KIRA

(Entering Right, a briefcase under her arm)
Stop acting like a damn coward!

BOY

(Waving to her)
Kira! Where have you been?

KIRA

In class.

SECOND GIRL

Today?

KIRA

Why not?

SECOND GIRL

But...

KIRA

What are you all doing here? Waiting, trembling, showing them how frightened you are?

COMRADE SONIA

Aren't you, Comrade Argounova?

KIRA

What?

COMRADE SONIA

Frightened.

KIRA

(Looks at her, says calmly)
I wouldn't confess that so openly if I were you, Comrade Sonia.

COMRADE SONIA

Confess what?

KIRA

That you'd enjoy hearing me say Yes.

Comrade Sonia

(Shrugging)

Well, we shall see what we shall see and we won't have long to wait.

2. Leo's Tuberculosis

From the end of act 1, scene 3, in Versions II B–D.[1]

Kira

(Tearing herself away from him, terrified)

Leo! Leo, what happened?

Leo

(Pulls himself together with an effort, speaks in a set, expressionless voice)

It happened long ago. In those cells of the G.P.U. that weren't heated very well. Only I didn't know it. But I've seen a doctor, Kira.

Kira

(Stares at him for a long moment. Then whispers, her voice choked.)

What...did...he...say?

Leo

Tuberculosis.

Kira

(After a long pause. Stares at him incredulously. Whispers impatiently.)

Well?...

(In a dead, flat voice)

Well, what did he say? What did he tell you to do?

Leo

Nothing.

Kira

(Screaming suddenly)

Leo! What did he say? What did he...

Leo

What he said doesn't matter, Kira. Because there's nothing to be done.

Kira

What did he say?!

---

[1] There are no variations among these three, though in Version II D the entire scene is crossed out.

LEO

Rest. Sunshine. Fresh air. Food. Human food. I need a sanatorium for this winter. In the south. The Crimea. One more winter in Petrograd will be as certain as a firing squad for me. That's what he said. But there's no point in torturing yourself and me by discussing the impossible.

KIRA

You mean...you're going to die?
(He shrugs. She looks at him. Then she laughs softly, almost soundlessly.)

LEO

What are you laughing at?

KIRA

(Quietly)
It's nonsense, Leo. You don't expect me to take it seriously, do you? You wouldn't stand there and tell me that you're going to cut your head off in a moment and expect me to be frightened, would you?

LEO

(Frightened)
Kira...!

KIRA

(With the calm of an insane stubbornness)
Well, you're sick. I'm sorry to hear that. But there's nothing to worry about. You'll go south and be cured. If they'd told me that you had to go through a long, painful illness, I'd be frightened. I'd cry, probably. But when they say you're going to die—it's just silly. They're laughing at me. You know they are.

LEO

Stop it, Kira. We won't talk about it.

KIRA

Don't look so serious. It's nonsense. Don't you see it's nonsense. You have no right to believe it. I love you. We all have to suffer. We all have things we want that are taken away from us. It's all right. But there's something in each of us, like the very heart of life condensed—and that shouldn't be touched. You understand, don't you? Well, you are that to me, and you can't tell me you're going to die, because you can't let me stand here, and look at you, and talk, and breathe, and move, and then tell me you're going to die—we're not insane, both of us, are we, Leo?

LEO

(Softly, tenderly, puts his arm around her, leads her to a chair, makes her sit down and sits beside her.)

You see, dear, why I didn't want to tell you. I thought something could be done. It can't. I've heard the last refusal today—the final one. I'm used to it now. You must get used to it too. And then we must forget about it—until it happens.

KIRA

What are you saying? You're going south.

LEO

(Shrugs, shakes his head)

Kira, where do you suppose I've been every evening, these last few weeks? Hospitals. State hospitals. Begging them for a place in a sanatorium in the Crimea. You know what they said? The first official I saw said: "You're not a member of the Party? You're not a member of a Trade Union? You're joking, Citizen." The second one said: "We have hundreds on our waiting lists. Trade Union members. We can't even register you." The third one ordered his secretary to throw me out.

KIRA

But you're going to die!

LEO

But I'm not a Trade Union member.

KIRA

Did you explain to them that you're going to *die?*

LEO

(Quietly)

I'm not alive for them now, Kira. They look at me as if they were staring at an empty office. They listen to me as if they heard a noise coming from nowhere. I'm not a man to them, Kira, because such a thing *as a man*—it doesn't exist.

KIRA

But...

LEO

Don't try to understand it. We can't. And they can't understand what we're begging them for and why we want to live. One single man who wants to live—it's only a blank sentence to them, only sounds without any meaning at all. You can repeat and repeat it to them, you can cry and scream it, but what's the use? They don't hear you. They don't understand.

KIRA

There are private sanatoriums in the Crimea. There are places where you can go without an order from them.

LEO

(In a dead voice)

There are.

KIRA

Well?

LEO

I've asked. I was told I could leave for the Crimea tomorrow. All I have to do is deposit a sum we couldn't earn in three years.

KIRA

We can borrow it.

LEO

From whom? Your mother?

KIRA

I know people. I'll ask at the office. I'll...

(Stops at a sudden thought)

I'll go to see Andrei Taganov. He can get you a place in a State sanatorium. If not—he'll loan me the money. He must get a big salary.

LEO

(Furiously)

You won't go near him! Do you hear? You won't breathe a word to him! I don't want my life as a present from that G.P.U. murderer!

KIRA

(Softly, incredulously)

Your life...Leo...

(Her whole attitude changes. There is no fear, no despair in her manner any longer. There is an inexorable determination. She is completely matter of fact.)

You must take your clothes off, Leo, and go to bed. I think your shoes are wet. I'll put them on the stove to dry. I'll get you some milk and fresh eggs. It will help—until you go to the Crimea.

LEO

Oh, Kira, I don't want you to try it all over again, and go through the hell I've been through—for nothing.

KIRA

(Inexorably)

You said we must forget about it. You were right. Don't let's talk about it anymore. *You're going* to the Crimea—and there's nothing else to discuss.

Leo

Give it up, Kira. You know, I think...I think I'm glad. I was frightened at first. But I'm not—now. Everything seems so much simpler—when there's a limit set. We can still be together—for a while. When it becomes contagious—well...

> (Shrugs. She stands looking at him. He whirls toward her suddenly.)

Let's borrow some vodka from our good neighbor Comrade Lavrova, and let's drink, drink and the hell with all of it!

Kira

Leo!

Leo

Don't stare at me like that!...It's a good old custom to drink at births and weddings and funerals...Well, we weren't born together, Comrade Argounova. And we've never had a wedding, Comrade Argounova. But we might yet see the other...We might...yet...the other...Kira...

> (And suddenly, with a despair that wipes off, like an explosion, all his previous calm resignation)

Kira! I want to live! I want to live!

3. *Kira and Syerov, Leo and Antonina*

The opening of act 2, scene 3, in Versions II B–D.[2] The scene is set in Leo's home. Kira is sitting before a mirror, preparing to go out to meet Andrei. Leo is out with Antonina. Pavel Syerov knocks, then enters before being let in. He is "very obviously drunk."

Syerov

Ah, good evening, Comrade Argounova!

Kira

> (Jumping up, startled, sharply)

What are you doing here?

Syerov

Where's Kovalensky?

Kira

He's out.

---

[2] The scene in Version II A is somewhat different. There are no variations among Versions II B–D, except that at the top of the opening page of the scene in Version II D, Rand wrote, "This scene is out."

SYEROV

All of them are out, the damn crooks! Stalling me off, are they? Hiding from me, the rotten...

KIRA

What do you want? Don't you know that you can't be seen here?

SYEROV

I don't give a damn! I gotta see Kovalensky. I stopped over at that hog Morozov's, and I rang the bell for five solid minutes, but nobody's in. I gotta find one of them.

KIRA

What happened? What are you after?

SYEROV

My money! That's what I'm after? My share. That damn hunk of pork Morozov is late again on the last deal. I told him I won't be kept waiting!

KIRA

Keep quiet! Do you want the whole house to hear you?

SYEROV

Let 'em hear me! Nobody can touch me. I can shut every damn mouth. I can buy them all, guts and souls!

KIRA

Have you lost your mind? Coming here and inviting G.P.U. on your trail...

SYEROV

I got a friend in the G.P.U. A friend who can cut anyone's head off like that...
    (Snaps his fingers)
...just like that! I can do as I please! And I'll be damned if I'll let your Kovalensky hold my share out on me!

KIRA

If you're dissatisfied, why don't you drop the whole business?

SYEROV

Huh?

KIRA

    (Eagerly)
Cancel the whole deal. Let us out of it. Tell Leo you don't want him and close his food store. Get yourself another partner.

SYEROV

Gone crazy, have you? Cancel it? *Now?* With the money rolling in? Not on your life, I won't cancel it! Look at me! I bet you never saw a suit like this in Leningrad! Five hundred rubles, genuine foreign cloth! I'm not one to run around in their sleazy cooperative burlap!...Think I'm gonna be just another stray mongrel eating outta slop pails all my life? A ration-card slave? Well, Pavel Syerov will show them! It's his day.

KIRA

(Quietly)

Get out of here.

SYEROV

(Incredulously)

Huh?

KIRA

I don't want to hear about your store. I'm glad you're in trouble. If I can break your dirty scheme, I'll break it. I'll get Leo out of it some day. And now, if you don't get out of here at once, I'll have you thrown out—and I don't care who'll see you.

SYEROV

(Edging toward the door)

You better tell him or I'll wring his neck one of these days. He can't treat me like that. I'm a great man. Some day, I'm going to make foreign capitalists look like mice. That's what: mice!...You just tell him...so long, Comrade!

(Exits slamming the door)

(KIRA stands looking after him. Then turns resolutely, walks to telephone, picks up receiver.)

KIRA

(In a low voice)

Twenty-one—eighty-one, please...Allo, Andrei?...Yes...Andrei, I can't come tonight...No...No...I can't tell you now, you know how difficult it is for me to phone you...Yes, my parents might hear...You know that I want to see you, but...

(Tries to sound more cheerful)

No, I'm not. Do I sound nervous?...Nothing, nothing at all...

(Breaking a little)

Oh, Andrei, if only I could...

(Controlling herself)

No, nothing...Tomorrow...Yes, dear, I promise I'll come tomorrow...Nine o'clock at your place...

> (Smiling)

Yes, I will...my red dress...Good night, Andrei...

> (Hangs up. Looks nervously at her wristwatch. There is the sound of a door thrown open offstage Left and voices approaching, dominated by LEO's gay, ringing laughter. ANTONINA PAVLOVNA and LEO enter. ANTONINA PAVLOVNA wears a resplendent, but considerably disarranged evening gown and a fur wrap slipping off one shoulder; strands of hair hang down her neck, with hairpins slipping out; powder is caked in white patches on her nose, lipstick smeared in a vague blot between her nose and chin. LEO wears immaculate dinner clothes, but his hair is disheveled. Both are slightly inebriated, particularly LEO.)

Leo

Allo, Kira...You're home? I thought you said you were going to visit your parents tonight?

Antonina Pavlovna

> (Trying to sound dignified)

Good evening, Kira Alexandrovna.

> (KIRA stands looking at them silently)

Leo

Don't frown like that, Kira. It's not becoming—and utterly ineffective.

Antonina Pavlovna

> (Falling down on a chair)

Phew!...That was one grand evening!...If only my shoes weren't killing me! Do you mind if I slip them off?

> (Kicks her pumps off and wiggles her toes)

That's much better.

Leo

> (Lighting a cigarette, staggering a little)

Really, Kira, you could say "Good evening."

Kira

> (Quietly)

Good evening, Leo. I should also say, sit down please. You're tired.

Leo

> (Falling down on the davenport, his head thrown back, his legs high on its arm)

I am tired. So utterly, totally, magnificently tired that I love the whole world. It's an exquisite feeling.

ANTONINA PAVLOVNA

Wasn't it a beautiful evening? You missed a great deal tonight, Kira Alexandrovna.

KIRA

Undoubtedly.

LEO

Oh, yes, a magnificent evening. Just the right kind to put you at peace with your fellow men. It's a difficult art, you know. At first, you merely loathe them. Every single one you pass on the street. You shrink to keep their skin from touching yours.

ANTONINA PAVLOVNA

Leo! What are you talking about?

LEO

(Pleasantly)

That's only the beginning. Then you come to the point when you clench your fists in your pockets not to leap at the first man before you, any man.

ANTONINA PAVLOVNA

Leo, for God's sake!

LEO

Oh, but you don't do it.

ANTONINA PAVLOVNA

(Bewildered and almost relieved)

No?

LEO

No. You do something worse. You become one of them.

ANTONINA PAVLOVNA

What on earth...

LEO

You smile and you throw your arm around their shoulders, and you drink with them, and you laugh, and they'd rather not hear it, but they smile back and drink to you.

KIRA

(Quietly)

Leo, please...

LEO

And then, then you come to the point when you're even beyond that. When you feel nothing. Nothing. It's a beautiful word, isn't it? You don't hate them any more. You can look at the world and love it. When you love the world like that—well…

(Shrugs)

Yes, we've had a beautiful evening, Kira.

4. *Pavel Syerov and Andrei Taganov*

This exchange, from the middle of act 2, scene 3, is unique to Version III. It occurs shortly after Comrade Sonia tells Syerov she is pregnant.

ANDREI

Good evening, Syerov.

SYEROV

(Brusquely)

Good evening.

ANDREI

Strange, finding you here. I haven't seen you at our Party Club very often lately.

SYEROV

(Gets up, then stops brusquely)

But I've seen you too often lately. I seem to run into you much too often. What's the matter, Comrade Taganov? Got an assignment to watch me?

ANDREI

No, Comrade Syerov.

SYEROV

Then you'd better watch your step. I might resent it one of these days.[3]

ANDREI

It's a nice suit you're wearing, Syerov.

SYEROV

Well, what of it? Think you're going to frighten me with that? I'm not one to run around in their sleazy cooperative burlap! Think I'm gonna be just another stray mongrel eating outta slop pails all his life? A ration-card slave? Well, I'll show you. I'll show you whose day this is. I'll show you what I've got.

---

[3] Everything following this line is crossed out.

ANDREI

Everything, Syerov. But self-respect.

SYEROV

(Sits down on the edge of the table. Looks at him, chuckles.)

Do you notice, Comrade Taganov, that you're using a certain word much more often than I do? Not a nice word. Not for a member of the Communist Party.

ANDREI

What word?

SYEROV

Self, Comrade Taganov. Self-respect, self-pride, self-admiration. Do you realize how much you think of your own precious self? You're worse than a capitalist. You're a capitalist of the spirit. A hoarder of your own soul. You don't give a damn for anything but your own purity.

(ANDREI turns to go.)

No, wait. I've wanted to say this to you for a long time. For your own good. As friend to friend. I'm done with trembling before you. You're much worse than I am. You're the real traitor. I'm only human. I live as others live around me. I don't want to be any better than my fellow men. Perhaps only a little smarter. I don't worry too much about my self-respect. I was taught not to think about my great self. It isn't great to me. But you're the real egotist, Andrei. Of the deadliest kind. And if you want to look beyond the surface, which of us is nearer to the ideal of actual selflessness? You or I?

(ANDREI doesn't answer.)

Well? Answer me. You or I?

ANDREI

Perhaps it's you, Syerov.

SYEROV

Well, at least you're honest. So don't you think that—philosophically speaking— I'm much more the man of our times than you are? And don't you think that you'd better leave me alone?

5. *Andrei Taganov and Stepan Timoshenko*

From act 2, scene 3, of Version IV A. Andrei has just been talking to Syerov. As Syerov is preparing to leave, Timoshenko enters.

TIMOSHENKO

Good evening, Andrei.

(Noticing Syerov)

Why, there's our own little Comrade Syerov in person! What's the matter, Comrade Syerov? You don't look very happy.

> (SYEROV moves to go.)

Wait a minute. Why such hurry? I want to speak to you.

> (SYEROV pushes him aside and exits, slamming the door. TIMOSHENKO shakes his head.)

I don't think Comrade Syerov likes me. Wonder why.

ANDREI

Where have you been, Stepan? I haven't seen you for months. I thought you had forgotten your old friends. What's happened to you?

TIMOSHENKO

Oh, nothing. Not a single little thing...

> (As an afterthought)

Well, yes, I've been seasick.

ANDREI

What?

TIMOSHENKO

Yep. Seasick. But not on board ship.

ANDREI

What are you talking about?

TIMOSHENKO

> (Pointing to the door)

This—is an example.

ANDREI

What?

TIMOSHENKO

Comrade Pavel Syerov. There are too damn many Pavel Syerovs around these days.

ANDREI

> (Interested)

What do you know about Pavel Syerov?

TIMOSHENKO

Have you ever seen him opening his wallet to pay for a whore's champagne? Have you wondered where he gets the money?...You don't visit the European

Roof Garden, I bet. I do. Very instructive. If you did, you'd see one Citizen Morozov getting indigestion on caviar. Who is he? Just assistant manager of the Food Trust. The Red Food Trust of the Union of Socialist Soviet Republics!

(Jumps up)

ANDREI

Where are you going?

TIMOSHENKO

Going. Anywhere. I don't want to stay here.

ANDREI

Stepan, don't you think that I see it too? But screaming about it won't help. One can still fight.

TIMOSHENKO

Fight? Whom? How?

ANDREI

What do you know about Citizen Morozov of the Food Trust?

TIMOSHENKO

Plenty. But it won't do us any good, Andrei.

ANDREI

How much can you prove?

TIMOSHENKO

That's the point. Nothing.

ANDREI

Listen, Stepan. I've watched Syerov for months. I know that there are strange things going on at his railroad station. But I can't get anything definite. I know that Syerov is in it—and Morozov.

TIMOSHENKO

And someone else.

ANDREI

Who?

TIMOSHENKO

Something damn peculiar happened to me yesterday.

ANDREI

What?

TIMOSHENKO

Well, about a week ago there was a shipment of canned cherries from the Crimea delivered at Syerov's station. But the experts said the cans were rotten. Packed improperly. Poisoned. Not fit to eat. So they dumped the whole lot. Or they said they did...Well, yesterday, I happened to walk into a little private food store near the Alexandrovsky market. I saw something on a shelf...I'm very fond of cherries, Andrei.

(Produces a can out of his pocket and hands it to Andrei)

ANDREI

(Seizing the can)

You bought this at a private store?

TIMOSHENKO

It was the first shipment of canned cherries from the Crimea this year, Andrei. There has been no other.

ANDREI

Who owns that store?

TIMOSHENKO

Their third partner. I don't know him. The name on the sign says "Leo Kovalensky".

ANDREI

Who?!

TIMOSHENKO

Do you happen to know him?

ANDREI

(In a hard, flat voice)

Yes...Yes, I happen to know him.

(He is silent for a moment, then he raises his head resolutely.)

Let me keep this, Stepan. Don't mention it to anyone else. Watch Citizen Morozov. Don't let him know it, but watch him from now on. I'll take on Syerov—and the other.

TIMOSHENKO

Sure, if you say so. I'll watch Morozov. Only what's the use?

ANDREI

Don't you see? It's our chance, Stepan. It's our test. We'll expose this case. We'll make a gift of it to the Party. This case will begin the end of all the Pavel Syerovs. It's we or they, Stepan.

TIMOSHENKO

It was. But the battle's been decided long ago. Why make new victims?

ANDREI

It's not too late. I don't care about the victims. I don't care who they are nor how many of them there are to be. We still have a chance, Stepan. It's we or they.

II. THE TRANSFORMATION OF ANDREI'S SPEECH

The following is meant as a detailed illustration of the kinds of editing that Ayn Rand employed in moving from the novel to the final version of the play. It also provides an example of the kind of evidence that supports the establishment of the chronology of the surviving typescripts.

1. *The 1936 Edition of the Novel* We the Living

Toward the opening of Part 2, chapter 13, we are told that Andrei Taganov will be making a report on the agrarian situation that night at the Party Club. Shortly thereafter, Kira confronts him and presents her "Airtight" speech. Andrei borrows from it in his own presentation, much of which makes up the second section of chapter 13 (pp. 499–502), all of which is presented here:

"...and you've locked us airtight, airtight till the blood vessels of our spirits burst! You've taken upon your shoulders a burden such as no shoulders in history have ever carried! You have a right to do it, if your aim justifies it. But your aim, Comrades? Your aim?"

The chairman of the Club struck his desk with his gavel.

"Comrade Taganov, I'm calling you to order!" his voice thundered. "You will kindly confine your speech to the report on the agrarian situation."

Down the long, dim hall a wave of motion rippled through the crowded heads, and whispers rose, and somewhere in the back row someone giggled.

Andrei Taganov stood in the speaker's pulpit. The hall was dark. One bulb burned over the chairman's desk. Andrei's black leather jacket merged into the black wall behind him. Three white spots stood out, luminous in the darkness: his two long, thin hands, and his face. His hands moved slowly over a black void; his face had dark shadows in the eye sockets, in the hollows of the cheeks. He said, his voice dull, as if he could not hear his own words:

"Yes, the agrarian situation, Comrades...Within the last two months, twenty-six Party members have been assassinated in our outlying village districts. Eight clubhouses have been burned. Also three schools and a Communal Farm storehouse. The counterrevolutionary element of village hoarders has to be crushed without mercy. Our Moscow chief cites the example of the village Petrovshino where, upon their refusal to surrender their leaders, the peasants were lined in a row and every third one shot, while the rest stood waiting. The peasants had locked three Communists from the city in the local Club of Lenin and boarded the windows on the outside and set fire to the house...The peasants stood and watched it burn and sang, so they would hear no cries...They sang and played harmonicas...They were wild beasts. They were beasts run amuck, beasts crazed with misery. Perhaps there, too—in those lost villages somewhere so far away—there, too, they have girls, young and straight, more precious than anything on earth, driven into the last hell of despair, and men who love them more than life itself, who have to stand by and see it and watch it and have no help to offer! Perhaps they too..."

"Comrade Taganov!" roared the chairman. "I'm calling you to order!"

"Yes, Comrade Chairman...Our Moscow chief cites the...What was I saying, Comrade Chairman?...Yes, the hoarders' element in the villages...Yes...The Party has to take extraordinary measures against the counterrevolutionary element in the villages, that threatens the progress of our great work among the peasant masses...Our great work...We came as a solemn army and forbade life to the living. We thought everything that breathed could live. Can it? And aren't those who can live, aren't they too precious to be touched in the name of any cause? We've killed thousands. In those thousands—were there three who could have lived? Is any battle worth the life of one good soldier? What cause is worth those who fight for it? And aren't those who can fight, aren't they the cause itself and not the means?"

"Comrade Taganov!" roared the chairman. "I'm calling you to order!"

"I'm here to make a report to my Party comrades, Comrade Chairman. It's a very serious report and I think they should hear it. Yes, it's about our work in the villages, and the cities, and among the millions, the living millions. Only there are questions. There are questions that must be answered. How can they be answered if they can't even be asked? Why should we be afraid if we can answer them? But if we can't...? If we can't?...Comrades! Brothers! Listen to me! Listen, you consecrated warriors of a new life! Are we sure we know what we are doing? No one can tell men what they must live for. No one can take that right if he doesn't want to face a monster, a horror which is not for human eyes to bear. Because, you see, there are things in men, in the best of us, which are above all states, above all collectives, things too precious, too sacred, things which no outside hand should dare to touch. Look into yourself, honestly and fearlessly. Look and don't tell me, don't tell anyone, just tell yourself: what are you living for? Aren't you living for yourself and only for yourself? For a higher truth which is your own? Call it your aim, your love, your cause—isn't it still *your* cause? Give your life, die for your ideal—isn't it still *your* ideal? Every honest man lives for himself. Every man worth calling a man lives for himself. The one who doesn't— doesn't live at all. You cannot change it. You cannot change it because that's the way man is born, alone, complete, an end in himself. You cannot change it any more than you can cause men to be born with one eye instead of two, with three legs or two hearts. No laws, no books, no G.P.U. will ever grow an extra nose on a human face. No Party will ever kill that thing in men which knows how to say 'I.' But you can try. Oh, you can try. You have tried. Now look at what you're getting. Look at those whom you allow to triumph. Deny the best in men—and see what will survive. Do we want the crippled, creeping, crawling, broken monstrosities we're creating? Are we not castrating life in order to perpetuate it?"

"Comrade Ta..."

"Brothers! Listen! We have to answer this!" The two luminous white hands flew up over a black void and his voice rose, ringing, as it had risen in a dark valley over the White trenches many years ago. "We have to answer this! If we don't—history will answer it for us. And we shall go down with a burden on our shoulders that will never be forgiven! Anything is permitted to us if we're right. But our aim? Our aim, Comrades? What are we doing? Do we want to feed a starved humanity in order to let it live? Or do we want to strangle its life in order to feed it?"

"Comrade Taganov!" roared the chairman. "I deprive you of speech!"

"I . . . I . . . ," panted Andrei Taganov, staggering down the pulpit steps. "I have nothing more to say . . . "

He walked out, down the long aisle, a tall, gaunt, lonely figure. Heads turned to look at him. Somewhere in the back row someone whistled through his teeth, a long, low, sneering, triumphant sound.

When the door closed after him, someone whispered: "Let Comrade Taganov wait for the next Party purge!"

2. Version I

Act 3, scene 4, includes Kira's confrontation with Andrei and a version of her "Airtight" speech (see pp. 149–51 above), but there is no speech by Andrei to his comrades in this or any other scene.

3. Version II A

End of act 3, scene 4.

CHAIRMAN

I declare this meeting of the All Union Communist Party Club of the Eleventh District of Leningrad open . . . First on the order of the day is a report on the agrarian situation by Comrade Andrei Taganov. Word is now given to Comrade Taganov.

> (ANDREI rises and mounts slowly the speaker's pulpit; stands looking at the room; then speaks, his voice dull, mechanical, as if he does not hear his own words.)

ANDREI

Comrades! The agrarian situation is the darkest spot on our future. Within the last two months, twenty-six Party members have been assassinated in our outlying village districts. The counterrevolutionary element of village hoarders has to be crushed without mercy. Our Moscow chief cites the example of the village Petrovshino where the peasants locked three Communists from the city in the ~~local~~ Club of Lenin and boarded the windows on the outside and set fire to the ~~house~~ *building*[4] . . . The peasants stood and watched it burn and sang, so they would hear no cries . . . They were wild beasts. They were beasts run amuck, beasts crazed with misery. Perhaps there, too—in those lost villages somewhere so far away—there too they have girls, young and alive, driven into the last hell of despair, and men who love them and have to stand by and see it and have no help to offer! Perhaps there too . . . "

---

[4] ~~Crossed-out words~~ and the *handwriting* font indicate handwritten edits by Ayn Rand.

CHAIRMAN

(Striking his gavel)

Comrade Taganov! I'm calling you to order.

(A wave of whispers runs through the room.)

ANDREI

Yes, Comrade Chairman...Our Moscow chief cites the...What was I saying, Comrade Chairman?...Yes, the hoarders' element in the villages...Yes...The Party must take extraordinary measures against them. There can be no mercy where our duty is clear...Our duty...The hoarders threaten the progress of our great work among the peasant masses...Our great work...We came and we forbade life to the living. We've closed all doors and we've locked them airtight, airtight till the blood vessels of their spirits burst!

CHAIRMAN

Comrade Taganov! I'm calling you to order!

ANDREI

I'm here to make a report to my Party comrades, Comrade Chairman. It's a very serious report and I think they should hear it. Yes, it's about our work in the villages, and the cities, and among the millions, the living millions. Only there are questions. There are questions that must be answered. How can they be answered if they can't even be asked? Why should we be afraid if we can answer them? But if we can't...? If we can't?...Comrades! Brothers! Listen to me! Listen, you consecrated warriors of a new life! Are we sure we know what ~~we are~~ *we're* doing? No one can tell ~~men~~ *man* what ~~they~~ *he* must live for. No one can take that right if he doesn't want to face a monster, a horror which is not for human eyes to bear. Because there are things in men, in the best of us, which are above all states, above all collectives, things too precious to touch in the name of any cause! A man's life, the highest, sacred heart of his life, is not the means to any end. It is the end ~~itself,~~ *and* the reason of all reasons! You cannot change it. You cannot change it because that's the way man is born, alone, complete, an end in himself. ~~No Party will ever kill that thing in men which knows how to say "I".~~ But we've tried. Now look at what we're getting. Look at those whom we allow to triumph. Deny the best in men—and see what will survive. Whom are we sacrificing—and to whom? Do we want the crippled, crawling, ~~broken~~ lying monstrosities that we're creating? Are we not castrating life in order to perpetuate it?

CHAIRMAN

Comrade Ta...

ANDREI

Brothers! Listen! We have to answer this! If we don't—we shall go down ~~with~~ *under* a burden ~~on our shoulders~~ that will never be forgiven. What are we doing? Do we want to feed humanity in order to let it live? Or do we want to strangle its life in order to feed it?

CHAIRMAN

Comrade Taganov! I deprive you of speech!

ANDREI

(Staggering down the pulpit steps)

I...I...I have nothing more to say.

(Walks to door and exits. Silence. *Someone in the room whistles through his teeth, a long, low, sneering, triumphant sound. Then* The CHAIRMAN says slowly)

CHAIRMAN

Let Comrade Taganov wait for the next Party purges!

4. Version II B

End of act 3, scene 1. Virtually identical to Version II A; but the handwritten revisions in Version II A are typewritten in Version II B, and there are further handwritten revisions as well.

CHAIRMAN

I declare this meeting of the All Union Communist Party Club of the Eleventh District of Leningrad open. First on the order of the day is a report on the agrarian situation by Comrade Andrei Taganov. Word is now given to Comrade Taganov.

(ANDREI rises and mounts slowly to the speaker's pulpit; stands looking at the room; then speaks, his voice dull, mechanical, as if he does not hear his own words.)

ANDREI

Comrades! The agrarian situation is the darkest spot on our future. Within the last two months, twenty-six Party members have been assassinated in our outlying village districts. ~~The counterrevolutionary element of village hoarders has to be crushed without mercy.~~ Our Moscow chief cites the example of the village Petrovshino where the peasants locked three Communists from the city in the ~~local~~ Club of Lenin and boarded the windows on the outside and set fire to the building...The peasants stood and watched it burn and sang, so they would hear no cries...They were wild beasts, ~~They were beasts run amuck,~~ Beasts crazed with misery...Perhaps there, too—in those lost villages somewhere so far away—there too they have girls, young and alive, driven into the last hell of despair, and men who love them and have to stand by and see it and have no help to offer! Perhaps there too..."

CHAIRMAN

(Striking his gavel)

Comrade Taganov! I'm calling you to order.

(A wave of whispers runs through the room.)

ANDREI

Yes, Comrade Chairman...Our Moscow chief cites the...What was I saying, Comrade Chairman?...Yes, the hoarders' ~~element~~ in the villages...Yes...The Party must take extraordinary measures against them. There can be no mercy where our duty is clear...Our duty...The hoarders threaten the progress of our great work among the peasant masses...Our great work...We came and we forbade life to the living. We've closed all doors and we've locked them airtight, airtight till the blood vessels of their spirits burst!

CHAIRMAN

Comrade Taganov! I'm calling you to order!

ANDREI

I'm here to make a report to my Party comrades, Comrade Chairman. It's a very serious report and I think they should hear it. Yes, it's about our work in the villages, and the cities, and among the millions, the living millions. Only there are questions. There are questions that must be answered. How can they be answered if they can't even be asked? Why should we be afraid if we can answer them? But if we can't...? If we can't?...Comrades! Brothers! Listen to me! Listen, you consecrated warriors of a new life! Are we sure we know what we're doing? No one can tell man what he must live for. No one can take that right if he doesn't want to face ~~a monster,~~ a horror which is not for human eyes to bear. Because there are things in men, in the best of us, which are above all states, above all collectives~~, things too precious to touch in the name of any cause~~! A man's life, the highest, sacred heart of his life, is not the means to any end. It is the end and the reason of all reasons! You cannot change it. You cannot change it because that's the way man is born, alone, complete, an end in himself. But we've tried. Now look at what we're getting. Look at those whom we allow to triumph. Deny the best in men—and see what will survive. Whom are we sacrificing—and to whom? Do we want the crippled, crawling, lying monstrosities that we're creating? Are we not castrating life in order to perpetuate it?

CHAIRMAN

Comrade Ta...

ANDREI

Brothers! Listen! We have to answer this! If we don't—we shall go down under a burden that will never be forgiven! What are we doing? Do we want to feed humanity in order to let it live? Or do we want to strangle its life in order to feed it?

CHAIRMAN

Comrade Taganov! I deprive you of speech!

ANDREI

(Staggering down the pulpit steps)

I...I...I have nothing more to say...

> (ANDREI walks to door and exits. Silence. Someone in the room whistles through his teeth, a long, low, sneering, triumphant sound.)

(The chairman says slowly)

Chairman

Let Comrade Taganov wait for the next Party purges!

5. *Version II C*

Identical to Version II B, except that it is a clean copy (no handwritten inserts or deletions) and has incorporated all of the handwritten revisions in Version II B. There is no need to reproduce it here.

6. *Version II D*

The typescript is identical to that of Version II C, except that there are two paragraphs (which I reproduce here) with handwritten revisions:

Comrades! The agrarian situation is the darkest spot on our future. Within the last two months, twenty-six Party members have been assassinated in ~~our~~ outlying village districts. Our Moscow chief cites the example of the village Petrovshino where the peasants locked three Communists from the city in the ~~local~~ Club of Lenin and boarded the windows on the outside and set fire to the building...The peasants stood and watched it burn and sang, so they would hear no cries...They were wild beasts. Beasts crazed with misery...Perhaps there, too—in those lost villages somewhere so far away—there too they have girls, young ~~and alive~~ *girls*, driven into the last *of hells* ~~hell of despair~~, and men who love them and have to stand by and see it and have no help to offer! Perhaps there too..."

....

I'm here to make a report to my Party comrades, Comrade Chairman. It's a very serious report and I think they should hear it. Yes, it's about our work in the villages, and the cities, and among the millions, the living millions. Only there are questions. There are questions that must be answered. ~~How can they be answered if they can't even be asked?~~ Why should we be afraid if we can answer them? But if we can't...? If we can't?...Comrades! Brothers! Listen to me! Listen, you consecrated warriors of a new life! Are we sure we know what we're doing? No one can tell man what he must live for. No one can take that right if he doesn't want to face a horror which is not for human eyes to bear. Because there are things in men, in the best of us, which *must not be touched.* ~~are above all states, above all collectives. A man's life, the highest, sacred heart of his life, is not the means to any end. It is the end and the reason of all reasons!~~ You cannot change it. You cannot change it because that's the way man is born, alone, complete, an end in himself. But we've tried. Now look at what we're getting. Look at those whom we allow to triumph. Deny the best in men—and see what will survive. Whom are we sacrificing—and to whom? Do we want the crippled, crawling, lying monstrosities that we're creating? Are we not castrating life in order to perpetuate it?

7. *Version III*

End of act 3, scene 3.

CHAIRMAN

I declare this meeting of the All Union Communist Party Club of the Eleventh District of Leningrad open...First on the order of ~~the day is a report on the agrarian situation by Comrade Andrei Taganov. Word is now given to Comrade Taganov.~~

> ~~(ANDREI rises and mounts slowly to the speaker's pulpit; stands looking at the room; then speaks, his voice dull, mechanical, as if he does not hear his own words.)~~

~~ANDREI~~

~~Comrades! The agrarian situation is the darkest spot on our future. Within the last two months, twenty-six Party members have been assassinated in our outlying village districts. The counter~~[5] the day is a thesis on the "Basic Philosophy of Communism" by Andrei Taganov. Word is now given to Comrade Taganov.

> (ANDREI rises and mounts to the speaker's pulpit. Stands looking at the room, then speaks, his voice dull, mechanical, as if he were unconscious of his own words.)

ANDREI

Comrades...In these days of struggle, when the eyes of the world are upon us, we hear many people condemning our methods, while admiring profoundly our ideals. It is, therefore, imperative for us to keep clear in our minds the basic principles of our great cause, the certainty of our ultimate good which shall justify all our actions...The rock upon which we build is our faith in the supremacy, the pre-eminence, the all-inclusive power of the Collective. The State, which is the symbol of men's general brotherhood, recognizes no right but its own right, no will but its own will. The Collective is our single god and the State is its single prophet. To this great conception all else must be sacrificed...To this great conception...all else...even the most precious woman on earth...even the lovely...the single...the unrepeatable...

CHAIRMAN

> (Striking his gavel)

Comrade Taganov! I'm calling you to order.

> (A wave of whispers runs through the room.)

---

[5] This page ends here, but the next page follows from the point before which this passage was crossed out. It seems Rand has put together two versions.

ANDREI

Yes, Comrade Chairman...To this great conception...What was I saying, Comrade Chairman?...Oh, yes. To this great conception all else must be sacrificed. Man does not exist save as a useful servant to all other men. The good of his brothers is paramount to any private thought, to any private wish he may conceive. The good of all is good for all. When this is reached, no man on earth shall go hungry. Such is our faith. Such is our great work...Our great work...We came and we forbade life to the living. ~~We closed all doors and we locked them air-tight, air-tight till the blood vessels of their spirits burst!~~

CHAIRMAN

Comrade Taganov! I'm calling you to order!

ANDREI

I'm here to read a thesis to my Party comrades, Comrade Chairman. It's a very important thesis and I think they should hear it. Yes, it's about our basic philosophy—and about the things to which it leads. Comrades! Look at the world we're facing! Do you see the seeds we planted sprouting abroad in new forms? In another country, close to us, there is a man, an obscure man who is rising. He is rising upon a principle he learned from us: Man is nothing, the State is all. What if he proclaims it under another color and another name? We were the first to say it! God forgive us, we were the first to say it! We brought a gift to the world, in which there lies the key to all the horrors such as had never been possible in the history of men! One key, one single phrase: Man is nothing, the State is all...

CHAIR

Comrade Taganov! I...

ANDREI

Comrades! Brothers! Listen to me! Listen, you consecrated warriors of a new life! No one can tell man what he must live for! No one can take that right, not in the name of any cause! For the best of mankind is the single, the irreplaceable, the unrepeatable man. He has a right which no brother, not even all his brothers together, can take away from him—the right to the aim and the meaning of his own life. All else can be doubted. But one thing is not to be questioned, not to be tempered, not to be touched—the only sacred conception on this earth—freedom. *Freedom*, Comrades!...For there are things in men, in the best of us, which must not be touched by others. You cannot change it. You cannot change it because that's the way man is born, alone, complete, an end in himself. But we've tried. Now look at those whom we allow to triumph. Deny men's ego—then look at those who will be able to survive. Whom are we sacrificing—and to whom? Do we want the crippled, crawling, lying monstrosities that we're creating? Are we not castrating life in order to perpetuate it?

CHAIRMAN

Comrade Ta...

ANDREI

Brothers! We have to answer this! What are we doing? Do we want to feed humanity in order to let it live? Or do we want to strangle its life in order to feed it?

CHAIRMAN

(Leaping to his feet)
Comrade Taganov! I deprive you of speech!

ANDREI

(Staggering down the pulpit steps)
I...I...I have nothing more to say...
(Exits)

8. Version IV A

End of act 3, scene 3.

~~CHAIRMAN~~ CHIEF

I declare this meeting of the All Union Communist Party Club of the Eleventh District of Leningrad open. First on the order of the day is a thesis on the "Basic Philosophy of Communism" by Andrei Taganov. Word is now given to Comrade Taganov.

(ANDREI rises and mounts to the speaker's pulpit. Stands looking at the room; then speaks, his voice dull, mechanical, as if he were unconscious of his own words.)

ANDREI

Comrades...In these days of struggle, when the eyes of the world are upon us, we hear many people condemning our methods, while admiring profoundly our ideals. It is, therefore, imperative for us to keep clear in our minds the basic principles of our great cause, the certainty of our ultimate good which shall justify all our actions...The rock upon which we build is our faith in the supremacy, the pre-eminence, the all-inclusive power of the Collective. The State, which is the symbol of men's general brotherhood, recognizes no right but its own right, no will but its own will. The Collective is our single god and the State is its single prophet. To this great conception all else must be sacrificed...To this great conception...all else...even the most precious woman on earth...even the lovely...the single...the unrepeatable...

~~CHAIRMAN~~ CHIEF

(Striking his gavel)
Comrade Taganov! I'm calling you to order.
(A wave of whispers runs through the room.)

ANDREI

Yes, Comrade Chairman...To this great conception...What was I saying, Comrade Chairman?...Oh, yes. To this great conception all else must be sacrificed. Man does not exist save as a useful servant to all other men. ~~The good of his brothers is paramount to any private thought, to any private wish he may conceive.~~ The good of all is good for all. When this is reached, no man on earth shall go hungry. Such is our faith. Such is our great work...Our great work...We came and we forbade life to the living.

~~CHAIRMAN~~

~~Comrade Taganov! I'm calling you to order!~~

ANDREI

~~I'm here to read a thesis to my Party comrades, Comrade Chairman. It's a very important thesis and I think they should hear it. Yes, it's about our basic philosophy—and about the things to which it leads. Comrades! Look at the world we're facing! Do you see the seeds we planted sprouting abroad in new forms? In another country, close to us, there is a man, an obscure man who is rising. He is rising upon a principle he learned from us: Man is nothing, the State is all. What if he proclaims it under another color and another name? We were the first to say it! God forgive us, we were the first to say it! We brought a gift.~~[6]

~~CHAIRMAN~~ *CHIEF*

Comrade Taganov! I'm calling you to order!

ANDREI

Comrades! Brothers! Listen to me! Listen, you consecrated warriors of a new life, you who seek the great and the sacred! Nothing is great but Man—the single, the irreplaceable, the unrepeatable Man. Nothing is sacred but his freedom. He is not the means to any end. He is the end and the reason of reasons. No one can tell him what he must live for! No one can take that right, not in the name of any cause! Man has a right which no brother, not even all his brothers together, can take away from him—the right to the aim and the meaning of his own life. All else can be doubted. This alone is not to be questioned. For there are things in men, in the best of us, which must not be touched by others. You cannot change it. You cannot change it because that's the way man is born, alone, complete, an end in himself. But we've tried. Now look at those whom we allow to triumph. Deny men's ego—then look at those who will be able to survive. Whom are we sacrificing—and to whom? Do we want the crippled, crawling, lying monstrosities that we're producing? Are we not castrating life in order to perpetuate it?

~~CHAIRMAN~~ *CHIEF*

Comrade Ta...

---

[6] This paragraph—completely crossed out—ends abruptly here, at the end of the page, and the next page begins with the words of the Chief that follow.

ANDREI

Brothers! We have to answer this! What are we doing? Do we want to feed humanity in order to let it live? Or do we want to strangle its life in order to feed it?

~~CHAIRMAN~~ CHIEF

Comrade Taganov! I deprive you of speech!

ANDREI

(Staggering down the pulpit steps)

I...I...I have nothing more to say.

(Exits)

9. *Version IV B*

Identical to the speech in Version IV A (with the same handwritten revisions), though there are further revisions to one paragraph:

Comrades! Brothers! Listen to me! Listen, you consecrated warriors of a new life, you who seek the great and the sacred! Nothing is great but Man—~~the single, the irreplaceable, the unrepeatable Man~~. Nothing is sacred but his freedom. He is not the means to any end. He is the end and the reason of reasons. ~~No one can tell him what he must live for! No one can take that right, not in the name of any cause! Man~~ *He* has a right which no brother, not even all his brothers together, can take away from him—the right to the aim and the meaning of his own life. ~~All else can be doubted. This alone is not to be questioned.~~ For there are things in men, in the best of us, which must not be touched by others. You cannot change it. You cannot change it because that's the way man is born, alone, complete, an end in himself. But we've tried. Now look at those whom we allow to triumph. Deny men's ego—then look at those who will be able to survive. Whom are we sacrificing—and to whom? Do we want the crippled, crawling, lying monstrosities that we're producing? Are we not castrating life in order to perpetuate it?

10. *Version V A*

End of act 3, scene 1. Basically the same as in Version IV, incorporating the handwritten revisions.

CHIEF

I declare this meeting of the All Union Communist Party Club of the Eleventh District of Leningrad open. First on the order of the day is a thesis on the "Basic Philosophy of Communism" by Comrade Andrei Taganov. Word is now given to Comrade Taganov.

(ANDREI rises and mounts the speaker's pulpit. Stands looking at the room; then speaks, his voice dull, mechanical, as if he were unconscious of his own words.)

ANDREI

Comrades...In these days of struggle, when the eyes of the world are upon us, we hear many people condemning our methods, while admiring profoundly our ideals. It is, therefore, imperative for us to keep clearly in our minds the basic principles of our great cause, which shall justify all our actions...The rock upon which we build is our faith in the supremacy, the preeminence, the all-inclusive power of the Collective. The State, which is the symbol of men's brotherhood, recognizes no right but its own right, no will but its own will. The Collective is our single god and the State is its single prophet. To this great conception all else must be sacrificed...To this great conception...all else...even the most precious woman on earth...even the lovely...the single...the unrepeatable...

CHIEF

Comrade Taganov!

(Strikes gavel)

I'm calling you to order.

(A wave of whispers runs through the room.)

ANDREI

Yes, Comrade Chairman...To this great conception...What was I saying, Comrade Chairman?...Oh, yes. To this great conception all else must be sacrificed. Man does not exist save as a useful servant to all other men. The good of all is good for all. When this is reached, no man on earth shall go hungry. Such is our faith. Such is our great work...Our great work...We came and we forbade life to the living.

CHIEF

Comrade Taganov! I'm calling you to order!

ANDREI

Comrades! Brothers! Listen to me! Listen, you consecrated warriors of a new life, you who seek the great and the sacred! Nothing is great but Man. Nothing is sacred but his freedom. He is not the means to any end. He is the end and the reason of reasons. He has a right which no brother, not even all his brothers together, can take away from him—the right to the aim and the meaning of his own life. For there are things in men, in the best of us, which must not be touched by others. You cannot change it. You cannot change it because that's the way man is born, alone, complete, an end in himself. But we've tried. Now look at those whom we allow to triumph. Deny Man's ego—then look at those who will be able to survive. Whom are we sacrificing—and to whom? Do we want the crippled, crawling, lying monstrosities that we're producing? Are we not castrating life in order to perpetuate it?

CHIEF

Comrade Taganov...

ANDREI

It was our own fault. Once, men were ruled with a god's thunder. Then they were ruled with a sword. Now they're ruled with a bread card. Once they were held by reverence. Then they were held by fear. Now they're held by their stomachs. But you don't hold heroes by their stomachs. It was our own fault...

CHIEF

Comrade Ta...

ANDREI

Brothers! We have to answer this! What are we doing? Do we want to feed humanity in order to let it live? Or do we want to strangle its life in order to feed it?

CHIEF

Comrade Taganov! I deprive you of speech!

ANDREI

I...I...I have nothing more to say.

(Staggers down the pulpit steps)

11. Version V B

Same as in Version V A, with two changes: (1) in Andrei's first passage, "clearly" is changed to "clear"; and (2) the Chief's line "Comrade Taganov..." and the passage of Andrei's that followed it (beginning "It was our own fault") are cut. See pp. 280–81 above.

III. TWO ALTERNATIVE ENDINGS

Ayn Rand had a difficult task before her in writing the final scene of the novel: as its theme was the fate of the individual under totalitarianism, Kira had to die; but at the same time, she wanted to project Kira's (and her own) conviction that the universe is benevolent. She handled this marvelously through descriptions of Kira's introspection while attempting to cross the border—interrupted by the "biography" of Ivan Ivanov, the soldier who eventually shoots her. Adapting such an ending for the stage proved impossible, however, and Rand found it difficult to determine just how to end the play. The two complete versions included in this volume take very different approaches. What follows are a further two attempts: the final scene in Version II D and in Version IV B. (The endings in the other versions all closely resemble one of the four included in this book.)

1. Version II D

TIME: A week later.[7]

SCENE: Frontier post on the Russian-Latvian border. A small crude log-cabin with bare rafters and unpainted log walls. One large window in Wall Center and a door by its side. A crude table, a few benches, a cast iron stove with fire flickering in it. Pictures of Lenin and Stalin, on the walls, red posters, a gilded sickle and hammer over the door. Night. Nothing can be seen beyond the window but total darkness. Only once in a while, at slow intervals, a bright, narrow searchlight, from somewhere beyond the cabin, sweeps across the room, from Right to Left, and reveals briefly an endless snow plain behind the window.

AT RISE: The FIRST SOLDIER, husky, lazy fellow, is sitting at the stove, warming his hands, singing the "Little Apple," softly, under his breath. The SECOND SOLDIER, a lean, nervous youth, stands looking out of the window.

FIRST SOLDIER

(Rubbing his hands)

I guess I froze my hands for good, yesterday.

SECOND SOLDIER

(Without turning)

Probably.

FIRST SOLDIER

(Rubbing his ears)

My ears, too... God, it's cold!

SECOND SOLDIER

Yes.

FIRST SOLDIER

Four hours in the snow yesterday...

SECOND SOLDIER

(Staring hopelessly at the window)

Snow... snow... snow... nothing but snow for miles and miles... I figure you could walk three days and you wouldn't see nothing but this damn white swamp around you.

FIRST SOLDIER

Uh-huh.

---

[7] That is, a week after Kira's last scene with Leo.

SECOND SOLDIER

I think I'll go blind if I got to look at it much longer...God, I'd give anything for a heap of horse dung to make it look alive!

FIRST SOLDIER

Get yourself a snort of vodka, and...

(A shot is heard in the distance.)

SECOND SOLDIER

What was that?

FIRST SOLDIER

Nothing...Just Grishka out there, shooting a rabbit most likely.

SECOND SOLDIER

(Listens nervously, hears nothing)

It'll get me, some day, I tell you. Sometimes I ain't sure I'm alive no more. I get a funny feeling, like that snow was stuffed down my throat, and I can't yell, and there ain't a living soul nowhere around to hear me!

FIRST SOLDIER

I wish there wasn't a living soul around. Then we wouldn't have to sit here. But there is. Seven of them counterrevolutionaries last week, trying to cross the border.

SECOND SOLDIER

Yeah, seven corpses in Moscow this time.

FIRST SOLDIER

Uh-huh. Serves 'em right for trying to sneak out.

SECOND SOLDIER

But they keep coming, the damn fools, they keep trying! Like ghosts, crawling in the snow, all in white, the fools, think we won't notice 'em. All wrapped up in flour sacks or bed sheets. They don't seem alive, either, they're dead, but still moving.

FIRST SOLDIER

Shut up! You're going daffy, all right.

(Dead silence)

Second Soldier

(Panicky)

D'you hear it?

First Soldier

What? I don't hear nothing.

Second Soldier

That's it: nothing. Nothing nowhere! Maybe we're dead already. Maybe we're dead and don't know it.

First Soldier

Oh, shut your mouth!

> (The door flies open. The third soldier, GRISHKA, a tall, awkward, rather good-natured looking man, enters, a bayonet over his shoulder, pushing KIRA into the room, ahead of him. She is dressed all in white; an old white coat, white felt boots, white mittens, a white scarf wound tightly around her head, hiding her hair. The TWO SOLDIERS jump up, startled. The SECOND SOLDIER gasps. KIRA stands still, her shoulders sagging, spent, exhausted, but preserving a hard, rigid immobility throughout the following scene, as if the men around her did not concern her at all.)

First Soldier

Where'd you get that, Grishka?

Grishka

Tried to cross the border, the damn counterrevolutionary. Had to shoot to stop her.

Second Soldier

> (Staring at Kira)

A child...Just a child...

Grishka

You never know what you'll catch these days. All trying to sneak out. What are they running from, the damn fools?

Second Soldier

How did she get this far? Must have walked all night.

First Soldier

> (To Kira)

What's your name? Where did you come from?

> (She does not answer, does not look at them.)

You better tell us now. They'll make you talk at headquarters.

> (She does not move.)

SECOND SOLDIER

Leave her alone.

GRISHKA

You two go on out. Your turn to make the rounds. I'll watch her. When the morning shift comes, we'll take her to headquarters.

FIRST SOLDIER

She'd better tell us...

SECOND SOLDIER

(Buttoning his coat)

Come on. Don't you see she's dead tired? Leave her alone.

(The TWO SOLDIERS pick up their bayonets and exit, closing the door. GRISHKA unbuttons his coat, walks to the stove.)

GRISHKA

(To Kira)

Don't stand there like a pole. Sit down. Rest. You have a whole night to wait.

(He turns his back to her indifferently, stretches his hands to the fire in the stove, rubbing them, blowing on his stiff, frozen fingers.)

(KIRA walks to a bench, Left, and falls, rather than sits down, slumped with ~~uncontrollable~~ weariness. Silence. The searchlight sweeps across the room. KIRA raises her body with an immense effort to an upright position, gathering her last strength, she looks out of the window.)

KIRA

What was that?

GRISHKA

What?

KIRA

The light.

GRISHKA

Oh, that? From the other side. The Latvian frontier post.

KIRA

From... *the other side?*

GRISHKA

Yes.

KIRA

From . . . *abroad*?

GRISHKA

Yes.

(The search light sweeps over them again. She jumps up, stands motionless, her face raised to the light, staring at it intently, as if her eyes could hold the swift ray. The light vanishes. She staggers to the window, looks into the darkness, to the Right, her body tense, as if ready to leap, her hands grasping the window sill for support.)

KIRA

(Pointing to the Right)
Those lights . . . over there . . . it's the border?

GRISHKA

Yes.

KIRA

(Staring ahead, insanely fascinated)
The border? . . . The border of the *U.S.S.R.*? . . . The *end* of it?

GRISHKA

Yes.

KIRA

And that's *abroad*—there—beyond the lights?

GRISHKA

Sure.

KIRA

So close . . . I . . . I could touch it with my hands . . .
(Stretches her hand out as the searchlight sweeps over her, bringing out for a swift second her white, convulsed, eager fingers)

GRISHKA

(Looking at her)
Well, what of it?

KIRA

(Whirling around suddenly, her two hands grasping the window sill for support *behind her*, her eyes wide, intent, her voice low, tense, husky)
Let me go!

GRISHKA

Huh?!

KIRA

Let me go. It's only a few steps now.

GRISHKA

Crazy, are you?

KIRA

What difference would it make to you? If you hadn't seen me, no one would know. No one has to know. Let me out. You'll go on as usual, your country will go on as usual, and I...I...I'll be out! Don't you understand?

GRISHKA

(Softening in spite of himself)

You crazy little fool! What do you want to be out for?

KIRA

(Softly, almost gently, without reproach)

I...I don't know. I can't tell you. I could have told you before...long ago...but I can't, now. I've stopped thinking of that. I can't tell anyone anything anymore...ever...I don't know. I don't remember. I know only that I have to get out. To get out. Only to get out.

GRISHKA

Honest, Citizen, don't you see I can't do it?

KIRA

(Softly, eagerly)

You're a human being, aren't you? You're alive, aren't you? Have you ever wanted something so much, so much that you couldn't stand for it? Have you?

GRISHKA

What are you talking about?

KIRA

What do you want? What do you want most on earth?

GRISHKA

Well, I...I don't know what I want anything much.

KIRA

You want to eat, don't you? You want to breathe? You couldn't live if you didn't breathe, could you?

GRISHKA

(Bewildered)

Well, I guess not.

KIRA

Then think! What if someone took you by the throat, and choked you, and you felt the air trickling down into your lungs slower and slower, drop by drop, slower, and you knew the drops were stopping, and your lungs were on fire, wouldn't you want to throw those fingers off your throat, wouldn't you forget everything else, wouldn't you become a beast with nothing left of your whole world but those fingers and your lungs and air, air, your last drops of air?

GRISHKA

(Staring at her, fascinated and frightened)

Honest, Citizen, I...

KIRA

Wouldn't you?

GRISHKA

Well, I would...I guess...

KIRA

Then don't you see? That's how I want it...this...

(Points at the search light sweeping the room)

...this light? Let me out!

GRISHKA

God, Citizen, I can't! The State don't allow it.

KIRA

Of what use am I to you or to your State? You have enough people left without me. There...behind us...a whole country...a whole nation...it's all yours...What do you want me for?...You have millions to rule. I have only my life...my one life...Why don't you let me go?

GRISHKA

(Breaking)

I wish to God I could!

(She looks at him, sees her victory, unbuttons her coat slowly, her eyes never leaving him, rips the lining open, takes out a roll of bills and hands it to him silently.)

(Indignantly)

You damn...

(Looks at the bills closer, stops short, gasps, his voice changes)

Lord Jesus Christ! *Foreign* money?!

KIRA

(Calmly, precisely)

English pounds. Fifty of them. Take it.

GRISHKA

(Making a sign of the cross)

Where...where did you get all that?

KIRA

I bought them. For...over there. But I won't need it. Take it. Just let me out.

(He hesitates, mopping his forehead.)

You won't have to share it with the others. No one will know. Just open the door.

(Throws the money down on the table)

GRISHKA

(His hand advances involuntarily toward the bills, but he stops, leans heavily with both hands on the table for support, speaks quietly, brokenly, his voice choked, almost a whisper.)

I...I can't take you...across the border...It would be...the firing squad for me...I can only...open the door...and then...

KIRA

Just open the door.

GRISHKA

But the others...they're out there...somewhere...if they see you...

KIRA

They must be far away by now.

GRISHKA

(His hand moving irresistibly toward the bills.)

I got to...warn you...I won't cheat you...It's a...big chance you're taking.

KIRA

(With a note in her voice that sounds almost like happy laughter)

I'm not afraid. I have nothing left. Nothing but that I know I'm still alive, and I can't give up. It's a sacred trust, to be alive. You can't betray it. You can't let it be taken away from you. I'm not afraid. So much is still possible!

(GRISHKA seizes the bills avidly and pockets them swiftly, furtively. He looks at her. She smiles, a bright smile of encouragement. He walks to the door, throws it open. There is nothing but a black void beyond the door. The searchlight sweeps over the scene, revealing the endless snow plain, and dies away, leaving total darkness. GRISHKA makes the sign of the cross with a trembling hand.)

GRISHKA

(In a low, faltering whisper)

Good luck... Comrade...

(KIRA turns to him at the door, waves goodbye with a high, exultant sweep of her arm, and disappears in the darkness beyond the door.)

(GRISHKA stands frozen to the spot, wide-eyed, staring after her. Silence. Then a shot rings out in the darkness outside. GRISHKA shudders with his whole body, but does not move. Silence. Nothing can be seen beyond the door. Then the searchlight sweeps over the scene. It reveals KIRA'S body in the snow, a few steps beyond the door, lying still, one arm outflung. The searchlight dies away, leaving darkness behind. GRISHKA sags, his head drooping, his hand, hanging onto the door for support, beginning to close the door slowly.)

CURTAIN

2. Version IV B

TIME: A week later.

SCENE: Snow plain on the Russian-Latvian border. Night.

AT RISE: When the curtain rises, nothing can be distinguished, but the bluish shadow of a snow hill, the black immensity of the sky beyond and dots of light twinkling far away, to the Right. Then a search-light sweeps slowly over the scene from somewhere off-stage Right. While the light is moving we can see the hill, a single tall, snow-laden fir-tree on its slope and, under the branches of the tree, an open shelter—a small, crooked, dilapidated lean-to, open on three sides. A furious snow storm is raging. We can see the glittering sparks of snow whirling in the ray of the searchlight. The ray vanishes and the stage is dark once more. The ray returns at regular intervals on its slow circle throughout the entire scene.

On the searchlight's second appearance, A SOLDIER is seen struggling through the snow, from Left toward the shelter. He is dragging KIRA after him. He is a tall, husky brute of a man, with a bayonet on his shoulder, with the peaked Soviet military cap on his head. KIRA is dressed all in white: old, white fur coat, white boots, a white kerchief wound over her hair; she can hardly be seen against the wall inside, sits down heavily on the ground. She falls, rather than sits beside him. When the searchlight is absent their two figures can be distinguished as dim shadows.

SOLDIER

Who are you? Where do you come from?

(She doesn't move or answer.)

You'd better talk. What's the difference to you now? You're caught, aren't you? They'll make you talk all right down at headquarters.

(She doesn't answer.)

They're used to handling people like you down there. Caught seven of them counterrevolutionaries last week trying to cross the border. Seven corpses in Moscow by this time. What are you running from, you damn fools?

(She doesn't answer them.)

How did you get this far? Walked all night?

(She doesn't answer. The searchlight sweeps over the scene. She raises her face to it, watches it disappearing.)

KIRA

What was that?

SOLDIER

What?

KIRA

The light.

SOLDIER

Oh, that? From the other side. The Latvian frontier post.

KIRA

From . . . *the other side?*

SOLDIER

Yes.

KIRA

From . . . *abroad?*

SOLDIER

Yes.

(She leans forward, looks off, Right, tensely. Asks, her voice trembling a little.)

KIRA

Those lights . . . over there . . . it's the border?

SOLDIER

Yes.

KIRA

The border?...The border of the U.S.S.R.?...The *end* of it?

SOLDIER

Sure.
> (She stretches her hand up as the searchlight sweeps over them, bringing out for a moment her white, eager, convulsed fingers that seem trying to seize the ray. The ray vanishes. She jumps up.)

Hey! Where are you going?

KIRA

> (Pointing Right, very simply)

Over there.

SOLDIER

> (Jumping up, seizing her arm)

Crazy, are you?

KIRA

Let me go. It's only a few steps now. I've walked all night. I'm very tired. But I'll get out.

SOLDIER

You damn fool! Do you think we allow it?

KIRA

Of what use am I to you? You have enough people left without me. There...behind us...a whole country...a whole nation...it's all yours...What do you want me for?...You have millions to rule. I have only my life...my one life...Why don't you let me go?

SOLDIER

You crazy little fool! What do you want to get out for?

KIRA

> (Softly, almost gently, without reproach)

I...I don't know. I can't tell you. I could have told you before...long ago...but I can't, now. I don't know. I know only that I have to get out. To get out. Only to get out.

SOLDIER

Shut up, you fool! They told us that it's people like you who've always oppressed people like me. So people like you gotta be destroyed for the sake of people like me. Who is nothing—who had been nothing, shall be all.[8]

> (She tears herself away and runs. She runs to the Left, up the hill, then crosses to disappear behind the fir-tree. He seizes his bayonet, starts after her, shouting.)

Come back here! Come back, God damn you!

> (He stumbles in the snow at the top of the hill. He raises his bayonet.)

Come back or I'll shoot!

> (In the ray of the searchlight, she is seen running Right, down hill, beyond the tree. He fires just as the ray vanishes, in the darkness. We see nothing for a moment. Then the ray comes back. As it sweeps slowly over the scene, it reveals KIRA's body in the snow, at the foot of the hill Right, lying still, one arm outflung. The ray moves on to the SOLDIER who stands high up on the hill, tall, husky, erect, bayonet in hand. The ray stops, or perhaps it only seems to us that it did stop, a brief pause which can be guessed rather than grasped, one brief instant which is over before it is fully perceived, one instant of the sharp white light focused upon the triumphant figure of the winner. Then the ray moves on and vanishes.)

CURTAIN

---

[8] The soldier is struggling with a line from the *Internationale* (*Nous ne sommes rien, soyons tout* in the original 1871 lyrics). Rand would later give this line to Gus Webb, a minor villain in *The Fountainhead* (pt. 3, ch. 6).

Adapting *We the Living* for the Stage*

Jeff Britting

By the mid-1930s, Ayn Rand was at the start of a promising career. She had written and sold three works: a screen scenario titled *Red Pawn*; a successful Broadway play, *Night of January 16th*; and a first novel, *We the Living*. The works showed promise and accomplishment, but they were not professional breakthroughs. *Red Pawn*, a story set in Russia, was sold to Universal Pictures in 1932. It never went into production and remains unproduced to this day. *Night of January 16th* ran successfully for 29 weeks on Broadway during the 1935–36 season, but Al Woods, its producer, disfigured the play with inappropriate changes.[1] In 1936 Macmillan published *We the Living*. Despite the novel's considerable coverage in the press and slow but accelerating sales, the book went out of print prematurely and vanished.[2]

Adapting *We the Living* was proposed shortly after the novel's publication in 1936, a time when Rand's early successes were most evident. The proposal did not originate with Rand; rather, Jerome Mayer, a producer and writer, originated the idea.[3] Mayer had read and admired *We the Living* and offered to option the novel while Rand adapted the work. Unlike Al Woods, producer of *Night of January 16th* and a successful producer of "hit" melodramas, including *The Trial of Mary Dugan*, Mayer was a modest producer of intellectually orientated plays with no major financial successes.[4] Nevertheless, the idea appealed to Rand as a way to stimulate the slow domestic sales of the novel. As she later said, her motive was legitimate but "it was not a literary motive. My primary goal and interest were not in the play as such."[5]

---

* This essay was originally published as the first half of "Adapting We the Living," in Robert Mayhew, ed., *Essays on Ayn Rand's* We the Living (Lanham, MD: Lexington Books, 2004). It has been revised for publication here (and is included with the permission of the author and publisher).

[1] Rand disavowed the play's amateur version and subsequent Hollywood film adaptation. For an explanation, see her 1968 introduction to the play, in Ayn Rand, *Night of January 16th*, final revised version (New York: Plume, 1987).

[2] Biographical interviews (Ayn Rand Archives).

[3] Biographical interviews (Ayn Rand Archives).

[4] Biographical interviews (Ayn Rand Archives).

[5] Ayn Rand, *The Art of Nonfiction: A Guide for Writers and Readers*, ed. Robert Mayhew (New York: Plume, 2001), 81. Rand is known primarily for her work as a novelist. However, she developed an early interest in theater, motion pictures, and, later in her life, television.

Rand was a successful Broadway playwright and published novelist and her next theatrical effort warranted newspaper coverage. A July 1936 headline in the *New York Mirror* announced, "Mayer Buys Play from Girl Who Fled Soviet."[6] *The New York Times* reported that Ayn Rand was spending the summer writing a play based on her novel, a "bitter attack of Soviet Russia," published that spring.[7] In a September follow-up report, *The New York Times* wrote, "Ayn Rand has been toiling through the summer on a dramatization of her own novel, 'We, the Living.' By this morning she should have finished two acts of it. By November, she expects, Jerome Mayer will be ready to produce it—a bitter and anti-Soviet note that will not make Union Square very happy."[8] By January 1937, *Publishers Weekly* reported that Ayn Rand had completed her adaptation.[9]

In March 1937, a year after the publication of the novel, the production was delayed. "First announced last July for production last February," *The New York Times* reported, "Ayn Rand's dramatization of her novel, *We the Living*, is now listed for a spring [1937] tryout. All being well, [Mayer] would bring it here in the autumn."[10] However, all was not well. Mayer's effort to raise sufficient money to capitalize his production proved daunting and casting the role of Kira Argounova caused further delays. In June 1937, theater columnist Jack Stinnett reported that Mayer was in Hollywood searching for actors for a spring 1938 production of *We the Living*. The play, he wrote, "will undoubtedly start a siege of picketing, being strongly anti-communist."[11] Casting troubles continued. A year later in July 1938, Leonard Lyons's column "Broadway Melody" reported, "Ayn Rand, author of *Night of January 16th* is having difficulty casting her new play. Its theme is anti-communist."[12]

Rand's own assessment of the situation concurred with the published reports. The underlying cause of Mayer's casting troubles was the play's openly anticommunist theme. It was the height of the 1930s "Red Decade," an aptly named period when American intellectuals sympathetic to Soviet Russia struggled to

---

[6] *New York Mirror*, July 10, 1936, found in "Press Book, Warner Bros. Pictures *The Unconquered*, November 24, 1939–February 1940, Books A and 1," available on microfilm, Billy Rose Theatre Collection, New York Public Library. (As a result of the press book's deteriorated condition, the authorship and publication information of some clippings have been lost.)

[7] *New York Times*, July 10, 1936, press book, *The Unconquered*.

[8] *New York Times*, September 6, 1936, press book, *The Unconquered*. The comma in the play's title reflects the original spelling of the book's name as used in promotional materials at the time of the novel's publication in 1936. The date and reason for the comma's discontinuation is not known. However, it remained a common journalistic practice until 1939.

[9] *Publishers Weekly*, January 1937, press book, *The Unconquered*. Rand's adaptation under Mayer is no longer extant, and the evolution of the drafts is unknown. Among the *Ayn Rand Papers* (at the Ayn Rand Archives) are 11 typescripts, which appear to have been prepared and/or revised under George Abbott, including extensive revisions in Rand's hand and miscellaneous notes on speeches.

[10] *New York Times*, March 13, 1937, press book, *The Unconquered*.

[11] Malone, New York *World-Telegram*, June 19, 1937, press book, *The Unconquered*.

[12] *Chicago Times*, July 13, 1938, press book, *The Unconquered*.

dominate Hollywood and Broadway.[13] Leonard Peikoff, Rand's literary executor, relates that there was

> a tremendous amount of opposition from Hollywood stars, who would profess to her—Bette Davis is one example—that they would be honored to do the part of Kira and suddenly, two weeks or two months later, they would say, "I'm sorry. My agent says [appearing in an anticommunist play] will destroy my career."[14]

Without Bette Davis or an equivalent star, Mayer was unable to capitalize his production and his option lapsed. Meanwhile, Rand focused on other writing projects, completing her novella *Anthem*, and the plotting of her next novel, *The Fountainhead*.

Rand was well into the writing of *The Fountainhead* when her agent called with news of yet another offer on *We the Living*, this time from the Broadway star Eugenie Leontovich.[15] Leontovich read the novel, learned that a theatrical adaptation existed, and requested a script. Leontovich then sent the play to George Abbott, a personal friend and onetime director, who was also a major Broadway producer.[16] Eager to direct a serious drama, Abbott read the play and agreed to proceed with Leontovich in the role of Kira Argounova.

Rand described Abbott as a "scrupulously" honorable man primarily interested in musical comedy and farce, but who aspired to a more serious type of theater. Financially speaking, Abbott was a significant advance over Mayer: he was one of Broadway's most successful producers and was backed financially by Warner Bros. Studios in Hollywood. Abbott's interest in *We the Living* was auspicious—a Broadway success might generate further interest on the part of Hollywood.[17] Meanwhile, in 1937, Rand had made a disturbing discovery, which underscored the urgency of a Broadway production. Much to Rand's surprise, Macmillan failed to keep *We the Living* in print, having destroyed prematurely the book's typeset. Abbott's theatrical venture, virtually the only way to keep the memory of the novel alive in the public's mind, could not be ignored.

Abbott scheduled *We the Living* for the 1939–40 New York theatrical season. By fall 1939, Abbott began casting *We the Living* around Eugenie Leontovich and preparing the play's out-of-town tryout in Baltimore. The play would open on Christmas evening and run for one week, thereafter coming to New York at the

---

[13] Biographical interviews (Ayn Rand Archives). See also Eugene Lyons, *The Red Decade* (New Rochelle, NY: Arlington House, 1971).

[14] Michael Paxton, *Ayn Rand: A Sense of Life* (Layton, UT: Gibbs Smith, 1998), 101.

[15] Biographical interviews (Ayn Rand Archives).

[16] George Francis Abbott (1887–1995). "Combining an astute business sense and a rare flair for the stage, George Francis Abbott has become one of the most remarkable men of the American theater. Thoroughly schooled in a dozen branches of stagecraft, he is an admitted expert playwright, actor, director and producer." Quoted from "Theatre," Cue [?], no date, press book, *The Unconquered*.

[17] Under the standard production contract, investors in Broadway plays earn a set percentage of the future market created by a successful theatrical run. Warner Bros. reportedly invested $50,000 in *The Unconquered* (New York *World-Telegram*, December 28, 1939) and provided the use of the Biltmore Theatre, which it owned at the time (Internet Broadway Database).

beginning of January 1940. *We the Living* would be Abbott's fourth Broadway production that season and his most costly, ambitious production ever.[18]

Meanwhile, Rand began revising *We the Living* under Abbott's supervision and, in the weeks before the Baltimore opening, came to realize at the last minute that the whole venture was a mistake. Abbott, she recalled, was a "very nice person" but "totally inept about drama." As a director, he was

> totally un-stylized. And he wanted the folks next door...[He] tried to suggest that if a line was simple, you must use ten words instead of three...[For instance] something as simple as Kira saying, "I will try to cross the border."...He wanted her to say...: "Well, if I have a chance, and I think I might try, what I really would like is to cross the border."...And I asked him, "What for?" And he said, "Because when it's too brief, people don't talk that way."

Unlike Woods, who sought to make script changes in *Night of January 16th* without her permission, Rand had final say over all changes in *The Unconquered*. Abbott requested changes and Rand refused constantly: "I usually like to permit them changes, if there's any reason for it, and even when it's dubious, once in a while to permit it, simply not to be too arbitrary about it, because he had to direct. But it was one succession of flat 'No's' after another."[19]

By November 1939, Rand and Abbott's script troubles surfaced publicly. Under the headline "Author, Actor Trouble Hits Coming Play," the press reported that

> Miss Rand's play, "We, The Living" was to go in rehearsal immediately under George Abbott's sponsorship. The play is an indictment of Soviet Russia and Abbott has decided that one character needs to be made more sympathetic. Miss Rand doesn't think so, and the contretemps threatens to become serious. Also, Eugenie Leontovich, the play's star, is reported in the throes of reconciliation with her husband, Gregory Ratoff, and is anxious to return to Hollywood and abandon her stage career.[20]

The controversy, however, was quickly diffused by the *News*. It reported that a story "floating around Broadway" concerning a disagreement between Abbott and Rand over a "leading character" was false. On the contrary, both producer and author were "in complete agreement and of equal enthusiasm as to the drama's chances." The play was "scheduled to go into rehearsals early next week."[21] In December 1939, the *News* announced a new cast member and a name change: "With John Emery as her leading man, Eugenie Leontovich is en

---

[18] "When the rest of Broadway was trembling before threats of war in Europe and staged a general walkout, Abbott calmly announced four productions for the new season with possibility of others to come. True to schedule, he opened *See My Lawyer* (starring Milton Berle), *Too Many Girls*, and *Ring Two*. *We the Living*, due in January, rounds out the list." Quoted from "Theatre," *Cue* [?], no date, press book, *The Unconquered*.

[19] Biographical interviews (Ayn Rand Archives).

[20] Author and publication unknown, ca. November 1939, press book, *The Unconquered*.

[21] Author unknown, *News*, November 23, 1939, press book, *The Unconquered*.

route East for 'The Unconquered,' new title of Ayn Rand's play George Abbott is doing."[22]

In November 1939, newspaper coverage of *The Unconquered* began to widen beyond casting and writing controversies. Several months earlier in August 1939, the U.S.S.R. signed a controversial nonaggression treaty with Nazi Germany. As a result, newspaper reports about the play began to include references to the Soviet Union and other current topics. The *World-Telegram* wrote that the "George Abbott show is going to be a local Ninotchka—ridiculing the pro-Soviet plotter... *The New Masses*, incidentally, stations men to guard its editorial offices against vandals."[23] The press also tied the play back to Hollywood. According to *Woman's Wear* [sic], the new Ayn Rand play in rehearsal "will mark the first time Mr. Abbott has given any actor or actress precedence in billing over the name of a play he has produced. Miss Leontovich's reputation, however, and the magnitude of her role in the forthcoming production have moved him to change his traditional attitude toward the star system."[24]

By mid-December 1939, the play left New York for its Baltimore tryout, and a major problem surfaced in Eugenie Leontovich's portrayal of Kira. Rand recalled,

You could do nothing with her. She would play it in the old Moscow Art Theater style, ham all over the place, and she wouldn't take direction. Abbott, literally, couldn't do anything with her. He would work and he'd explain and he would show lines. She would say yes, and when it comes time to perform, she does it her way.[25]

Despite leading-lady problems, the press remained oddly silent. Instead, the press appeared diverted by the enormous size of the production loading into the Maryland Theatre and the elaborate theatrical vision of scenic designer Boris Aronson. The *Baltimore Sun* announced that the new Abbott show was "one of the most elaborate productions he has ever presented" and reported that "fourteen van loads of equipment, properties, electrical fixtures and setting were hauled to the theatre Tuesday night and Wednesday" in anticipation of a Christmas opening.[26]

As described by the *Baltimore Evening Sun*, the production was enormous:

The twin turntables, each eighteen feet in diameter, have been placed side by side on stage. Although each of the play's seven major scenes is being played

---

[22] Author unknown, *News*, December 1, 1939, press book, *The Unconquered*. John Emery (1905–64) portrayed Leo Kovalensky in *The Unconquered*. Completing the principal cast of *The Unconquered* was Dean Jagger (1903–91) in the role of Andrei Taganov.

[23] G. Ross, New York *World-Telegram*, November 27, 1939, press book, *The Unconquered*.

[24] *Woman's Wear* [sic], December 6, 1939, press book, *The Unconquered*.

[25] Biographical Interviews (Ayn Rand Archives).

[26] Boris Aronson (1900–1980) was a native of Russia who studied art and design in Kiev and Moscow before coming to New York in 1923. He became one of the leading scenic designers in American theater history. His work was featured in such productions as *Awake and Sing* (1935), *Cabin in the Sky* (1940), *Bus Stop* (1955), *The Diary of Anne Frank* (1955), and *Cabaret* (1966).

out front, stagehands at the rear will be setting up the backdrops and properties for the next scene on the rear halves of the two turntables. A curtain will drop momentarily, the twin tables will spin then halt with the new set facing the proscenium and the action will be resumed with but the briefest of delays.

As to the set design, the report continued, "The action takes place in and around the Kremlin [*sic*], the massive and gloomy stone citadel of Czarist origin in Moscow, and the massive sets were designed by Boris Aronson, to recreate the atmosphere that surrounds that grim building."[27]

In an interview with Aronson, the *Baltimore Sun* reported extensively on the designer's vision:

> Aronson uses the color red as the predominant theme in the sets for *The Unconquered*..."Of course red is the revolutionary color," Mr. Aronson explained, "but it is used here as the connecting theme between the two regimes." Its backgrounds are a rich, wine red velour and against them he projects the splendor of Czarist palaces, and the upsurge of the proletariat. For one, red symbolizes richness of color and decoration; for the other, red symbolizes a movement overtaking an older one.
>
> Even the last scene, an exterior, has the same red background, except that the red is black. Better let Mr. Aronson explain this: "Plain black is flat," he said, "but red-black is different from green-black. Look at the difference...the use of emulsions of the lights changes the red to black, only it's red-black and carries out the artistic sense of red which runs through the other scenes." He doesn't believe in making sets the duplicates of actual rooms. Sets, to him, should express the mood of the play, the essence of the environment. He takes special interest in the current production because it is Russian. Most of his other plays have been 100% American..."I got so I knew more about American hotel bars than I did about Russian houses so I had to study up before I started this one."
>
> There are seven sets in the latest Abbott play and thirteen changes, any of which can be done in forty seconds. Eight men came with Mr. Abbott, and about two dozen from Baltimore are needed to operate the sets. Three banks of switches—where one alone sufficed for the other Abbott shows—are used..."Nineteen hundred and twenty-four was a dynamic period," he said. "It was the time I last remembered Russia. The old was being taken over by another order. That's what I tried to do in the sets. Show the former period and contrast it sharply with the new." Executed on a massive scale by Boris Aronson...[t]heir decadent tone is in keeping with the author's underlying inference—the decay of the human character and the destruction of the human soul by the Moloch of the all-powerful state, which denies even the primary rights to humanity.[28]

In addition to press mentions of the sets, a Baltimore paper reported on a new production aspect, "Special music is being arranged by Alexander Haas to be played during performances of *The Unconquered*...The selections will be made

---

[27] *Baltimore Evening Sun*, December 22, 1939, press book, *The Unconquered*.

[28] *Baltimore Sun*, December 23, 1939, press book, *The Unconquered*.

from post-revolutionary music now popular in Russia...Mr. Haas is also preparing an unusual program of music to be played during the entr-actes [*sic*]."[29]

In a summary statement, another Baltimore paper wrote that *The Unconquered* will be "Mr. Abbott's first appearance hereabout as a director of romantic drama...an impassioned love story [that] deals with the way in which individual liberty was crushed by the tyranny of communist bureaucracy."[30]

The Unconquered opened on the evening of December 25, 1939. The curtain rose upon a massive production, which included its own artificial snow—as well as a flurry of theatrical jinxes. The *Baltimore Sun* reported that

> Howard Freeman, character actor in the cast of George Abbott's *The Unconquered*, fell fifteen feet from a second-floor tier of the dressing rooms at the Maryland Theater just before the curtain was scheduled to rise on the world premiere of the play...
>
> John Parrish, who had never rehearsed Freeman's role, went on in his place and read the part from the script. The accident was not announced before the play began...
>
> A wondering Baltimore audience, many of whom could not remember a read performance at a premiere in this city, at first received the substitute coldly. There was much grumbling when the curtain fell on the first act...In the lobby outside, the news of the accident spread quickly. And as the audience awoke to the situation the whole feeling changed from distaste to warm sympathy. This spirit was evident throughout the rest of the play.[31]

Unfortunately, the Baltimore critics were not of a unanimously warm spirit. Norman Clark wrote that one "hesitates to pass judgment upon George Abbott's newest play, *The Unconquered*, after viewing the hesitant, out-of-key performance given at the Maryland Theatre last evening." The play was

> a jerky melodrama—there are thirteen scenes—with its locale in Red Russia. But, barring some jibes at the inefficiency and hypocrisy of Communism, the plot could have been laid anywhere at all...Whether or not *The Unconquered* presents a true picture of affairs in Russia, we honestly cannot say. We once had dinner in a Russian cafe in New York, but that hardly qualifies us to pose as an expert on Soviet conditions.

In conclusion, Clark wrote, "may we wish Mr. Abbott a most happy and prosperous New Year."[32]

The *Baltimore Evening Sun*, however, disagreed and referred to *The Unconquered* as a "Gripping Abbott Tragedy." The review said the producer of "'Brother Rat' and 'Room Service'...has taken an excursion into heavy drama—powerful, gripping tragedy with a trio of emotional stars whose Herculean wrestling with

---

[29] *Baltimore* [?], n.d., "Abbott Play at Maryland Dec. 25," press book, *The Unconquered*.

[30] Author and publication unknown, ca. 1939, press book, *The Unconquered*.

[31] *Baltimore Sun*, December 16, 1939, press book, *The Unconquered*.

[32] Norman Clark, "*Unconquered*, New Abbott Play, Now at Maryland," press book, *The Unconquered*.

their several cosmic problems present some of the most effective dramatic acting seen here in many months." Calling the play a "ringing indictment of communism," the reviewer referred positively to the plot, especially "Andrei's speech on Communistic principles after his disillusionment in which a wooden repetition of Reed platitudes becomes a ringing indictment of Sovietism."[33]

The mixed Baltimore reviews had a sobering effect. Abbott now explained to Rand that if they went to New York, they would have to fire Leontovich. Rand agreed completely. However, Abbott's dilemma was how to fire Leontovich—after all, the entire production had been developed with her in mind. Rand recalls Abbott's solution:

> He asked me: Would I permit him to tell her that it's my decision, not his? And since I have the okay on the cast, he can do nothing about it. And I said, "Most certainly," kind of [astonished]. And it took me several days to realize what a cowardly thing it was on his part. He had said, "You see, we're old friends with her, and can I tell her that it's you, and that I'm giving in." I said, "By all means." ... [And] that's how he got rid of Eugenie Leontovich.[34]

When the Baltimore tryout closed, the *Journal-American* reported that Leontovich had "retired gracefully from the recent Abbott play when it was discovered she wasn't the type, [and] will retire from the stage, too, and resume as Gregory Ratoff's hausfrau."[35] Immediately, Abbott began to revise his production. The *Sun* reported, "Broadway won't see its first production of 1940 until the second week in January due to the shelving by George Abbott of Ayn Rand's play *The Unconquered*, which has been due to come to the St. James a week from this evening."[36]

Anticipating the next round of battles between producer and author, the Baltimore *Eagle* reported that the play was "not without its comic situations."[37] In early January, the *News* announced, "George Abbott has made up his mind to go ahead with the revised edition of Ayn Rand's *The Unconquered*. The drama already has been drastically rewritten with Abbott submitting several ideas and sequences. The producer is searching for an actress to replace Eugenie Leontovich."[38] The revisions, recalled Rand, resulted in "sacrificing everything for comedy": "There was a scene in the Home of the Peasant, with Comrade Bitiuk and Kira ... And he played it for a farce in the most ridiculous way, with the girls marching in and out of the office almost in goose step ... It's the only kind of thing that he felt at home in."[39]

---

[33] R. B. C., *Baltimore Evening Sun*, press book, *The Unconquered*.
[34] Biographical Interviews (Ayn Rand Archives).
[35] D. Kilgallen, *Journal-American*, January 29, 1940, press book, *The Unconquered*.
[36] *Sun*, "The Holiday Stage" column, December 27, 1939, press book, *The Unconquered*.
[37] "Abbott Play," *Eagle*, December 19, 1939, press book, *The Unconquered*.
[38] *News*, January 7, 1940, press book, *The Unconquered*.
[39] Biographical Interviews (Ayn Rand Archives).

Abbott's direction, according to Rand, was "miserable." However, during the recasting of Kira Argounova in New York, Abbott at last discovered "how to really direct" the play:

There was one English actress that some agent had sent insisting very much that he wanted us to hear her. She was sort of late thirties, very homely. She was really a young character woman type that would have done much better for Comrade Sonia than Kira, so that Abbott had not even wanted to give her a reading but did it as a courtesy for the agent. She was marvelous. Now that was really heartbreaking, in a way, for both Abbott and me. The reading was magnificent. But she was just so much not the type that it was impossible. She was short, stocky, somewhat piano legs or on that order or, you know, which would have been really impossible. Why the incident remains in my mind is this: Abbott told me afterwards, he said, "Do you know," in a kind of a sad manner, "I only now realized what your writing is like or how this play should have been done." He said "that actress made me realize." He said, "You know, your style is the same as Bernard Shaw's. Bernard Shaw is considered very difficult to stage, for the same reason. I only realized it by the way she read it." ... [Abbott] didn't mean style in the full literary sense of the word. He meant the method, the purposeful and intellectual. In other words, lines that had to be understood and not projected emotionally. That's what he got out of that girl. But imagine a director telling you that, when it's too late. I don't think he could have done it, anyway.

Helen Craig was cast as the new Kira. Although not ideally suited for the part, Rand considered Craig, an admirer of *We the Living*, a hard-working, "rather good," and politically conservative actress.[40]

With script changes completed and a new Kira in place, Abbott announced his opening date: Tuesday, February 13. A reporter noted, "Tuesday is a departure for Mr. Abbott, who has long favored Wednesday openings on Broadway. Now he has picked not only a Tuesday, but a Tuesday the 13th!"[41] During February 1940, seven new and competing Broadway productions would open, including plays by Clifford Odets and Ernest Hemingway.[42]

By February 11, 1940, the week of *The Unconquered*'s Broadway opening, over three hundred blurbs, column mentions, preview pieces, and feature articles including photographs and drawings of cast members had prepared the New York theatergoing public for the premiere.[43] On February 11, two days before

[40] Biographical Interviews (Ayn Rand Archives). Helen Craig (1912–86), an aspiring actress since childhood, created the role of the deaf-mute in the Broadway production of *Johnny Belinda*.

[41] Author and publication unknown, press book, *The Unconquered*.

[42] In addition to *The Unconquered*, they were as follows: *The Taming of the Shrew*, starring Alfred Lunt and Lynn Fontanne; *For the Show*, by Nancy Hamilton and Morgan Lewis; *Another Sun*, by Dorothy Thompson and Fritz Kortner; *Night Music*, by Clifford Odets; *The Burning Deck*, by Andrew Rosenthal; *Leave Her to Heaven*, by John van Druten; and, *The Fifth Column*, by Ernest Hemingway. Listed in "News of the Theatre," *New York Herald Tribune*, February 2, 1940, press book, *The Unconquered*.

[43] Press book, *The Unconquered*.

the opening, *The New York Times* placed an Al Hirschfeld caricature announcing *The Unconquered* across page one of the Sunday arts section. The headline read, "This Week Gives Broadway Only One Drama Opening." The pen and ink drawing foretold a drama involving the Soviet state, the proletariat, propaganda posters, and a defiant girl.[44]

On Monday, February 12, the first preview performance hosted a fund-raising event for the Young Folks Auxiliary of the Home for Hebrew Infants.

On February 13, *The Unconquered* opened at the Biltmore Theatre.

On February 14, roughly between the hours of midnight and early morning, the New York critics completed 26 full-length reviews of *The Unconquered*.

On February 17, George Abbott closed *The Unconquered* after six performances.[45] The production was a complete failure.

The reviews were almost entirely negative. The critics were unanimous in their negative assessment of the play's structure, Abbott's direction, the comedy-satire, and the character motivations. The critics praised the acting, especially performances by Dean Jagger as Andrei Taganov and Helen Craig as Kira Argounova, and the settings of Boris Aronson. Politically, the reviewers were divided into three camps: those on the Left, who rejected the play's politics; those in the middle, who rejected the play's lack of entertainment value; and those on the Right, who rejected what they considered the play's diluted attack on the evil of Soviet Russia.

Leading the attack from the political Left was Alvah Bessie, screenwriter and future member of the Hollywood Ten. Under the headline "One for the Ashcan...," Bessie wrote in the *New Masses*,

> If you were a smart, capitalistically inclined impresario and were anxious to produce a vicious and effective diatribe against the U.S.S.R., wouldn't you hire the finest playwright you could lay your hands on, who could write a brilliant, incisive, subtle, and above all *moving* play, that would damn the hell out of all those awful Bolsheviks? Or would you toss onto the stage a deadly dull 10–20–30 meller written by a fourth-rate hack?

After summarizing the play, Bessie concludes with a nod to his fellow reviewers,

> To quote the capitalist press: "Not only does Miss Rand's melodrama make a G.P.U. man its most attractive character, but its loudest eloquence seems devoted to the contention that what the Russians needed (in 1924–25) was more and better purges. The idealistic agent of the secret police is surrounded by shrewd, Tosca-like heroines, decadent aristocrats, corrupt politicians and fat speculators, and the most violent charge the play brings against the Communist regime is that the G.P.U. refuses to shoot more of them." (New York *Herald Tribune*) Soviet papers please copy[46]

---

[44] *New York Times*, Sunday, February 11, 1940, press book, *The Unconquered*.

[45] Press book, *The Unconquered*.

[46] Alvah Bessie, *New Masses*, February 27, 1940, press book, *The Unconquered*.

Theatre Arts expressed a more politically liberal viewpoint: "*The Unconquered* by Ayn Rand, a dramatization of her novel, *We the Living*,...suffered from the lack of perspective that recent experience makes inevitable. Reputed to be founded on actual events, Miss Rand's story of life in present day Russia smacked more of nineteenth-century melodrama, French Revolutionary style, than reality," by which was meant the current events involving the U.S.S.R.[47]

The nonpolitical, nonintellectual, middle-of-the-road commentators included the following: a gossip column in the *Post* wrote, "*The Unconquered* is a story of a White Russian in a Red Sea of trouble, and if Mr. Abbott cares, or doesn't, I like him better when he's in more of an 'Abbott' and Costello mood."[48] The *Bronx Home News* wrote that although "*The Unconquered* was heralded as an expose of the terrible GPU, Ayn Rand O'Connor actually has written about poor Russians in the dreadful clutches of SEX."[49]

From a politically more sympathetic but still theatrically critical mode is the *Morning-Telegraph*'s review. After apologizing to George Abbott for attacking his efforts to fill a "feeble" season with an "astounding" four new plays, the reviewer wrote, "The truth of the matter is Mr. Abbott should stick to his last [comedy] and Miss Rand should stick to her knitting. For not only is the play an absurd and improbable one, but it is produced and directed" without any subtlety, which makes the play's "gem of an idea" a "gross caricature of Miss Rand's philosophy and an immense bore to the public at large." Conceding that a play about a philosophy that "refuses to recognize the importance, or even the existence of individual desires" is a valid theme, the paper writes that the only valid way to attack the wrongness of such a philosophy "is to demonstrate that even under ideal conditions such a philosophy only brings disastrous results, while Miss Rand, on the contrary does her best to convince us that all Soviet officials are venal and self-seeking grafters, and that idealism has been corrupted by the basic pettiness of human nature, which is unable to use power for constructive purposes." The *Morning-Telegraph* repeated objections expressed by the critical establishment: the play's "characters are completely unreal; the comedy is unbearably caricatured; its plot is melodramatic and unconvincing. The tale of a couple who because of bourgeoisie descent and a desire for personal freedom are unable to exist under the Soviet Government, turns into a lurid story of a pair of food speculators."[50]

From the other side of the country, Hollywood's representative in New York filed the following with the *Hollywood Reporter*:

> George Abbott unveiled Ayn Rand's anti-Soviet play, *The Unconquered*, at the Biltmore Theatre last night, and no matter how you look at it politically, dramatically it's sabotage, Comrades.

---

[47] Review, *Theatre Arts*, April 1940, press book, *The Unconquered*.

[48] Dixie Righe [?], "George Abbott Presents," *Post*, February 14, 1940, press book, *The Unconquered*.

[49] The Playviewer, "New Plays, The Unconquered," *Bronx Home News*, February 14, 1940, press book, *The Unconquered*.

[50] "The Stage Today" column, "Ayn Rand's Play at Biltmore Theatre Came, Was Seen, Failed to Conquer," *Morning-Telegraph*, February 15, 1940, press book, *The Unconquered*.

In adapting this bit of anti-entertainment to the stage from her novel, "We, the Living," Miss Rand has succeeded only in boring from within—for [its] three acts are as interminable as the five-year plan. Neither John Emery's noble struggle with a plot that thickens every time it should be liquidated, nor Boris Aronson's eye-blinking settings can save *The Unconquered* from being an anti-Red excursion that will put Mr. Abbott in the red.[51]

The regional *Philadelphia Record* took a broader, more cultural viewpoint. The paper noted that the "isms" sweeping Europe and spreading into this country periodically transformed Broadway into "a rostrum either to defend our form of democracy, or to reveal the flaws of the ideologies of dictators." Writing that *The Unconquered* might have been "inspired by the front pages" and by a recent speech by President Roosevelt about "the dictatorial qualities of the Soviet Government," the play was "far more a political document than it is entertainment expected from a night in the theatre."[52]

Lewis Nichols of *The New York Times* wrote that the drama was "confusing, not going into the matter of the individual man in Russia, 1924—where there would be a play—and not adding to the theatre's already expert knowledge of the state of romance." Abbott tried to "pull together the sentimental melodrama that was almost old Hoboken and the discussion of the rights of man, of which there was not nearly enough."[53]

Completing the spectrum of political commentary was the voice of the political Right. Sidney B. Whipple criticized the play because it diluted the presentation of Soviet Communism's evil with trivializing theatrics. Whipple wrote that, opposing Andrei Taganov, a character who

is tragic and noble rather than a symbol of Bolshevik ruthlessness, [Ayn Rand] gives us [in Leo] a decadent aristocrat, a weakling whose liquidation would not be a matter of concern to the bitterest of Red-baiters. Certainly this cannot be the "civilization" Miss Rand hopes to save!...The other characters are too petty—too unimportant, in fact, to be considered horrifying examples of the rotten fruits of Stalinism.

Whipple concludes that the "unadorned facts are stronger than any of the imagined situations created by dramatists however sincere they may be and however hotly they burn with crusading fervor."[54]

Virtually the only semi-sympathetic review came from *Woman's Wear* [sic], which wrote that the play is "an anti-Soviet melodrama with scattered moments of compelling interest" and that the "play is well acted in the main...Dean

[51] "The New York Play" column, *Hollywood Reporter*, February 14, 1940, press book, *The Unconquered*.

[52] Mark Barron, "Spying on Gotham—'Unconquered' Changes Stage into 'Antiisms' Rostrum," *Philadelphia Record*, February 18, 1940, press book, *The Unconquered*.

[53] Lewis Nichols, "The Play" column, "The Unconquered," *New York Times*, February 14, 1940.

[54] Sidney B. Whipple, "Events Too Rapid for Dramatist," press book, *The Unconquered*.

Jagger is a bit stagy in his portrayal of Taganov, until his big scene where he addresses the Marxist club. The scene he plays brilliantly."[55]

Within days of *The Unconquered*'s closing, the production's physical properties were dispersed, its personnel dismissed, and the play slipped into theatrical obscurity.[56]

What was Ayn Rand's own critical reaction to the production? On this she commented at some length. She regarded the venture as a total and expensive disaster. First of all, the book was not proper play material. Its plot involved too much well-connected action and was better suited for film adaptation.[57] By the Baltimore tryout, she also realized Abbott's production, including her own script, was bad. Even the expensive sets were wrong for the play. Abbott, to his credit, had expended his best, most honorable effort, which made the failure worse.[58]

"It was," Rand recounts, "a total flop...I had a terrible time writing the play, and I disliked every version of it, from the original to the many rewrites. I became acutely aware of the fact that my purpose in writing it did not originate with me."[59]

The Abbott production marked the end of Ayn Rand's career as a playwright.[60] The promising decade of the 1930s—which included her first financial successes—ended in professional disappointment. In 1940 Rand returned to freelance employment, reading and summarizing stories for the film industry. But most importantly, she returned to writing and securing a publisher for *The Fountainhead*.

---

[55] Kelcey Allen, "The Unconquered," *Woman's Wear* [sic], February 14, 1940, press book, *The Unconquered*.

[56] Certain records of organizations involved with the production are on deposit with the New York Public Library. Besides a small collection of Van Dame Studio promotional photographs, Boris Aronson's set renderings, and a Warner Bros. Pictures press book on *The Unconquered* and related ephemera, nothing of the production is known to remain.

[57] Biographical Interviews (Ayn Rand Archives).

[58] Biographical Interviews (Ayn Rand Archives).

[59] Rand, *The Art of Nonfiction*, 80–81.

[60] *Ideal*, a novella written by Rand during her first Hollywood period, was subsequently adapted for the stage in New York City and revised intermittently until 1941. A second play, *Think Twice*, was written in the years 1939–40. Neither work was produced in Rand's lifetime. Both plays are included in Leonard Peikoff, ed., *The Early Ayn Rand: A Selection from Her Unpublished Fiction* (New York: New American Library, 1984; Signet paperback edition, 1986).

Appendix 1: Sources

There survive 12 copies of Ayn Rand's attempts at adapting her novel *We the Living* for the stage: 11 were saved by her and now reside in the Ayn Rand Archives, and 1 is in the New York Public Library (Billy Rose Theatre Division). Of the 12, 2 are identical and the others range from nearly identical to vastly different; 1 copy is incomplete.

In what follows, I use the term "version" loosely to refer to either a broad class of drafts of the play, which have been grouped together because of their similarity to one another (e.g., Version II), or to a particular typescript (e.g., Version II A). Note that Ayn Rand once said that "there were at least five or seven [versions], all together" and that the "first one was for Jerome Mayer."[1]

Here is a list of the versions of the play, presented in chronological order:[2]

Version I

Two identical copies (ARP 075-01x and ARP 076-04x)[3] and a third copy (ARP 075–08x), which is identical except for a revised and shortened act 3, scene 3.

We the Living (in the present volume) is a transcription of ARP 075-01x/076-04x.

Version II

    A. ARP 076-06x
    B. ARP 076-03x
    C. ARP 077-09x
    D. ARP 076-05x

---

[1] Biographical interviews (1960–61), in the Ayn Rand Archives.

[2] The order was determined by a detailed comparison of all versions. Especially important were handwritten revisions, and their incorporation into later versions. For some of the evidence supporting this chronology (as well as examples of the differences in these versions), see "The Transformation of Andrei's Speech" (pp. 309–22) and Appendix 3, "Scene Synopses and Casts of Characters."

[3] Ayn Rand Archive box numbers (ARP = Ayn Rand Papers).

Version II A is something of a transitional version between versions I and II B–C, sharing features of each. Versions II B–D are all essentially the same play, with Versions II C–D containing further layers of editing.

Version III

The first scene is missing. The remainder comes from two sources in the Ayn Rand Archives: act 1, scene 2–act 2, scene 3, p. 9, is out of place in ARP 076-02x (which in addition to this material contains Version IV A); act 2, scene 3, p. 10–act 3, scene 5 is the sole content of ARP 168-01t.

Version IV

A. ARP 076-02x
B. ARP 076-07x

Version IV B is identical to Version IV A, but with many handwritten revisions.

Version V

A. New York Public Library, call no. "NCOF+ (Rand, A. Unconquered)"
B. ARP 077-11x

Version V B is the same as Version V A, but with handwritten revisions and 22 retyped pages. *The Unconquered* (in the present volume) is a transcription of ARP 077-11x.

I consider this chronology to be established with certainty. Two other certainties are as follows: (1) Version IV B (or one like it) was the version performed at Maryland Theatre (Baltimore), December 1939; (2) Version V (A or B or one like them) was the version performed at Biltmore Theatre (Broadway), February 1940.[4]

I consider it probable that Version I was the one written for Jerome Mayer (completed in January 1937).[5] Finally, I also consider it probable that Version II A—a transitional version between versions I and II B–D—was the first one Ayn Rand sent to George Abbott.[6]

---

[4] This is based on a comparison of these versions with the scene synopses in the playbills for these two performances (copies of which are in the Ayn Rand Archives, ARP 073–06x).

[5] For a different view, see Jeff Britting's essay, above, p. 336, note 9.

[6] See Appendix 3, "A Note on George Abbott."

Appendix 2: Scene Synopses and Casts of Characters

I here present the scene synopses and the casts of characters for the different versions of the play, as found in the typescripts.[1] I have indicated handwritten revisions.

This material was crucially important in determining the chronology of the various versions of the play. For example, consider the transformations, from the earliest version to the last, of (1) the synopses descriptions of act 1, scene 1, and (2) the border guard in most of the casts of characters (sometimes called "Grishka," sometimes simply "soldier"):

1. Act 1, scene 1:
   - I: November 1923. Street in Petrograd.
   - II A: ~~November~~ *Fall* of 1923. ~~Street~~ *Leo's home* in Petrograd.
   - II B/C: Fall of 1923. Leo's home in Petrograd.
   - II D: ~~Fall of 1923~~ *Winter of 1924*. Leo's home in Petrograd.
   - *III:*   *Winter of 1924. Leo's home in Petrograd.*[2]
   - IV/V: Winter of 1924. Leo's home in Petrograd.

2. Soldier(s)/Grishka:
   - I: ...soldiers [includes the border guards in the final scene]
   - II A: *Grishka* [one of the border guards in the final scene]
   - II B/C: Grishka
   - II D: ~~Grishka~~ *Soldier* [one of the border guards in the final scene]
   - *III:*   *Soldier* or *A Soldier [the one border guard in the final scene]*
   - IV A: A Soldier [the one border guard in the final scene]
   - IV B: Soldier [the one border guard in the final scene]
   - V A: A Soldier [does not refer to a border guard; the final scene is set in Leo's home]
   - V B: ~~A~~ Soldier [does not refer to a border guard; the final scene is set in Leo's home]

---

[1] Version III is missing its scene synopsis, cast of characters, and act 1, scene 1. I reconstructed its synopsis and cast from its content.

[2] This scene is missing, but both versions II D and IV A (between which Version III is a transition) have "Leo's home in Petrograd."

Version I

ARP 075–01x, 076–04x, 077–08x

Title: *We the Living*

Synopsis

Act 1
Scene 1:   November 1923. Street in Petrograd.
Scene 2:   Spring of 1924. Technological Institute in Petrograd.
Scene 3:   Same evening. Leo's home in Petrograd.
Scene 4:   Fall of 1924. "The House of the Peasant."
Scene 5:   Same evening. Andrei's home.

Act 2
Scene 1:   Summer of 1925. Leo's home.
Scene 2:   Three weeks later. Andrei's home.
Scene 3:   Winter of 1925. Syerov's home.
Scene 4:   Same evening. Restaurant.

Act 3
Scene 1:   A few days later. Office of the G.P.U.
Scene 2:   Same evening. Leo's home.
Scene 3:   Same night. Andrei's home.
Scene 4:   Two days later. Leo's home.
Scene 5:   A week later. Frontier post on the Russian-Latvian border.

Characters

Pavel Syerov
Comrade Sonia
Kira Argounova
Andrei Taganov
Leo Kovalensky
Galina Petrovna Argounova
Citizen Lavrova
Olga Ivanovna
Comrade Bitiuk
Comrade Voronov
Antonina Pavlovna
Karp Morozov
G.P.U. Official
G.P.U. Chief
Students, Clerks, Guests, Speculators, Soldiers

VERSION II A

ARP 076–06x

Title: *We the Living*

Synopsis

Act 1

Scene 1:	~~November~~ *Fall of* 1923. ~~Street~~ *Leo's home* in Petrograd.
Scene 2:	Spring of 1924. Technological Institute ~~in Petrograd~~.
Scene 3:	Fall of 1924. Leo's home ~~in Petrograd~~.
Scene 4:	Fall of 1924. "The House of the Peasant."
Scene 5:	Same evening. Andrei's home.

Act 2

Scene 1:	Summer of 1925. Leo's home.
Scene 2:	Three weeks later. Andrei's home.
Scene 3:	Winter of 1925. ~~Syerov~~ *Leo*'s home.
Scene 4:	~~Same~~ *Next* evening. Restaurant.

Act 3

Scene 1:	A few days later. Office of the G.P.U.
Scene 2:	Same evening. Leo's home.
Scene 3:	Same evening. Andrei's home.
Scene 4:	Two days later. Leo's Home. *Same evening. Party Club.*
Scene 5:	*A week later. Leo's home.*
Scene ~~5~~ 6:	A week later. Frontier post on the Russian-Latvian border.

Characters

Leo Kovalensky
Olga Ivanovna
Kira Argounova
Pavel Syerov
Andrei Taganov
Citizen Lavrova
Galina Petrovna Argounova
Comrade Bitiuk
Comrade Voronov
Antonina Pavlovna
Karp Morozov
G.P.U. Chief
His Assistant
Grishka
Students, Clerks, ~~Guests~~, Speculators, Soldiers

Version II B

ARP 076–03x

Title: *We the Living*

Synopsis

Act 1

Scene 1:	Fall of 1923. Leo's home in Petrograd.
Scene 2:	Spring of 1924. Technological Institute.
Scene 3:	Fall of 1924. Leo's home.
Scene 4:	Three days later. Andrei's home.

Act 2

Scene 1:	Spring of 1925. Leo's home.
Scene 2:	Three weeks later. Andrei's home.
Scene 3:	Winter of 1925. Leo's home.
Scene 4:	Next evening. Restaurant.
Scene 5:	A few days later. Office of the G.P.U.
Scene 6:	Next evening.[3] Leo's home.

Act 3

Scene 1:	Same evening. Party Club.
Scene 2:	A week later. Leo's home.
Scene 3:	A week later. Frontier post on the Russian-Latvian border.

Characters

Leo Kovalensky
Olga Ivanovna
Kira Argounova
Pavel Syerov
Andrei Taganov
Citizen Lavrova
Galina Petrovna Argounova
Antonina Pavlovna
Karp Morozov
G.P.U. Chief
His Assistant
Grishka
Students, Speculators, Soldiers

---

[3] The play itself has "Same evening."

Version II C

ARP 077–09x

Title: *We the Living*

Synopsis

Act 1

Scene 1:	Fall of 1923. Leo's home in Petrograd.
Scene 2:	Spring of 1924. Technological Institute.
Scene 3:	Fall of 1924. Leo's home.
Scene 4:	Three days later. Andrei's home.

Act 2

Scene 1:	Spring of 1925. Leo's home.
Scene 2:	Three weeks later. Andrei's home.
Scene 3:	Winter of 1925. Leo's home.
Scene 4:	Next evening. Restaurant.
Scene 5:	A few days later. Office of the G.P.U.
Scene 6:	Next evening.[4] Leo's home.

Act 3

Scene 1:	Same evening. Party Club.
Scene 2:	A week later. Leo's home.
Scene 3:	A week later. Frontier post on the Russian-Latvian border.

Characters

Leo Kovalensky
Olga Ivanovna
Kira Argounova
Pavel Syerov
Andrei Taganov
Citizen Lavrova
Galina Petrovna Argounova
Antonina Pavlovna
G.P.U. Chief
His Assistant
Grishka
Students, Speculators, Soldiers

---

[4] The play itself has "Same evening."

VERSION II D

ARP 076–05x

Title: *We the Living*

Synopsis

Act 1

Scene 1:	~~Fall of 1923~~ *Winter of 1924*. Leo's home in Petrograd.
Scene 2:	Spring of 1924. Technological Institute.
Scene 3:	Fall of 1924. ~~Leo's home~~ *Various scenes of Petrograd*.
Scene 4:	~~Three~~ *A few*[5] days later. Andrei's home.

Act 2

Scene 1:	Spring of 1925. Leo's home.
Scene 2:	~~Three weeks~~ *A month* later. Andrei's home.
Scene 3:	Winter of 1925. ~~Leo's~~ *Syerov's* home.[6]
Scene 4:	A week later. Syerov's home.[7]
Scene 4~~5~~:	Next evening. Restaurant.
Scene 6:	*A few days later. Andrei's home.*[8]
Scene ~~5~~7:	A few days later. Office of the G.P.U.
Scene ~~6~~8:	~~Next~~ *Same* evening. Leo's home.

Act 3

Scene 1:	Same evening. Party Club.
Scene 2:	A week later. Leo's Home.
Scene 3:	A week later. ~~Frontier post~~ *Snow plain*[9] on the Russian-Latvian border.

Characters

Leo Kovalensky
~~Olga Ivanovna~~
Kira Argounova
Comrade Sonia
Pavel Syerov
Andrei Taganov
Comrade Bitiuk
Alexander Argounova
~~Citizen Lavrova~~
Galina Petrovna Argounova
Antonina Pavlovna
Karp Morozov
Stepan Timoshenko
Glieb Presniakov
G.P.U. Chief
His Assistant
~~Grishka~~ *Soldier*
Students, ~~speculators~~ *Guests*, Soldiers

---

[5] The play itself still has "Three days later."
[6] The play itself still has "Leo's home," though the entire scene has been crossed out.
[7] There is no such scene in the play itself.
[8] There is no such scene in the play itself.
[9] The play itself still has "Frontier post."

Version III

ARP 076–02x (out of place files) and ARP 168–01t

The front matter is missing from this version. What follows is extracted from the play itself.

Title: *We the Living*

Synopsis

Act 1
Scene 1:   Winter of 1924. Leo's home in Petrograd.[10]
Scene 2:   Spring of 1924. Technological Institute in Petrograd.
Scene 3:   Fall of 1924. Railroad office.
Scene 4:   Same evening. Leo's home.
Scene 5:   Next evening. Andrei's home.

Act 2
Scene 1:   Spring of 1925. Railroad office.
Scene 2:   Same evening. Leo's home.
Scene 3:   Winter of 1925. Party Club.
Scene 4:   Next evening. Restaurant.
Scene 5:   Next evening. Andrei's home.

Act 3
Scene 1:   A few days later. Office of the G.P.U.
Scene 2:   Same evening. Leo's home.
Scene 3:   Same evening. Party Club.
Scene 4:   A week later. Leo's Home.
Scene 5:   A week later. Snow plain on the Russian-Latvian border.

Characters

Leo Kovalensky
Kira Argounova
Comrade Sonia
Pavel Syerov
Andrei Taganov
Comrade Bitiuk
Comrade Voronov
Karp Morozov
Antonina Pavlovna
Stepan Timoshenko
G.P.U. Chief
His Assistant
A Soldier
Students, Clerks, Profiteers, Soldiers

---

[10] This scene is missing, but both versions II D and IV A have "Leo's home in Petrograd."

VERSION IV A
ARP 076–02x

Title: *We the Living*

Synopsis

Act 1

Scene 1:	Winter of 1924. Leo's home in Petrograd.
Scene 2:	Spring of 1924. Technological Institute in Petrograd.
Scene 3:	Fall of 1924. Railroad Office.
Scene 4:	Same evening. Leo's home.[11]
Scene 5:	Next evening. Andrei's home.[12]

Act 2

Scene 1:	Spring of 1925. Railroad Office.
Scene 2:	Same evening. Leo's home.
Scene 3:	Winter of 1925. Party Club.
Scene 4:	Next evening. Restaurant.[13]
Scene 5:	A few days later. Andrei's home.[14]

Act 3

Scene 1:	A few days later. Office of the G.P.U.
Scene 2:	Same evening. Leo's home.
Scene 3:	Same evening. Party Club.
Scene 4:	A week later. Leo's Home.
Scene 5:	A week later. Snow plain on the Russian-Latvian border.

Characters

Leo Kovalensky
Kira Argounova
Comrade Sonia
Pavel Syerov
Andrei Taganov
Comrade Bitiuk
Comrade Voronov
Karp Morozov
Antonina Pavlovna
Stepan Timoshenko
G.P.U. Chief
A Soldier
Students, Clerks, Guests, Soldiers

---

[11] There is no such scene in the play itself.

[12] This is scene 4 in the play itself.

[13] There is no such scene in the play itself.

[14] This is scene 4 in the play itself. The scene description reads, "~~Next evening~~ *A few days later*. Andrei's room."

VERSION IV B

ARP 076–07x

Title: ~~We the Living~~ *The Unconquered*

Synopsis

Act 1
Scene 1:   Winter of 1924. Leo's home in Petrograd.
Scene 2:   Spring of 1924. Technological Institute.
Scene 3:   Fall of 1924. Railroad Office.
Scene 4:   Same evening.[15] Andrei's home.

Act 2
Scene 1:   ~~Spring~~ *Summer* of 1925.[16] Railroad office.
Scene 2:   Same evening. Leo's home.
Scene 3:   Winter of 1925. ~~Party Club.~~ *Railroad office*[17]
Scene 4:   A few days later.[18] Andrei's home.

Act 3
Scene 1:   A few days later. Office of the G.P.U.
Scene 2:   Same evening. Leo's home.
Scene 3:   Same evening. Party Club.
Scene 4:   A week later. Leo's Home.
Scene 5:   A week later. Snow plain on the Russian-Latvian border.

Characters

Leo Kovalensky
Kira Argounova
Pavel Syerov
Comrade Sonia
Andrei Taganov
Comrade Bitiuk
Comrade Voronov
Stepan Timoshenko
Karp Morozov
Antonina Pavlovna
G.P.U. Chief
Soldier
Students, Clerks, Soldiers

---

[15] The play itself has "Next evening."

[16] The play itself has "Spring of 1925."

[17] ARP 076–07x contains two versions of act 2, scene 3: one is set in the Party Club, the other (which represents a transition between versions IV B and V A) is set in the Railroad office.

[18] The play itself has "~~Next evening.~~ *A few days later.*"

VERSION V A

New York Public Library, call no. "NCOF+ (Rand, A. Unconquered)"

Title: *The Unconquered*

Synopsis

Act 1
Scene 1:   Winter of 1924. Leo's Home in Petrograd.
Scene 2:   Spring of 1924. Technological Institute.
Scene 3:   Fall of 1924. Railroad Office.

Act 2
Scene 1:   Spring of 1925. Railroad Office.
Scene 2:   Winter of 1925. Railroad Office.
Scene 3:   A few days later. Andrei's Home.
Scene 4:   A few days later. Office of the G.P.U.
Scene 5:   Same evening. Leo's Home.

Act 3
Scene 1:   Same evening. Party Club.
Scene 2:   A week later. Leo's Home.

Characters

A Soldier
Leo Kovalensky
Upravdom
Kira Argounova
A Student
Pavel Syerov
Older Examiner
Andrei Taganov
Attendant at Institute
Malashkin
Comrade Sonia
Comrade Bitiuk
Girl Clerk
Boy Clerk
Comrade Voronov
Stepan Timoshenko
Karp Morozov
Antonina Pavlovna
G.P.U. Chief
Assistant G.P.U. Chief
Neighbor
Party Club Attendant

Version V B

ARP 077–11x

Title: *The Unconquered*

Synopsis

Act 1
Scene 1:   Winter of 1924. Leo's Home in Petrograd.
Scene 2:   Spring of 1924. Technological Institute.
Scene 3:   Fall of 1924. Railroad Office.

Act 2
Scene 1:   Spring of 1925. Railroad Office.
Scene 2:   Winter of 1925. Railroad Office.
Scene 3:   A few days later. Andrei's Home.
Scene 4:   A few days later. Office of the G.P.U.
Scene 5:   Same evening. Leo's Home.

Act 3
Scene 1:   Same evening. Party Club.
Scene 2:   A week later. Leo's Home.

Characters

A Soldier
Leo Kovalensky
Upravdom
Kira Argounova
A Student
Pavel Syerov
Comrade Sonia
Older Examiner
Andrei Taganov
Attendant at Institute
Malashkin
Comrade Sonia
Comrade Bitiuk
Girl Clerk
Boy Clerk
Comrade Voronov
Stepan Timoshenko
Karp Moroszov
Antonina Pavlovna
G.P.U. Chief
Assistant G.P.U. Chief
Neighbor
Party Club Attendant

APPENDIX 3: A NOTE ON GEORGE ABBOTT

In early January 1940, after *The Unconquered* closed in Baltimore after a week-long run, it was reported that George Abbott, owing to dissatisfaction with the production, had "asked Miss Rand to rewrite the muddled piece."[1] Another newspaper, however, went beyond this and claimed that "the drama already has been drastically rewritten *with Abbott submitting several ideas and sequences*" (emphasis added).[2]

There were certainly some significant revisions to Version IV B, the one performed in Baltimore. The most "drastically rewritten" part was the ending.[3] Should we be concerned about the extent to which the "final" version of *The Unconquered* is actually the product of George Abbott's influence, and to that extent not the work of Ayn Rand? I don't think so.

Rand made two comments about working with George Abbott that are relevant here:[4]

(1) [Abbott was] totally un-stylized. And he wanted the folks next door...[He] tried to suggest that if a line was simple, you must use ten words instead of three...

(2) I usually like to permit [directors] changes, if there's any reason for it, and even when it's dubious, once in awhile to permit it, simply not to be too arbitrary about it, because he had to direct. But it was one succession of flat "No's" after another.

I would like to address both Abbott's unstylized verbosity and Rand's resistance to his editorial suggestions generally.

---

[1] Donald Kirkley, "'Unconquered' Unconquered," in the Theater section of *The Baltimore Sun*, January 7, 1940, p. M8. Cf. "Plans of George Abbott," *The New York Times*, January 18, 1940, p. 27 (no byline): the play "had been extensively rewritten by Ayn Rand."

[2] *News*, January 7, 1940, press book, *The Unconquered*. (A fuller quote from this piece is included in Jeff Britting's essay, p. 342.)

[3] The entire ending from Version IV B is included in the excerpts section (see pp. 331–34 above), and this should be contrasted with the ending of *The Unconquered* included in full in this volume (see pp. 281–89). One may also wish to compare, as typical of the kinds of line-editing involved, the two relevant versions of Andrei's speech (see pp. 318–22).

[4] Biographical interviews (Ayn Rand Archives).

There exists evidence of Abbott's attempt to get Ayn Rand to "use ten words instead of three"—and of her resistance to such suggestions. Version II A (which I believe is the first version Rand sent to Abbott), contains well over one hundred circled numbers next to lines of dialogue, in some cases followed by additional comments, all written in pencil (but not in Rand's handwriting). Further, there is a file in the Ayn Rand Archives (ARP 078-18x) containing miscellaneous *We the Living–Unconquered* materials, including an "Analysis of Speeches," which is of great interest in the present context. This document contains numbered typewritten comments or suggestions, corresponding to the penciled numbers in Version II A.[5] Though no author's name is included, I think Abbott is the most likely candidate. As far as I can tell, these comments are descriptions of the state of mind of the speaker—perhaps included with a view to revising stage directions in the text or aiding the actual direction of the actor whose lines they were to be—and suggested revisions of the spoken lines themselves. In the case of the latter, they fit perfectly Rand's description of Abbott's proposed revisions. Here are two examples.

(1) In act 1, scene 2, Andrei says to Syerov, who is acting outside his authority in questioning Kira, "Go back to work." A number 4 is penciled in next to this line, and the corresponding item in the "Analysis of Speeches" document is:

"I won't argue the point, Syerov. I'm giving the order and you'll obey." Quietly, assured, commanding.

(2) In act 2, scene 2, in response to Kira's statement that the Party would not approve of their marriage, Andrei says simply, "I don't care." A number 104 is written above this line, and the corresponding item in the "Analysis of Speeches" document is:

"My Party! I don't give a good god-damned what my Party might think about it!"

So far as I can tell based on a comparison of the relevant lines in both versions II A and II B, and with an eye on the "Analysis of Speeches" document, Rand made no changes based on Abbott's comments or suggestions (if these did come from him), despite the fact that she made a number of revisions in moving from Version II A to II B.

But among these revisions, is there any evidence relevant specifically to revisions to Version IV B? There is indeed one piece of evidence that is relevant and quite revealing. In the original novel, Timoshenko says to Morozov,

Once, they were held by reverence. Then they were held by fear. Now they're held by their stomach. Men have worn chains on their necks, and on their

---

[5] They do not correspond exactly: the document goes up to no. 203, and covers all three acts; the penciled numbers in Version II A, however, go up to 159, but not beyond act 2. Further, the last few numbers in Version II A do not exactly match the numbered items in the document. I suspect that the later items on this list of comments referred to a slightly different draft of act 3 (and the end of act 2) that is no longer extant.

wrists, and on their ankles. Now they're enchained by their rectums. Only you don't hold heroes by their rectums.[6]

In act 2, scene 4, of Version IV B, Timoshenko addresses these identical words[7] to Andrei. However, Ayn Rand made the following handwritten revisions to this passage in the typescript (in response to Abbott's request for revisions, as my comment following this quote makes clear):

> Once, they were held by reverence. Then they were held by fear. Now they're held by their stomachs. ~~Men have worn chains on their necks and on their wrists and on their ankles. Now they're enchained by their rectums.~~ Only you don't hold heroes by their ~~rectums~~ *stomachs*.[8]

And in the margin, running perpendicular to this passage, she wrote, "My greatest sacrifice to Abbott—I hope he appreciates it!"

That Ayn Rand would regard replacing "rectums" with "stomachs" as not only a concession to Abbott, but as her greatest sacrifice, suggests that he had very little influence on the ultimate script of *The Unconquered*—whatever else he may have done in directing that script.

---

[6] Ayn Rand, *We the Living* (New York: Macmillan, 1936), part 2, ch. 10 (p. 457).

[7] With one exception: "stomach" is changed to "stomachs."

[8] This passage, so revised, appears in act 2, scene 3, of *The Unconquered* (see p. 254).

CPSIA information can be obtained
at www.ICGtesting.com
Printed in the USA
LVHW081423140620
658038LV00019B/1113